ASSEMBLING AND TROUBLESHOOTING MICROCOMPUTERS

ASSEMBLING AND TROUBLESHOOTING MICROCOMPUTERS
SECOND EDITION

James Perozzo

DELMAR PUBLISHERS INC.®

NOTICE TO THE READER

Cover Photo courtesy of International Business Machines Corporation

Delmar Staff
Administrative Editor: Wendy W. Jones
Project Editor: Eleanor Isenhart
Manufacturing Supervisor: Larry Main
Design Supervisor: Susan C. Mathews
Art Coordinator: Michael Nelson

Delmar Publishers' Online Services
To access Delmar on the World Wide Web, point your browser to:
http://www.delmar.com/delmar.html
To access through Gopher: gopher://gopher.delmar.com
(Delmar Online is part of "thomson.com", an internet site with information on more than 30 publishers of the International Thomson Publishing organization.)
For information on our products and services:
email: info@delmar.com
or call 800-347-7707

For information, address Delmar Publishers Inc.
3 Columbia Circle, PO Box 15015
Albany, New York 12212-5015

COPYRIGHT © 1991
BY DELMAR PUBLISHERS INC.

Printed in the United States of America
Published simultaneously in Canada
by Nelson Canada
A Division of The Thomson Corporation

10 9 8 7 6 5

Library of Congress Cataloging-in-Publication Data

Perozzo, James.
    Assembling and troubleshooting microcomputers / James Perozzo. —
2nd ed.
        p.   cm.
    Rev. ed. of: Microcomputer troubleshooting.
    Includes index.
    ISBN 0-8273-3986-0
    1. Microcomputers—Maintenance and repair.   I. Perozzo, James.
Microcomputer troubleshooting.   II. Title.
TK7887.P47   1991
621.39'16—dc20   90-35812
                                                                  CIP

Contents

Preface xv

Acknowledgments xvii

About the Author xix

part one **An Overview of Computers** **1**

chapter one **How Microcomputers Work and
What They Can Do** **3**
Chapter Objective 3
What is a Microcomputer? 3
The Normal Operation of a Microcomputer 7
The Operating System 10
What a Microcomputer Can Do 10
  Word Processing Programs 11
  Data Base Programs 12
  Spreadsheet Programs 12
  Computer-Aided Drafting Programs 14
  Communications Programs 14
  Small Utility Programs 14
  Writing Your Own Programs 16
Chapter Summary 20
Review Questions 22

part two **When a Problem Develops in a
Working Microcomputer** **23**

chapter two **A Computer Problem or Not?** **25**
Chapter Objective 25
Operator Problems 25
External Power Problems 26
Diskette Problems 32
Hard Disk Problems 33
  Lack of Hard Disk Rotation 34
  Hard Disk Crash 34
  Normal Power Unavailable 34
System Board Problems 35
Is It a Hardware or Software Problem? 36
  Representative ROM Diagnostic Error Codes 37

Parity Errors 37
Boot-Up Troubleshooting Review 38
Diskette Drive File Access Problems 38
Chapter Summary 39
Review Questions 39

chapter three   **Troubleshooting to the Unit and Board Level**   **41**
Chapter Objective 41
Board- or Component-Level Troubleshooting? 41
Electrostatic Discharge and Other Cautions 43
Typical Computer Problems 48
    Complete Failures 48
    Tampered Equipment 48
    Intermittent Problems 48
    Application of Voltage in the Wrong Place 50
    Multiple Problems 51
    The Tough Problems 52
    Overheated Parts Failures 53
Check the Simple Things First 53
Which Part of the Computer is at Fault? 54
    Troubleshooting the Power Supply and Fan 54
    Printer and Monitor Cable Problems 55
    Printer Problems 55
    Monitor Problems 57
    Keyboard Problems 59
    Localizing Problems Within the System Unit 61
To Repair or Not to Repair? 66
Learning and Loading the Diagnostic Program 67
    A Word to the Wise 67
    A Summary of Diagnostic Programs 67
    Loading the Diagnostic Program 68
Completing the Service Call 69
    Reassembling the Equipment 69
    Necessary Paperwork 69
    Packing for Shipment 70
Chapter Summary 70
Review Questions 70

part three   **Assembling and Adding Options
to a Microcomputer**   **73**

chapter four   **Assembling a Microcomputer from Modules**   **75**
Chapter Objective 75
Microcomputers Are Modular 75

An Overview of Minimum Hardware Required 77
  Case 77
  Control Panel 77
  Speaker 78
  System Board 79
  Video Adapter and Monitor 82
  Keyboard 83
  Power Supply 84
  Floppy Diskette Controller/Diskette Drive(s) 84
Additional Hardware Options 86
  Additional Memory 86
  Math Coprocessors 90
  Clock 90
  I/O Ports 91
  Multifunction Cards 92
  Additional Monitors 92
  Printers 92
  Hard Disk Controller/Hard Disk 93
  Modems 93
Putting It All Together 93
  Installing the System Board 94
  Installing the Power Supply 95
  Installing the AT Clock and
    Setup Memory Battery 96
  Installing a PC/XT Clock Card 96
  Installing a Control Panel 97
  Installing the Video Card and Monitor 97
  Installing a Floppy Diskette Drive
    and Adaptor 98
  Installing a Hard Disk Drive and Controller 98
  General Notes on Installing Option Cards 98
  Installing a Modem 98
  Installing Additional I/O Ports 99
Checking Out the Final Assembly 99
  Configuring a PC or XT Computer 99
  Configuring an AT Computer 99
Chapter Summary 100
Review Questions 100

chapter five **Adding Options to an Existing Microcomputer** **102**
Chapter Objective 102
A Caution to Observe 102
Adding More Memory 102
Adding Additional I/O Ports 103

Adding a Multifunction Card   104
Upgrading an XT to an AT   105
Upgrading an XT with a Turbo Board   106
Installing a Math Coprocessor   106
Installing a Better Monitor   106
Installing an Additional Floppy Drive
      or Hard Disk   107
Installing a Larger Power Supply   107
Installing a Light Pen   107
Installing a Mouse   107
Installing a Digitizer Pad   108
Installing a Joystick   108
Chapter Summary   109
Review Questions   109

chapter six   **Installing and Troubleshooting**
                Floppy Diskette Drives   **110**
                Chapter Objective   110
                Floppy Diskette Drive Mechanics and Terms   110
                Data Storage on the Floppy Diskette   114
                Kinds of Floppy Diskette Drives   115
                  The "Standard" 360K Floppy Drive   115
                  The Quad-Density Floppy Drive   116
                  The High-Density Floppy Drive   116
                  The 3½ Inch Floppy Drive   117
                Writing Data on a Floppy Diskette   118
                The Floppy Drive Controller   119
                Cautions for Handling Floppy Diskettes   119
                Cautions for Handling a Floppy Drive   120
                Cautions for Handling a Floppy Drive Controller   121
                What a Floppy Drive FORMAT Does   121
                Floppy Drive Hardware Installation   121
                Symptoms of a Bad Floppy Diskette Drive   123
                Localizing a Problem to a Floppy Diskette Drive   123
                Check the Simple Things   124
                Troubleshooting the Floppy Drive Controller   124
                Floppy Diskette Drive Preventive Maintenance   128
                Repairing Floppy Diskette Drives   129
                Chapter Summary   129
                Review Questions   130

chapter seven   **Installing and Troubleshooting Hard Disk Drives**   **131**
                Chapter Objective   131
                Cautions for Handling Hard Drives   131

Power Required for a Hard Drive 132
Hard Drive Construction 133
  Hard Drive Capacity 133
  Hard Drives Are Sealed Units 133
  The Drive Number 134
  Tracks or Cylinders 134
  Sectors 134
  Platters 135
  Number of Heads 135
  Data Recording Methods 135
  Hardcards 136
Internal Operation of a Hard Drive 136
  Write Precompensation 136
  Reduced Write Current 137
  Error Correction Code 137
  CCB Option Byte (Step Pulse Rate) 137
  Landing Zone—The PARK Program 137
  Interleaf 138
Things to Know About a Particular Drive
    to Install It 138
  Bad Tracks on the Hard Drive 138
  Using Commercial Primary
      Formatting Programs 139
  Using the Controller Primary
      Formatting Program 139
Hard Drive Hardware Installation 141
  Configure the Controller Jumpers 141
  Configure the Hard Drive Hardware 142
  Mount the Hard Drive 143
  Install the Controller 144
Hard Drive Software Installation 146
  A Little Background Information 146
  The Primary (Low-Level) Format 147
  Using FDISK 152
  Using FORMAT 153
Checking the Hard Drive Installation 153
Tuning Up the Computer for Hard Drive Use 154
Installing Applications and Data 156
Troubleshooting Hard Disk Drives 156
Chapter Summary 158
Review Questions 159

chapter eight   Troubleshooting and Replacing the Power Supply   160
Chapter Objective 160

The Typical Microcomputer Power Supply 160
A Word About Safety 160
Power Supply Specifications 162
  Input Voltage Regulation 162
  Output Voltage Regulation 163
Connectors and Voltages 163
  The System Board Connector 164
  The Drive Power Connectors 164
Typical Power Supply Problems and Symptoms 165
  The Inadequate Power Supply 165
  Internal Power Supply Failures 165
To Repair or Replace, That is the Question 166
Symptoms of Power Supply Failure 166
  Did the Fuse Blow? 166
  If the Fuse Has Blown 166
  If the Fuse Has Not Blown 167
  Eliminating Power Supply Loads 167
Replacing the Power Supply 168
Chapter Summary 169
Review Questions 169

chapter nine   **Installing and Repairing Computer Monitors**   **170**
Chapter Objective 170
What a Computer Monitor Does 170
A Comparison of Video Adapters and Monitors 174
  The Monochrome Display Adapter (MDA) 174
  The Television Monitor 175
  The Color Graphics Adapter (CGA) 175
  The Enhanced Graphics Adapter (EGA) 176
  The Multicolor Graphics Array (MGCA) 176
  The Video Graphics Adapter (VGA) 176
Getting the Signals to the Monitor 177
  Composite Video Monitors 177
  Direct-Drive Monitors 178
Dual-Monitor Operation 179
Troubleshooting Video Adapters and Monitors 180
  Check the Obvious 180
  Try Substitution Next 180
  The Defective Video Adapter 180
  The Defective Monitor 181
Chapter Summary 186
Review Questions 187

chapter ten   **Installing and Repairing Computer Printers
and Plotters**   **188**
Chapter Objective 188
A Word About Safety 188
Types of Printers 189
   The Dot-Matrix Printer 189
   The Fully Formed Character Printer 192
   The Laser Printer 194
   Other Printer Types 196
Computer Data Output Concepts 197
   DOS-Level Outputs to a Printer 197
   "Dumb" Printers 198
   "Smart" Printers 199
   Control Codes and Escape Sequences 199
   Sending Printer Escape Codes
      at the DOS Level 200
   Applications Programs Run Printers Best 200
The Mechanics of Printers 201
   Printheads 202
   Paper Feeds 203
   Carriage Mechanisms 204
   Ribbon Feeds 206
   Interlock Switches 208
Installing a Printer 209
Installing a Plotter 210
Printer Spoolers 211
   Installing an External Printer Buffer 211
Troubleshooting Printer Problems 212
Printer Preventive Maintenance 213
Chapter Summary 213
Review Questions 214

chapter eleven   **Installing and Using a Modem**   **216**
Chapter Objective 216
An Overview of Modem Communications 217
The Hayes Modem Standard 218
   How a "Smart" Modem Works 218
Modem Hardware Installation 219
   Internal Setup Switches 220
Configuring Communications Software
      for Data Transfers 222
Originating a Modem
      Communications Connection 223

Answering a Modem
    Communications Connection 227
Passing Data Down the Line 228
Communications Protocols 229
  Half-Duplex Communication Protocols 229
  Full-Duplex Communication Protocols 231
  Special Communications Protocols 231
  Protocols Without Error Detection 232
File Archiving 232
Communications Problems 233
  Modem Hardware Problems 233
  Modem Software Problems 233
  The Initializing String 234
  Other Important Configuration Items 234
  If All Else Fails 235
Computer Viruses 236
Chapter Summary 236
Review Questions 237

part four   **Troubleshooting Computer Software Problems**   **239**

chapter twelve   **Troubleshooting Computer Software Problems**   **241**
Chapter Objective 241
Some Necessary Definitions 241
  Program Files 241
  Data Files 242
Defining the Problem—Hardware or Software 243
Hardware Failures 243
  Power Supply Failures 243
  Hard Drive Failures 244
  Hard Disk Operating System Won't Boot 244
  Prevention of Data Loss 245
  Restoring Data to a New Hard Drive 245
  Hard Disk Data Recovery 246
Floppy Drive Failures 247
  Symptoms 247
  Prevention of Floppy Diskette Data Loss 248
Memory Failures 248
Software Failures 248
  Symptoms 248
  Old Software 249
  New Software 249
  Manual Software Installation 249
  Batch Files 249
Chapter Summary 250
Review Questions 250

appendix A   Microcomputer Interconnection Standards   252

appendix B   DOS Commands for the Technician   261

appendix C   An Explanation of the ASCII Chart   264

appendix D   Microcomputer Error Codes   268

appendix E   Standard Hard Drive Types   275

appendix F   Hard Drive Types by Manufacturer   278

appendix G   Hayes 2400 Modem Commands   287

appendix H   Epson Printer Control and Escape Sequences   290

appendix I   Standard RS-232C Explained   296

appendix J   Answers to Odd-Numbered Questions   304

Glossary   309

Index   326

Preface

This second edition of *Microcomputer Troubleshooting* has been renamed *Assembling and Troubleshooting Microcomputers*. It has been expanded to include most of the technical information needed by both the microcomputer technician and the serious computer operator.

New features of this edition include the following:

- Information needed to evaluate a customer's requirements for computer hardware, such as the right kind of monitor, keyboard, or input/output ports to recommend for a specific use
- An explanation of how to assemble a computer from modules, such as floppy diskette drives and controllers, multifunction cards, and add-on memory cards
- Detailed information on how to prepare a hard disk drive for use, including new terminology and how to perform a low-level format, the use of FDISK, and high-level formatting
- Explanations, where appropriate, of the differences between and advantages of the IBM® AT® computer compared with the PC® and XT® computers
- Suggestions and justifications for adding additional hardware to a working system, such as a joystick, additional memory, and a math coprocessor
- Explanations of the capacities and relative merits of the several different floppy diskette drives available today
- Explanations of the differences and relative merits of the various kinds of monitors
- Understanding, installing, and troubleshooting of modems and their communications problems
- Expanded software troubleshooting chapter, including suggestions for regaining lost data
- Appendices that contain useful information on repairing or building damaged or missing cables.

The emphasis in this edition has moved way from component-level troubleshooting toward board-level replacement. This is real-world economics, justified by the decreasing cost of hardware, including floppy diskette drives.

The operating system used in this book is MS-DOS™ version 3.3. Most of the information applies to versions as early as 3.0; DOS 4.0 is also mentioned where appropriate, particularly in regard to hard disk configuration. System boards with less than 128K of RAM may not work for many applications; thus, the "standard" 640K of RAM is assumed unless otherwise specified.

This text is intended for second-year electronics students and for those who, having the necessary background, wish to assemble, repair, or maintain microcomputers. It is assumed that the reader is familiar with basic and digital electronics. My books *Systematic Electronic Troubleshooting* and *Practical Electronic Troubleshooting* are recommended for those interested in more detailed information on troubleshooting to the component level.

The block and schematic diagrams in this book are representative of microcomputers. These diagrams may not be accurate for all computers: The service and maintenance manuals for the computer under repair are the final authority.

This book is generic in its approach and is not equipment specific. It is, however, intended to give information for IBM-compatible computers only, not for Apple, Commodore, Atari, or other "non-compatible" computers.

James Perozzo

Acknowledgments

A special thanks is extended to John Curran, Spokane Community College, for his early, valuable input on text improvements. Thanks also to those who have encouraged me throughout my writing efforts, particularly my wife Sandi, and my friends Robert Dudley, David Malland, and Bud Abbey, photographer for most of the photographs in this text.

Len Boscarine, Al Pierce, and Gary Davidson of Mannesmann Tally, printer manufacturers, provided valuable information on state-of-the-art printers. Logical Micros, Albany, NY provided their equipment and expertise for many of the photographs.

The following reviewers provided valuable feedback during the development of this book: Ray Dong—Foothill College, Ronald DeBoy—St. Petersburg Vocational Technical Institute, Thomas W. Gerwatowski—N.E.C. Livonia, John Hamilton—National Education Centers, Tim Goulden—Southwest Technical College, Don Forbes—National Education Center, Westwood Campus, Willard Waters—RETS Electronic Institute, George Sappington—formerly of Lyons Institute, John Amico—Renton Vocational-Technical Institute, Daniel Moore—North Carolina State University, Reddy Talusani—Houston Community College, Ralph Masciulli—Franklin Institute of Boston, James King—Joliet Junior College, Glenn Buck—Pitt Community College, Edward Hartwick—Johnson City Community College.

About the Author

James Perozzo has over 30 years' experience repairing electronic equipment of many different types. After 20 years' service as a technician and officer in the Coast Guard, he broadened his experience by working in marine and aviation electronics, microwave voice carriers, and computer repair. A native of the Pacific Northwest, his qualifications include an FCC General Radiotelephone Certificate, Amateur Extra Class License, FAA Avionics Certification, and an Electronics Teaching Certificate. He currently teaches computer repair and robotics at Renton Vocational-Technical Institute in Renton, Washington. He has also written *Practical Electronics Troubleshooting*, (Delmar), 1985, and *Systematic Electronic Troubleshooting*, (Delmar), 1989.

part one

An Overview of Computers

chapter one

How Microcomputers Work and What They Can Do

CHAPTER OBJECTIVE

HOW MICROCOMPUTERS WORK AND WHAT THEY CAN DO gives the technician background information on the uses for and the capabilities of a microcomputer. Comparisons with game computers and mini- and mainframe computers put the microcomputer into proper perspective. A brief description of the major kinds of software that are used on microcomputers gives the technician a working knowledge of the purposes of each.

WHAT IS A MICROCOMPUTER?

All computers operate in basically the same way, regardless of size, although the capability and speed of operation of the computer generally improve as the cost of the system increases (see Figure 1.1). Game computers

Figure 1.1 Even a small computer can be capable of printing and other basic computer tasks. (Abbey Enterprises)

costing less than a hundred dollars can process a limited amount of information and output it to a printer. A microcomputer, on the other hand, is a computer system designed to meet the needs of the professional who uses one at home or at the office, the small business operator, and the serious computer hobbyist. The microcomputer is often used to type reports and letters using word processing software, to manipulate complex figures involving many variables using electronic spreadsheet software, and to keep track of multiple records using data base management software. Although the microcomputer can certainly be used to play games, this is not its primary purpose.

The tremendous popularity of microcomputers has led to the standardization of several interface connections such as driving signals and plugs for disk drives and plug-in cards, and standardized keyboards and monitors that are interchangeable between computers of different manufacture. This is a big advantage to the servicing technician because a single item such as an option card or monitor can often be used as a spare for several different makes of computer. The usual configuration of a microcomputer system is shown in block diagram form in Figure 1.2 and in a photo in Figure 1.3.

Microcomputers, the subject of this book, lie somewhere between the small computers shown in Figure 1.1 and the large mainframe computers used by large corporations (Figure 1.4). Mainframe computers have much more extensive data storage capability than microcomputers do. They also usually have more RAM memory and are able to service inputs from many operators at essentially the same time.

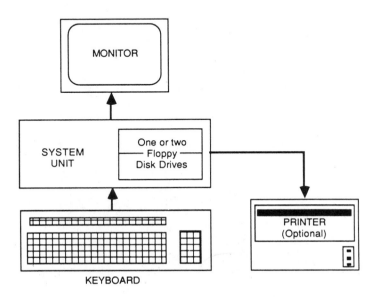

Figure 1.2 Block diagram of a typical microcomputer installation.

Knowledge of the details of microcomputer operation will enable you to understand the operation of complex computers more easily. The trouble-shooting techniques presented in this book, with appropriate modification, can be used to service any computer system. This book assumes the use of the very popular MS-DOS™ operating system for the operation of the microcomputer. With appropriate modifications of the commands, troubleshooting procedures can be translated into commands for other operating systems, such as CP/M™.

Figure 1.3 A typical microcomputer installation, representative of the kind of computer to be covered in detail in this text. (Tom Carney)

Figure 1.4 The mainframe computer processes information at a high rate of speed and can service the needs of many operators working at separate terminals. (Courtesy of IBM)

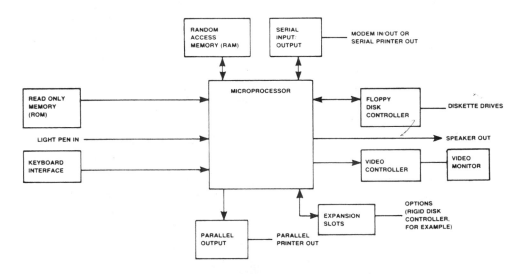

Figure 1.5 Basic block diagram of the internal circuitry of a microcomputer. (Courtesy of Corona Data Systems)

A personal computer (PC) is, generically speaking, a basic microcomputer with two disk drives. Although a PC could be operated with a single diskette drive, a diskette-based computer needs two drives for convenience. Operations such as file transfers from one diskette to another and whole-disk copying are much more easily accomplished if two drives are available. Earlier PC system boards, internal to the computer, often had only five expansion slots for adding optional plug-in cards.

An XT computer, on the other hand, is understood to have at least one diskette drive and a hard disk. With the hard disk, there is no compelling reason for also having two diskette drives, other than the conveniences previously mentioned. An XT with two drives is a very definite convenience, a configuration desired by anyone who uses computers to any great extent. A computer with a hard disk and two diskette drives can be thought of as a "standard" computer configuration. These newer computers usually have eight expansion slots.

An AT computer is a later generation computer that uses a newer, higher speed central processing unit (CPU), the 80286. The AT runs programs faster and has some sophisticated features not available in a PC or XT computer. The AT requires a special keyboard and special adapter cards for the floppy disk and hard disks, but the rest of the hardware is the same as a PC or XT.

THE NORMAL OPERATION OF A MICROCOMPUTER

Most computer repair jobs require a certain minimum knowledge to effectively localize the problem. The block diagram in Figure 1.5 presents graphically the internal workings of the computer.

When a computer is first turned on, it executes a program found in the computer's read-only memory (ROM) chip, seen in Figure 1.6. This ROM program provides the following functions, shown in Figure 1.7:

Figure 1.6 The ROM chip that contains the program to get the computer started. (Abbey Enterprises)

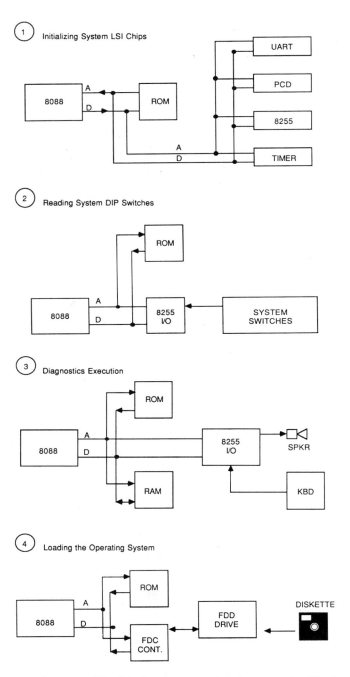

Figure 1.7 Steps usually accomplished during power-up of a microcomputer. (Stephanie Enterprises)

1. Initializing the large-scale integration (LSI) chips used in the system such as the 8255 peripheral input/output (PIO) chip and the 8253 timer chip, which is necessary to set them up for later use. For example, the 8255 PIO chip is initialized for appropriate directions of data flow—in on some pins, out on others.

2. A PC or XT computer then reads the system peripheral switches and puts this information into random access memory (RAM) where it is readily available to the computer. An AT computer is different in that the RAM on the system board is used to store configuration information. This special block of RAM is provided with a battery so that it retains information when the main power is turned off. This step lets the computer know what resources are accessible, such as the kind of monitor (color or monochrome) that is connected and the number and kind of disk drives that are installed.

3. The power-on diagnostics then tests up to 14 items, among them checks of the CPU, ROM, RAM, video display card, keyboard, and floppy disk drive system.

    Errors detected during this phase of the operation may result in an *error code* being displayed on the monitor. This code is a great help to the servicing technician. See Appendix D for a listing of the errors that might occur.

4. Normal execution of this part of the ROM diagnostic program results in the *no-error signal* of a single beep from the computer and an attempt to load the operating system from the A diskette drive. The LED on the A drive should come on at this time. If there is a diskette in the A drive with the proper operating system files, the operating system is loaded into memory.

5. If the diskette in the A drive does not have the operating system files, an error message indicates that there is a "boot failure" and the computer will stop. Some ROM software allows the insertion of the proper diskette and a single keystroke to load the operating system at this point, while other ROM software requires the computer to be rebooted before it will again attempt to read the operating system files on the A drive.

6. If a hard disk is present, the computer first attempts to load the operating system from the A drive as described. It then gives up and accesses the hard disk for the same files. If they are found, the computer loads the operating system and the computer is ready to go, showing the normal DOS prompt. If the hard disk drive does not have the operating system in the proper place, the error code will show as previously described.

Some IBM machines have the BASIC programming language built into their ROM. If one of these machines cannot boot up on the floppy diskette or the hard disk drive, it will come up with the BASIC prompt of "Ok."

THE OPERATING SYSTEM

Although not necessary for some computer games, the operating system is necessary to provide the basis for most applications programs such as word processors and data base programs. The operating system enables the CPU to pass information between the disk drives and the rest of the computer system in a standard manner that other programs can use efficiently. Part of this operating system, the BIOS, establishes the means of passing data among the keyboard, the printer, the monitor screen, and the serial communications port. Another part of the operating system, the DOS portion, provides the software necessary to read and write information to the disk drives. Different operating systems are available for microcomputers, notably Microsoft MS-DOS and CP/M from Digital Research. The details of ROM programming may be available in assembly language format in the computer instruction book.

After the operating system has been loaded into RAM, the CPU begins execution of that program directly from RAM. When the computer is then ready for keyboard input, it exhibits on the monitor the DOS prompt, the letter A followed by a "greater than" math symbol, the " > ". This prompt shows which disk drive is the default drive and also signifies that the computer is operating at the DOS level. (Programs other than DOS use different prompts such as a dash [-] or an asterisk [*]).

At this point, the computer may be used for such housekeeping tasks as looking at the directory of a diskette, changing the name of a file on a diskette, copying or erasing files, and the like. This is also the point at which more advanced programs such as word processing or data management programs may be loaded into the computer.

A problem occurring *prior to* reaching the DOS prompt means that the technician will initially rely on the numerical error codes and audio cues provided by the ROM diagnostics to localize a problem in the computer. If, however, a problem appears only *after* the computer reaches the DOS prompt, the diagnostics diskette becomes the primary troubleshooting tool.

WHAT A MICROCOMPUTER CAN DO

Microcomputers have enjoyed phenomenal acceptance in our society. They are rapidly becoming as commonplace as automobiles. This popularity is due mostly to the reprogrammability of the microcomputer: It can be used for many different purposes simply by loading a different program into the memory, where it is then executed.

There are an almost unlimited number of uses for the computer. The following are some of the more common uses for the microcomputer in business and the home.

Word Processing Programs

Anyone who has typed a letter several times in an attempt to eliminate errors or change awkward wording will appreciate the fantastic ease with which a letter can be **edited**, or changed, with a word processor after having been typed into the computer. Diskettes are beginning to replace the filing cabinet for document storage. Add to this the ability to type multiple copies with a few keystrokes. Then consider how some word processors check for correct spelling. Some word processors have the full capability of a thesaurus to help those needing a better word than the one that first comes to mind. Some word processors even make it possible to put drawings into a document and will keep track of tables of contents, footnotes, etc. The end result is a very powerful tool for producing, editing, duplicating, and otherwise efficiently managing text. Comparing a sophisticated word processor to a typewriter is much like comparing a Cadillac to a skateboard! See Figure 1.8 for a typical sheet of word processor output.

```
              THE TELEGRAPH - "AN EXPEDITIOUS METHOD
                   OF CONVEYING INTELLIGENCE"
                         Speech Outline

   I.  INTRODUCTION

  II.  EARLY ATTEMPTS

       A. The first written record suggesting the use of electricity as a means
of communication

       B. When the word "telegraph" was first used

       C. Static (Frictional) Telegraphs
          1. Ronald's Telegraph
          2. Dyar's Telegraph

       D. The Galvanic Telegraph
          1. Cooke's Chronometric System

 III.  THE ELECTROMAGNETIC TELEGRAPH

  IV.  SAMUEL FINLEY BREEZE MORSE

   V.  MORSE AND ALFRED VAIL

  VI.  CONCLUSION

       A. From Simplex to Duplex
^Z
```

Figure 1.8 A typical sheet of word processor output. (Courtesy of Karen Braunstein and Ann Woods, RVTI)

Data Base Programs

Keeping track of many related items is the job of the data base program. In its most basic form, the data base manipulates many individual records. Each record within the data base can be quickly sorted, chosen by one or more fields, or selected by greater-than or less-than criteria. For instance, an inventory of electronic parts can be sorted so that they are printed out in alphabetical order by name or by part number; parts can be printed out according to a particular range of dates when they were ordered; or they might be printed out only if they cost more or less than a specified price. Data bases are used extensively for inventory control and data collation. See Figure 1.9 for a typical data base printout.

Spreadsheet Programs

The spreadsheet is used to solve "what-if" problems, which are often encountered in financial situations. Information is entered into the program in the row-and-column format of an account's bookkeeping system. For example, the months of the year might be listed along the top of the spreadsheet, with individual accounts listed along the left margin of the form. Each intersecting cell could then be used to hold data about that particular account in any given month. Totals can then be automatically calculated at the right side of the sheet, with a grand total at the bottom of the right column. The real advantage of this format when used with a computer is that, should any of the values in any of the cells change, the totals can "instantly" and automatically change. See Figure 1.10 for a typical spreadsheet printout.

Page No.   1
03/04/90

MY ADDRESS FILE

NAME	ADDRESS	CITY-STATE	PHONE
VICKI	123 MAIN STREET	SEATTLE WA	345-6789
JOE	67 ELM STREET	SEATTLE WA	543-2345
MARY	752 245th STREET	RENTON WA	782-9945
LYLE	8345 OSCAR BLVD	SEATTLE WA	432-2331
GEORGE	2341 LAKEVIEW WAY	SEATTLE WA	432-7865
KAREN	654 112TH AVE	TACOMA WA	345-6221
DEBBIE	12 VIEWRIDGE DRIVE	SEATTLE WA	989-7762
TIMOTHY	9876 BIRCH DRIVE	SEATTLE WA	543-3443

Figure 1.9 A typical data base printout.

ATTENDANCE RECORD - SEPTEMBER, 1988

Student Name		1	2	3	4	5	6	7	8	9	10	11	12	13	14	15	16	17	18	19	20	21	22	23	24	25	26	27	28	29	30	31
Kaiser, Deborah	Reg. Hrs.						6	6	6	6		6	6	6	6	6	6			6	6	6	6	6			6	6	6	6	6	
	M/U Hrs.																																
	Coop.Hrs.						6	6	6	6		6	6	6	6	6	6			6	6	6	6	6			6	6	6	6	6	
Kaiser, Roger	Reg. Hrs.																															
	M/U Hrs.																																
	Coop.Hrs.						6	6	6	6		6	6	6	6	6	6			6	6	6	6	6			6	6	6	6	6	
Martinez, Ken	Reg. Hrs.																															
	M/U Hrs.						6	6	6	6		6	6	6	6	6	6			6	6	6	6	6			6	6	6	6	6	
	Coop.Hrs.																																
McCashland, Wa_	Reg. Hrs.						6	6	6	6		6	6	6	6	6	6			6	6	6	6	6			6	6	6	6	6	
	M/U Hrs.																																
	Coop.Hrs.						6	6	6	6		6	6	6	6	6	6			6	6	6	6	6			6	6	6	6	6	
Monk, Vicki	Reg. Hrs.																															
	M/U Hrs.																																
	Coop.Hrs.																							6									
Paynter, Jon	Reg. Hrs.						6	6	6	6		6	6	6	6	6	6		6	6	6	6	6	6			6	6	6	6	6	
	M/U Hrs.																																
	Coop.Hrs.																																
Petrin, Tom	Reg. Hrs.						6	4	6			6					6							4								
	M/U Hrs.																																
	Coop.Hrs.																																
Post, Jade	Reg. Hrs.						6	6	6	6		6	6	6	6	6	6			6	6	6	6	6			6	6	6	6	6	
	M/U Hrs.																																
	Coop.Hrs.																																
Rosenborg, Karl	Reg. Hrs.							6	6	6		6	6	6	6	6	6			6	6	6	6	6			6	6	6	6	6	
	M/U Hrs.																																
	Coop.Hrs.																																
Sasal, Marilyn	Reg. Hrs.							6	6	6		6	6	6	6	6	6			6	6	6	6	6			6	6	6	6	6	
	M/U Hrs.																																
	Coop.Hrs.																																
Sparks, Steven	Reg. Hrs.							6	6	6		6	6	6	6	6	6			6	6	6	6	6			6	6	6	6	6	
	M/U Hrs.																																
	Coop.Hrs.																																
Vines, Bernadette	Reg. Hrs.							6	6	6		6	6	6	6	6	6			6	6	6	6	6			6	6	6	6	6	
	M/U Hrs.																																
	Coop.Hrs.																																
Walter, David	Reg. Hrs.						6	6	6	6		6	6	6	6	6	6			6	6	6	6	6			6	6	6	6	6	
	M/U Hrs.																																
	Coop.Hrs.																																

Figure 1.10 A typical spreadsheet printout. (Courtesy of Pends)

Computer-Aided Drafting Programs

Mechanical drawings originally done by hand on paper are becoming obsolete. The principal reason for this is that editing of a hand drawing necessitates either erasures or complete redrawing, both of which are time-consuming and less than desirable. While drawing with a computer-aided drafting (CAD) program may only be approximately as fast as drawing by hand, the precision of a computer-generated drawing can be simply flawless. A very big advantage to doing a drawing this way is that many copies can be made, each of which is an original. No blueprints are necessary. Advanced programs can also quickly and painlessly compute area, perimeter, and dimensions with surprising speed and accuracy. See Figure 1.11 for a typical CAD drawing.

Communications Programs

While not astounding in itself, communications software opens new possibilities for our digital age. With a modem and the gargantuan worldwide telephone network, information of many different kinds can be sent quickly over any distance. A letter can, of course, be sent between modems from coast to coast in a matter of seconds. A mechanical drawing can be sent just as easily. Large volumes of material can be sent using the telephone during the night, when rates are lowest, if a computer is left on and is receptive. A computer can be programmed to allow access only to selected persons. With the proper code, an incoming call can be answered, the caller identified, and, if appropriate, the caller can then have access to any of the files available to the computer. This is a very real advantage to the businessperson on the road, because data in the computer at the home office can be accessed. Information can also be sent from a small laptop computer in a motel room back to the home office for immediate processing.

Small Utility Programs

There are a great number of programs available to solve specific problems. Some examples are as follows:

Programs that enable a teacher to easily keep track of student grades or to make the computer generate test questions

Programs to make the computer a super calculator for financial analysts, mathematicians, statisticians, and computer programmers, each of whom uses a different type of calculator

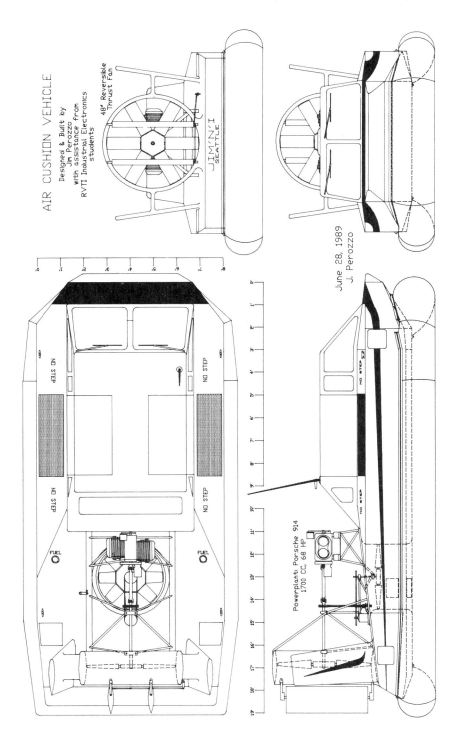

AIR CUSHION VEHICLE

Designed & Built by
Jim Perozzo
with assistance from
RVTI Industrial Electronics
students

48" Reversible
Thrust Fan

JIM'N'I
SEATTLE

June 28, 1989
J. Perozzo

Powerplant: Porsche 914
1700 CC, 68 HP

Figure 1.11 A typical CAD drawing.

Programs to take care of the details of running a "computer desk," a program that makes instantly available a notebook, clock, daily schedule, addresses, and telephone numbers. These programs can often even dial your number for you, if you have a modem

Programs to help you learn just about any topic, including tutorials for applications programs, such as word processors and data base programs, and for things like spelling and grammar in foreign languages.

These are only a few examples of the thousands of practical, useful programs available.

Writing Your Own Programs

If you have a unique need and a computer to accomplish the task, you can instruct the computer to solve the problem. This is a particularly appealing solution if there is a great deal of recalculating to be done. You could, for instance, program a computer to figure the exact amount of your house payment for each month until your contract is finished, a listing for many years. For each payment, you could have a listing of the principal, interest, remaining payment, and the date of each payment all calculated and printed out.

The computer must be told exactly, down to the very finest detail, just how to accomplish any given task. It does not think for itself in the slightest. Even a misplaced or missing comma or period can make a program totally useless. To do this programming, you have the choice of many different programming languages. The following is a very brief summary of some of them and their uses.

Assembly Language. A difficult language to learn, assembly is used mostly by professional programmers for use internal to microcomputers, for routines that are used often and that must run as quickly as possible. The strength of assembly language is its great speed of execution. See Figure 1-12 for a typical sheet of assembly language programming.

BASIC. One of the oldest computer languages, this is probably the easiest language to learn. Its instructions are somewhat evident, even to the first-time user. Although BASIC usually runs fairly slowly, there are tricks that can be used to speed up its operation. Programs are very easily written and **debugged** using BASIC. See Figure 1.13 for a typical sheet of BASIC programming.

"C". This language is very portable; a program written in this language can be

```
;Code sample courtesy Arthur Thompson
              Assume       CS:CODE_HERE
CODE_HERE   SEGMENT

START:        WAIT          ;WAIT WHEN TEST LINE LOW
                            ;SO THAT YOU CAN CHECK ADDRESS
                            ;LINES. (REQUIRES TEST E.T.)
              MOV AX, 0h    ;SET RAM AS DATA SEGMENT
              MOV DS,AX
              MOV SS, AX
              MOV SP, Ram1_top ;SET STACK TO TOP OF FIRST 2K

;INITIALIZE 8251 SERIAL PORT

              OUT Ser_control,AL ;SEND THREE 0'S TO ENSURE
              OUT Ser_control,AL ;8251 CAN RESET TO MODE
              OUT Ser_control,AL
              MOV CX, 4
DELAY0:            LOOP DELAY0
              MOV AL,01000000b    ;RESET 8251 TO MODE SET
              OUT Ser_control,AL
              MOV CX, 4           ;SET DELAY COUNT TO 4
DELAY1:           LOOP DELAY1     ;DELAY 4 INSTRUCTION CYCLES
              MOV AL, Serial_mode ;SEND SERIAL MODE TO COMMAND
              OUT Ser_control, AL ;PORT
              MOV CX, 4
DELAY2:           LOOP DELAY2
              MOV AL, Xceiv_command    ;SEND COMMAND BYTE TO 8251
              OUT Ser_control, AL
              MOV CX, 4
DELAY3:           LOOP DELAY3

;Set up interrupt vector table for NMI to address 0:400h

              MOV BX, 08h  ;SET OFFSET OF RAM TO
                           ;BEGINNING OF VECTOR TABLE
              MOV [BX], BYTE PTR 00     ;INPUT IP (LOW BYTE FIRST)
              INC BX
              MOV [BX], BYTE PTR 00
              INC BX
              MOV [BX], BYTE PTR 40h    ;INPUT CS (LOW BYTE FIRST)
              INC BX
              MOV [BX], BYTE PTR 00h
              MOV BX, 0400h    ;SET BX TO STARTING ADDRESS

;Poll RxREADY to determine when to INPUT CHARACTERS

PRESET:           MOV CX, 05h  ;SET COUNTER FOR 5 NOP SEARCH
BEGIN:        CALL POLL
              CALL GETCHAR    ;GET CHARACTER FOR MESSAGE
```

Figure 1.12 A typical sheet of microcomputer assembly language programming. (Courtesy of Arthur Thompson, RVTI)

easily made to run on unrelated computers. For instance, a "C" language program can be written on a PC, then taken to a VAX computer and run there. Only minor changes are necessary for the change of hardware. The "C" language is more difficult to learn than BASIC, but it is more powerful—you can do more hardware manipulation with it—and it can even be used with embedded

```
130 PRINT "For your information, the pressurized area of your ACV equals";INS;" square
inches or";FT;"square feet."
140 PRINT
150 INPUT "What is the estimated empty weight of your finished craft, with fuel?";W1
160 INPUT "What is the weight of ALL passengers and baggage?";W2
170 WT=W1+W2
180 PRINT "Total weight is calculated at ";WT;" pounds."
190 PRINT
200 PRINT
210 PRES=WT/INS
220 PRINT "This will require a cushion pressure of at least";PRES;" PSI."
230 PRINT
240 PRINT
250 PRINT "Now let's consider the LIFT FAN first:"
260 PRINT
270 INPUT "What lift fan diameter did you have in mind? (In INCHES)";LD
280 PRINT
290 REM: Calculate Fan Area
300 A1=3.14*LD/24*LD/24
310 REM: Calculate Power Loading
320 T1=A1*PRES*144
330 TBL=35*(1/SQR(PRES*144))
340 HP1=T1/TBL
350 PRINT "At least";HP1;" horsepower will be necessary to lift this load."
360 PRINT
370 REM: Calculate Total Fan Thrust
380 PL1=HP1/A1
390 REM: Calculate
400 TF1=T1/HP1
410 REM: Calculate Disk Loading
420 DL1=PRES*144
430 PRINT
440 PRINT
450 PRINT "The following data for the lift fan may be of interest to you:"
460 PRINT
470 PRINT
480 PRINT ;"POWER LOADING";,,"THRUST FACTOR";,,"DISK LOADING"
490 PRINT " ";PL1;," ";TF1;," ";DL1
500 PRINT "Horsepower/Sq. Ft.","Pounds Thrust/Horsepower","Thrust/Sq. Ft."
510 PRINT
520 PRINT
530 INPUT"If you would like to re-calculate the lift fan, enter Y.";LFT$
540 IF LFT$="Y" THEN 260 ELSE 550
550 CLS
```

Figure 1.13 A typical sheet of BASIC programming.

modules of assembly language code for enhancement of the overall speed of execution. See Figure 1.14 for a typical sheet of "C" programming.

FORTRAN. This language was originally developed to assist scientists with their number-crunching—the processing of great quantities of numbers and involved calculations. The average microcomputer user probably does not use this

```
*/
        printf("Please enter a small positive number, less than \n");
        printf("20, or else the first lines of output will scroll\n");
        printf("off the screen.\n");
/*
        Accept user input
        *****************
*/
        scanf("%d",&number_input);
/*
        Print message
        *************
*/
        printf("Here is the Fibonacci Sequence in\n");
        printf("%d",number_input);
        printf(" numbers:\n");

        while (number_input > 0)


/*      Start of loop
        ************
*/

        {
        printf("\t%d\n",fib_number);
        fib_number = first_number + second_number;
        second_number = first_number;
        first_number = fib_number;
        number_input--;
        }
/*      End of loop
        **********
*/
```

Figure 1.14 A typical sheet of "C" programming. (Courtesy of Karen Braunstein and Ann Woods, RVTI)

```
        PROGRAM CALCST

C       Program written by Ann Woods
C       April 11, 1990

C       This is a simple fortran program that reads the sale price in data
C       statements contained in an external JCL program.  This program adds
C       sales tax to price and writes the cost on a printed report.

   .    REAL PRICE, TAX, COST
   10     READ (5,1000,END=500) PRICE
          TAX = .06 * PRICE
          COST = PRICE + TAX
          WRITE (6,2000) COST
          GO TO 10
   500  STOP
   1000 FORMAT (F7.2)
   2000 FORMAT (' ',"Cost is $",F10.2)

        END
```

Figure 1.15 A typical sheet of FORTRAN programming. (Courtesy of Karen Braunstein and Ann Woods, RVTI)

language often, but it is available if needed. See Figure 1.15 for a typical sheet of FORTRAN programming.

COBOL. This language was developed to meet the needs of business and industry. Calculations and data base management are the main features of this language. Such abilities are needed to meet the requirements of inventory control and personnel and payroll management. See Figure 1.16 for a typical sheet of COBOL programming.

CHAPTER SUMMARY

HOW MICROCOMPUTERS WORK AND WHAT THEY CAN DO shows that the microcomputer is an extremely versatile tool for the professional in almost any field. It can be used to write text, produce drawings, keep track of multitudes of numerical and text information, and manipulate numbers with extreme precision. With the proper training and practice, one can custom program the microcomputer to perform any task within its capabilities by using one or more of the many different computer programming languages available.

```
/
PROCEDURE DIVISION.

A000-CREATE-WEEKLY-SALES-REPT.

    ACCEPT CURRENT-DATE FROM DATE.
    MOVE CORR CURRENT-DATE TO HEADING-DATE.

    OPEN INPUT  TRANSACTION-INPUT-FILE
         OUTPUT GUYS-REPORT-FILE
                GALS-REPORT-FILE.

    READ TRANSACTION-INPUT-FILE INTO TRANSACTION-INPUT-AREA
         AT END
             MOVE "NO " TO ARE-THERE-MORE-RECORDS.
    PERFORM UNTIL THERE-ARE-NO-MORE-RECORDS
      IF VALID-GENDER
        IF STUDENT-GENDER = "F"
          MOVE CORR TRANSACTION-INPUT-AREA TO
              GALS-REPORT-OUTPUT-AREA
          IF LINES-PRINTED IS EQUAL TO PAGE-SIZE OR > PAGE-SIZE
            MOVE FEMALE-CONSTANT TO GENDER-CONSTANT
            MOVE PAGES TO HEADING-PAGE-NO
            WRITE GALS-REPORT-LINE FROM FIRST-HEADING-LINE
                AFTER ADVANCING PAGE
            MOVE SPACES TO GALS-REPORT-LINE
            ADD 1 TO PAGES
            MOVE DOUBLE-SPACING TO PROPER-SPACING
            MOVE ZERO TO LINES-PRINTED
          END-IF
          MOVE SPACES TO GALS-REPORT-LINE
          WRITE GALS-REPORT-LINE FROM GALS-REPORT-OUTPUT-AREA
          MOVE SPACES TO GALS-REPORT-OUTPUT-AREA
        ELSE
          MOVE CORR TRANSACTION-INPUT-AREA TO
              GUYS-REPORT-OUTPUT-AREA
          IF LINES-PRINTED IS EQUAL TO PAGE-SIZE OR > PAGE-SIZE
            MOVE MALE-CONSTANT TO GENDER-CONSTANT
            MOVE PAGES TO HEADING-PAGE-NO
            WRITE GUYS-REPORT-LINE FROM FIRST-HEADING-LINE
                AFTER ADVANCING PAGE
            ADD 1 TO PAGES
            MOVE DOUBLE-SPACING TO PROPER-SPACING
            MOVE ZERO TO LINES-PRINTED
          END-IF
          MOVE SPACES TO GUYS-REPORT-LINE
          WRITE GUYS-REPORT-LINE FROM GUYS-REPORT-OUTPUT-AREA
          MOVE SPACES TO GUYS-REPORT-OUTPUT-AREA
        END-IF
      END-IF
      READ TRANSACTION-INPUT-FILE INTO TRANSACTION-INPUT-AREA
          AT END
              MOVE "NO " TO ARE-THERE-MORE-RECORDS
      END-READ
    END-PERFORM.
    CLOSE TRANSACTION-INPUT-FILE
          GUYS-REPORT-FILE
          GALS-REPORT-FILE.
```

Figure 1.16 A typical sheet of COBOL programming. (Courtesy of Karen Braunstein, Penelope McCashland and Ann Woods, RVTI)

REVIEW QUESTIONS

1. Where is the first program that a microcomputer executes stored?
2. What is the configuration of a PC, as generally understood?
3. What is the configuration of an XT?
4. How is a PC or XT programmed for the kinds of peripherals installed?
5. How is an AT microcomputer programmed for the kinds of peripherals installed?
6. What is the no-error audible signal that a microcomputer sounds when the internal diagnostics are completed successfully?
7. If diskette drives and a hard disk are both installed, from where will the computer attempt to "boot up"?
8. Programs are actually executed from what part of the computer?
9. When is the operating system of a microcomputer used?
10. Name three kinds of generic applications programs.
11. What computer programming language is the fastest in execution?
12. What is the most portable programming language?

part two

When a Problem Develops in a Working Microcomputer

chapter two

A Computer Problem or Not?

CHAPTER OBJECTIVE

A COMPUTER PROBLEM OR NOT? helps the technician eliminate the possibility of problems with a computer that are not located within the computer at all. External power problems, operator errors, and errors caused by faulty diskettes are discussed. Hardware problems such as memory errors and hard disk failures are also covered. The use of diagnostic software is introduced.

OPERATOR PROBLEMS

Many computer problems are nothing more than human error. The operator may not be striking the right keys to make the computer operate properly, may have expectations that are not realistic, may not have the software set up properly for the computer's hardware, or may have software settings within the program that are not correct.

One of the simplest examples involves a keyboarding error. The program will refuse to load if the program called

COMPUT-0.EXE

is invoked by the command

COMPUT-O

It is not the omission of the file extension (.EXE) that causes the program load failure, but rather using an "O" instead of the proper "zero" in the file name.

Unrealistic expectations are the problem if the operator expects a printer to type italics just because that is what the word processing document calls for. The printer may not be capable of printing italics in the first place.

Improper setup of software is a frequent problem that the technician is called upon to correct. This kind of problem can be very frustrating for both the operator and the technician. A technician may not be familiar with the specific program being used, yet may be asked to help configure that software. A typical example of this kind of problem is when a word processor program does not print to a newly arrived printer. This kind of problem is very similar to the following type of problem.

Incorrect software setting can cause some strange results. A word processor also provides a good example of this kind of problem. If the document on the screen looks just fine with a "ragged right" edge, yet the printer tries to make the right margin of the document a straight line, the printed document may be very different from that on the computer monitor. The difference? The word processing software is set for RIGHT JUSTIFICATION. The operator may not be aware of this as a software option that must be changed.

Operator problems can be solved by familiarity with the software being used and/or a great deal of study of the documentation that comes with the software program.

EXTERNAL POWER PROBLEMS

Computer malfunctions may be the result of power problems. Power is usually supplied to microcomputers by 120VAC power mains—a wall outlet— by no means a 100% reliable source. Computers require constant power to avoid the malfunction called a *computer crash*. Some computers are more tolerant than others with regard to short power interruptions because they have large capacitors in the power supply. Large filter capacitors can store enough energy to ride through the missing cycles of input AC power (see Figure 2.1).

Such power interruptions, if long enough, are detectable by the computer operator, who may report, "The lights blink and then the computer keyboard locks." Longer power interruptions are obvious, since the lights in the working area usually go out for some time. There can also be a power interruption in the computer supply line and not in the power lines supplying lighting. In this case, the computer screen may go dark for a moment, or it may blink off and then bloom momentarily when the power comes back on again. At the other extreme, a power interruption may be so short that the operator is not aware of the outage and knows only that the computer has ceased to function properly. At any rate, the interruption of input power is a major concern for computer operators.

The ultimate cure for power problems is to provide a backup battery power source. The computer operates on a battery supply during periods of

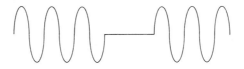

Figure 2.1 Short-term power shortages of a few cycles may or may not affect the computer, depending on their duration and the capacity of the computer's power supply filters.

low or no AC from the power lines. In normal operation, the battery is charged continuously from the power line (Figure 2.2). Another way of accomplishing the same result is to trickle-charge the battery at a low rate sufficient to maintain a full charge without any load on the batteries. An alternate path for power to operate the computer is provided through the contacts of a fast-acting switching arrangement such as a special relay. When the power line input drops to an unacceptable level, the power source for the computer immediately switches to the battery circuit for continued operation. The switching time should be less than the period of a 60-Hz cycle, or 16.6 milliseconds. Typical switching times are from 6 to 12 milliseconds. Figure 2.3 is a block diagram of this type of backup power supply.

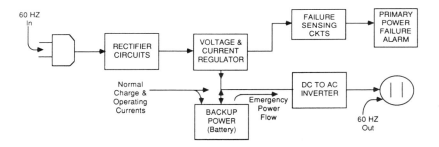

Figure 2.2 This type of battery backup system provides a no-break power capability.

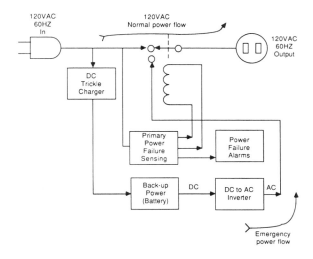

Figure 2.3 This type of power supply trickle-charges the battery and switches rapidly to use the battery power if the 120V lines fail. The switching time from 120V to the battery power must be very short to avoid disturbing the computer.

If for any reason the AC lines should fail to provide acceptable power, an alarm sounds to alert the operator, whose proper response is to immediately put whatever data is in the computer's RAM onto storage media such as diskettes. As much as 15 minutes or more of operation may be available to accomplish this, depending on the power requirements of the computer and the amount of energy stored in the batteries (Figure 2.4).

Another common power line problem is a temporary increase of line voltage, called a *voltage transient*. This is caused by other loads on the line such as heavy loads being connected, electric motors starting up, or lightning strik-

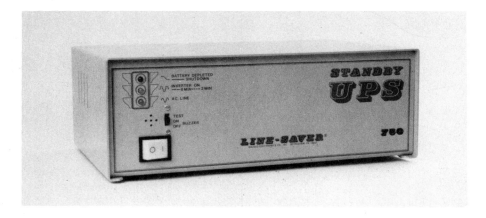

Figure 2.4 A commercial battery backup power supply for computer use. (Courtesy of Kalglo Electronics Company)

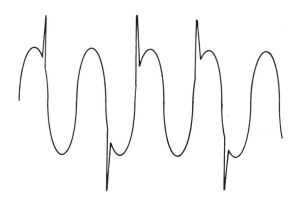

Figure 2.5 Voltage transients on the incoming 120VAC power lines can be very damaging to computers.

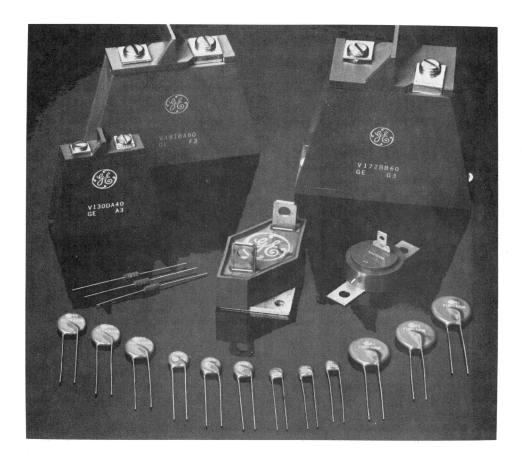

Figure 2.6 Commercial power line voltage spike suppressors often use MOVs to clip voltage transients to safe levels. (Photo reprinted with permission of GE Semiconductors, General Electric Company)

ing power lines in the vicinity (see Figure 2.5). These transients (also called *spikes*) can be especially damaging to electronic equipment. While a momentary loss of power may only cause a computer to crash, an overvoltage situation can cause overstressing of the power supply components, stressing of the chips within the computer, and in severe cases, damage that must be corrected by a technician.

An economical method of providing transient overvoltage protection is to use a special outlet attachment that has internal components designed to absorb supply line overvoltages. The component that does the actual work is a metal oxide varistor (MOV) (see Figure 2.6). The MOV is connected directly

Figure 2.7 A commercial unit that moves MOVs to protect a computer against line voltage transients. (Courtesy of Kalglo Electronics Company)

across the AC supply line. With normal voltages, the MOV is effectively an open circuit. If the supply voltage exceeds normal levels, the MOV will immediately conduct heavily, loading the power line severely, thus protecting the computer from the surge (Figure 2.7). Varistors have power limitations, however, and a sustained overvoltage condition can cause them to fail by opening, thus no longer providing protection.

Typical equipment failures that may point to possible transient damage include shorted rectifier diodes and bridges. Most well-designed equipment operated from 120 or 240VAC lines includes some form of transient suppression. These suppression components should be tested for proper operation if other semiconductors may have been damaged by transients, as the suppressors may be open or otherwise not performing their intended function. See Figure 2.8.

Installation of a battery backup unit is simple. The backup unit plugs into the wall, and the computer then plugs into it rather than the wall socket. Be sure to maintain the battery within the backup unit exactly according to the manufacturers' instructions! It would be a pity to have an expensive battery backup unit fail just when it was needed simply because no one checked or maintained the battery.

The battery backup power supply of Figure 2.2 can also provide a computer a great deal of protection from overvoltage. In the event of a severe

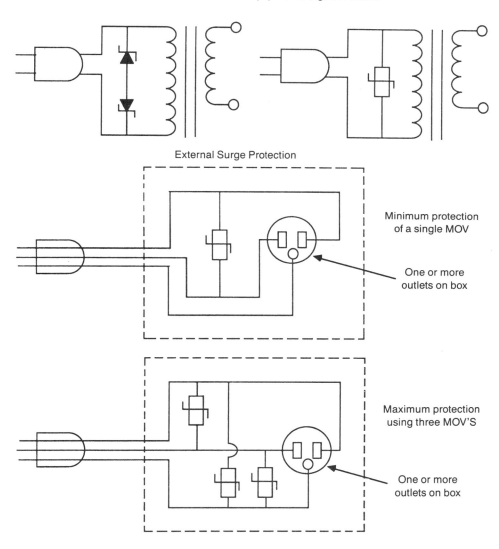

Internal Equipment Surge Protection

External Surge Protection

Minimum protection
of a single MOV

One or more
outlets on box

Maximum protection
using three MOV'S

One or more
outlets on box

Figure 2.8 Schematics of circuits using transient voltage protection components.

enough surge, the backup supply might be damaged but the computer itself will probably not be harmed, since the computer is effectively isolated from the surge by the very low impedance of the battery. The backup supply of Figure 2.3 does not provide this isolation from surges.

DISKETTE PROBLEMS

Another source of possible problems that may not be a fault within the computer itself is the floppy diskette. Since information is stored on diskettes by tiny magnetic fields, any disruption of these fields can hopelessly scramble the recorded information (Figure 2.9).

There are two different types of diskette information: the program you are running and the data required by that program. These diskettes are usually placed in the A and B drives, respectively. An example would be a word processing program that is inserted in the A drive. All of your typed correspondence, on the other hand, might be accessed in the B drive. If a program from a diskette used in the A drive becomes damaged, the computer ceases to operate or behaves very strangely; often the computer will not respond to keystrokes at the keyboard. Bad data (usually from the diskette in the B drive), in contrast, is usually indicated by a failure of the drive to access data from the diskette or perhaps the appearance on the screen of inappropriate characters. If a diskette

DO NOT WRITE ON THE JACKET WITH PEN OR PENCIL. USE A FELT TIP PEN.

DO NOT TOUCH PRECISION SURFACE WITH YOUR FINGERS.

TO AVOID DAMAGE TO THE DISKETTE AND TO YOUR DRIVE, INSERT DISKETTE CAREFULLY UNTIL BACKSTOP IS ENCOUNTERED.

RETURN THE DISKETTE TO ITS JACKET WHEN NOT IN USE.

KEEP THE DISKETTE AWAY FROM MAGNETIC FIELDS.

DISKETTES SHOULD BE STORED AT
10°C to 52°C
50°F to 125°F

HANDLE WITH CARE; BENDING AND FOLDING MAY DAMAGE DISKETTE.

Figure 2.9 Mishandling of the diskette can cause apparent computer problems. (Courtesy of Tandon Corporation)

Keep all dirt, dust and smudges
away from the diskette access slot.
Even a finger print can cause a
loss of data.

Figure 2.10 Keep fingers and any other contamination away from exposed portions of the diskette.

is the likely cause of a problem and if a backup diskette had been made of the now-suspect diskette, recopy the backup onto the suspected diskette. (Backup copies should be made on a routine basis for all important data and for all purchased applications software such as word processing and data base programs.) In the event that the diskette data must be recovered from a damaged diskette at any cost, the DOS utility program CHKDSK with a /F option or RECOVER should be investigated.

Diskettes may have been damaged by being placed near magnetic sources. A diskette dropped onto a pair of scissors, for instance, can be damaged by the magnetic field often present in such an instrument, and even paper clips can damage diskettes. Keep steel objects away from diskettes. Another cause of diskette problems is the contamination of the diskette surface through carelessness (see Figure 2.10).

Floppy diskettes should never be bent. It is easy to bend a diskette by forcibly inserting it into the computer disk drive. Handle diskettes carefully—and take your time inserting them. Store diskettes at normal office temperatures. Keep them out of direct sunlight, where they might overheat and warp. Remember that the interior of a closed car on a hot day may become hot enough to warp diskettes. (Chapter 12 discusses software problems in more detail.)

HARD DISK PROBLEMS

As noted in Chapter 1, the computer normally attempts to load the operating system from a diskette in the A drive. Failing that, the computer then looks for the operating system on the hard disk. If the hard disk has failed mechanically, it may be due to one of several possibilities.

Lack of Hard Disk Rotation

The rotation of the hard disk is usually quite evident to the operator under normal circumstances. The sound of the drive accelerating to normal speed is most noticeable during the first few seconds after the computer is turned on.

Lack of hard disk rotation can be caused by bad bearings in the drive. This might be the problem in an older drive, one that may have developed a whine over the previous months, and the bearings are now bad enough that the disk may not even get started. The starting torque of the hard disk drive motor is very low and may be insufficient to get the disk running again.

Another possible cause for the disk not rotating is that the heads have come to rest on the outer periphery of the disks, acting like a small brake and preventing the low-torque motor from getting the disk rotating. To prevent this, the computer operator should ALWAYS "park" the hard disk before turning off the main power to the computer. In doing so, the heads are taken from the outer to the inner tracks of the disks, where they have much less leverage as a brake. This makes it easier to start the drive when power is reapplied.

It may be possible to get a stuck hard drive running again, as explained in Chapter 7. If the hard disk persists in getting stuck, it should be repaired or replaced. Don't forget to park the hard disk before powering down!

Hard Disk Crash

If a hard disk suddenly and completely refuses to access for either the reading or writing of data, it has probably been damaged too badly for you to recover any of the data on it. A "crash" occurs when the read/write heads of the drive strike the recording media while the drive is running. These heads normally "fly" a few *microinches* (20 microinches is typical) above the disk's surface, which rotate at 3600 rpm. Such an accident can easily result if the computer is jarred while it is running. Rough treatment during transportation of a computer can also cause this problem. BE ABSOLUTELY SURE THAT THE HARD DISK HEADS ARE "PARKED" BEFORE MOVING A COMPUTER. This action will at least put the heads in a little-used area of the disk, where data is least likely to be damaged. Also, HANDLE A HARD DISK DRIVE, IN OR OUT OF A COMPUTER, LIKE EGGS!

If there were valuable data on a crashed hard disk, there is a small chance that a professional hard disk repair facility might be able to retrieve some of the data. The hard disk must be removed and taken there for analysis. It is this contingency that the computer operator anticipates when important data and programs have been previously and periodically "backed up." See Chapter 12 for more information on this procedure.

Normal Power Unavailable

The cable feeding power or signals to and from the hard disk drive may have come loose within the computer. It is necessary to remove the cover and be sure the cables are firmly seated on both the drive and the controller ends.

Another remote possibility is that the switching power supply within the computer is on the very edge of having sufficient power to run the hard disk. If operated in this condition, the power supply can suddenly and mysteriously cease to function. A few years ago, hard disks took a substantial amount of current, and the power supplies were barely large enough for the task. Today, power supplies are readily available that have plenty of reserve current capability to handle two hard disk drives and a couple of floppy drives, too. Add to this the increased efficiency of some of the later models of floppy and hard drives with their lower current requirements compared to older models. This makes the lack-of-power problem rare in late model computers.

If the hard disk has failed other than mechanically, there may be a software problem. See Chapter 12 for more help.

SYSTEM BOARD PROBLEMS

Since the circuitry on the main board is the very heart of the computer, almost any failure on the system board will cause major problems. If the computer refuses to boot up, even on a floppy disk, there is a good chance that there is a system board problem.

One of the first things to do when a system board problem is suspected is to reduce the computer system to the bare minimum of hardware and see if the computer then boots up properly. This means removing all expansion cards that are not absolutely necessary for the computer to operate. Such cards as extra serial ports, multifunction cards, and any special cards such as networking cards should be removed. The hard disk adapter can be removed. If provided, switches can be used to reduce the amount of memory that is being used, thus eliminating the higher banks of memory as a possible problem. Try to boot up on a floppy diskette. If this does not work, replace all of the memory chips in the active bank(s) with chips from the switched-out banks, thus eliminating the original bank of memory as a possible cause of the system crash. If the computer then boots, one of the cards or memory chips removed was the problem. One by one, replace the hardware and again attempt the reboot to localize the problem. If the problem persists at the minimum hardware level, one must look further.

The best thing to do when a computer refuses to boot with minimum hardware is to replace, one at a time, the socketed chips on the board. There are probably only a half-dozen such chips, the rest being soldered into the board. Chips that are soldered in are generally not worth unsoldering and replacing. Be sure to at least replace the system ROM chip, which probably has a small window in it that is covered with a sticker marked with the BIOS version number, among other things. You must substitute a chip with the exact same version number from the same exact system board for a substitution test of the ROM to be valid. Sometimes these ROM chips fail, resulting in the complete failure of the system.

As a last resort, replace the system board to verify that the old one was defective. Component-level troubleshooting of the bad system board will seldom be practical, so replacement of the board is the most common fix.

Once a new system board is operating properly, the removable chips from the old system board can be substituted, one at a time, into the good system to verify that these chips are good, thus making these chips available as replacements in case of future problems.

IS IT A HARDWARE OR A SOFTWARE PROBLEM?

When a computer malfunctions, it is first necessary to determine whether the problem is one within the computer (a *hardware* problem) or whether it is a matter of providing a correct program and data (a *software* problem) to the computer. Put a known good diskette with the operating system on it into the A drive and turn on the computer. Note whether the problem occurs before or after the A> prompt appears.

Problems occurring *before* the DOS prompt A> are usually hardware problems. Many microcomputers have an internal self-test, executed each time the computer is turned on, called the power-up diagnostic, power-on self-test, or ROM diagnostic. Execution of these routines is normally evident from a pause after turning on the computer's power, followed by a short beep at the successful conclusion of the tests. Indications other than the short beep mean that a problem has been detected and must be corrected before using the computer. The ROM diagnostic program may take from a few seconds up to a minute, depending on the amount of installed RAM memory.

For the IBM PC only, if there is no DOS diskette the IBM will load BASIC from special ROM chips and display the following:

```
The IBM Personal Computer BASIC
Version XXXX Copyright IBM Corp 198X
XXXX Bytes free
Ok
```

Note: A failure of the A diskette drive to load DOS results in the previous display and is a very good indication of an A disk drive malfunction. See Chapter 7 for disk drive repair.

Problems detected by the ROM diagnostics may, depending on the computer manufacturer, produce error codes similar to the following, which are those used by IBM.

Representative ROM Diagnostic Error Codes

Normal Indication. The following indicates normal operation:

Cursor appears somewhere on the monitor.

One beep sounds.

Drive A is accessed as shown by the activity light on the drive.

DOS prompt A> is displayed.

Note: If the DOS diskette in drive A has a file on it called AUTOEXEC.BAT, the computer automatically loads and executes the programs listed within that file. Testing a computer for proper operation is best done with as simple a program as possible, preferably the operating system alone.

Abnormal Indications. These indications may be audio or numerical codes:

1. Audio Error Codes

    No beep and no display indicate a probable power supply problem. Check the plug and the wall outlet for power availability. See Chapter 8.

    Continuous or repeating short beeps indicate that a power supply problem is likely. See Chapter 8.

    One long and one short beep indicate a problem with the system board. See Chapter 3.

    One long and two short beeps indicate a problem with the monitor circuits. See Chapter 9.

    A normal beep with no display indicates a probable monitor problem. See Chapter 9.

    Two short beeps indicate a possible problem reading the keyboard. See Chapter 3.

2. Numerical Codes

    Numerical codes may be provided to indicate specific problems within the computer. Appendix D lists codes that may be produced during power-up.

Parity Errors

PARITY CHECK ONE indicates a RAM memory failure on the system board. PARITY CHECK TWO indicates a RAM memory failure on one of the memory expansion boards. Either of these error messages may be preceded *momentarily* by a numerical code that indicates the bank in which the error occurred. Watch carefully for this code and write it down when it appears. The code may appear for only a second and then be replaced by one of the previously mentioned messages. See Chapter 4 for help in troubleshooting memory problems.

Boot-Up Troubleshooting Review

If the normal indications occur, you may assume several things. If the beep sounds, the RAM has passed a test that should show any permanent gross defects in the RAM chips. Operation to this point also confirms that the power supply is producing the necessary voltages, mainly +5V, to operate the computer. Depending on the kind of RAM chips used, other voltages required by those chips are also present. If the A> prompt shows, the computer has been able to find and load the necessary software, usually from the A diskette. (Some systems have other sources for loading system software, such as hard disks.) The presence of the prompt also indicates that the source for the data, usually the A drive, is working properly.

A computer working to the DOS prompt has eliminated the majority of common problems, those of the bad power supply, bad RAM memory chips, and the bad or out-of-alignment diskette drive (only the drive used to boot up the computer). It also clears the possibility of a bad copy of the operating system in the A drive.

Diskette Drive File Access Problems

Computer problems occurring *after* the DOS prompt A> are largely disk drive, peripheral, or software problems. An error code on the CRT screen such as READ ERROR, BAD COMMAND OR FILE NAME, or CANNOT OPEN FILE means that the information expected to be on a diskette is not available for one reason or another. In addition to mistyping a command, these errors may be shown if the requested file is simply not present on the diskette specified: You cannot expect a computer to find something that is not there. There are two hardware causes for this kind of failure: (1) The diskette drive is defective and unable to retrieve data properly recorded on the diskette or (2) the diskette has been damaged or improperly recorded upon by a misaligned drive. The problem must be examined further to determine which possibility is the actual problem.

To determine whether a problem is in the hardware or the software, substitute another diskette as the next logical step in troubleshooting. Assume that data on a diskette cannot be read, but putting a different diskette in the same drive produces normal indications. (For instance, the word processing files on one diskette cannot be read but a second diskette works normally, with all files apparently accessible after you have performed several random reads from the "new" diskette.) It is reasonable to assume that the first diskette has been damaged somehow and that the diskette drive is all right.

A caution is in order in making such an assumption, however. In time, a diskette drive may slowly drift out of mechanical alignment. If an out-of-alignment drive is used to format and record information, the diskette used is readable with the out-of-alignment drive. As the alignment gets worse, if the drive is still used to record and read, the information on the diskette can still be readable *with that drive*. Repeated problems reading with a particular drive strongly indicate an alignment problem with that drive. The possibility of a misaligned drive can be checked by using a diskette in known good condition, such as a diskette that has been recently purchased with a program or data already recorded on it by a drive assumed to be in good condition. Such a diskette can be used as a standard for this test. Insert it into the suspect drive and attempt to read the files. If there is still a problem in reading the diskette, the drive must be suspected to be too far out of alignment to read properly recorded information even though it may still read information recorded by itself. The correction of floppy drive problems is covered in Chapter 7.

Software problems are covered in Chapter 12.

CHAPTER SUMMARY

A COMPUTER PROBLEM OR NOT? shows that the microcomputer service technician must be aware that a reported problem with a computer is often not a hardware problem at all, but can be caused by operator misunderstanding or lack of training or perhaps "dirty" AC power applied to the computer. Failure to configure (set up) new software is also a common problem in operating a microcomputer. Other common failures include floppy diskette and hard disk drive failures, called "crashes." The use of diagnostic software can save hours of other troubleshooting techniques in localizing a problem in a microcomputer, if the computer can be operated up to the point of getting a DOS prompt. Lacking the ability to boot to a DOS prompt, the technician can still use the numerical error codes if displayed on the screen, or the audio cues from the speaker. Two important points to be made are (1) problems occurring *before* reaching the normal DOS prompt mean that the technician will probably have to rely on the numerical codes and audio cues provided by the ROM diagnostic software routines to localize a problem in the computer, and (2) problems occurring *after* the computer reaches the DOS prompt can be best localized using a diagnostic program on a diskette, which becomes the primary troubleshooting tool. See Chapter 3 for more information.

REVIEW QUESTIONS

1. Name two causes of a reported computer problem that are NOT hardware problems within the computer.

2. What is the ultimate cure for power problems?
3. What component is effective in limiting the amplitude of power line voltage spikes?
4. What does a parity error message indicate?
5. What is indicated when two floppy diskette drives work well when diskettes are used on individual drives, but one drive cannot use diskettes written to by the other?
6. Problems that occur before the computer reaches a DOS prompt usually mean a hardware problem. What is available to help the technician localize the problem?
7. What is the best tool to find computer problems if the computer will boot up to the DOS prompt?

chapter three

Troubleshooting to the Unit and Board Level

CHAPTER OBJECTIVE

TROUBLESHOOTING TO THE UNIT AND BOARD LEVEL explains the dangers of electrostatic discharge damage while localizing a problem that has been determined to be in the hardware within the computer. Emphasis is on locating the defective printed circuit board causing the problem. While a few chips may be in sockets, making them reasonably easy to test by substitution, the main objective is to replace a defective board, return it to the manufacturer for replacement or repair, or discard it. Completion of this chapter will enable the technician to localize a problem within the computer or in one of the peripheral equipments or cables.

BOARD- OR COMPONENT-LEVEL TROUBLESHOOTING?

There is a marked difference between troubleshooting electronic equipment such as stereo or radio equipment and treating computer problems. Almost anyone can operate stereos and radios, and very little audio equipment has the modularized construction (plug-in circuitry) that most microcomputers do.

Most computer problems are the result of operator error or software problems, with only a very small percentage involving electronic failures. Computer hardware repairs, perhaps all but 10%, are accomplished simply and rapidly. Repairs of computer hardware problems involve isolating the problem to a certain circuit or possibly a disk drive and then replacing that card or disk drive (Figure 3.1). Chapter 2 will help you decide whether there is a problem within the computer or whether it lies elsewhere.

A defective card should be sent back to the factory for replacement or repair if the card is still under warranty. If the warranty period has expired, the cost of technician time versus that of getting a new card from the manufacturer

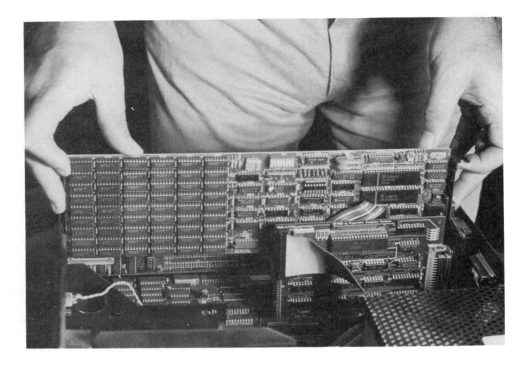

Figure 3.1 Most internal computer repairs are accomplished by the simple replacement of a defective card or disk drive. (Abbey Enterprises)

will affect the decision. On those few occasions when a replacement card is not available and continued operation of the computer is extremely important, it may be necessary to troubleshoot to the component level (Figure 3.2).

It is not difficult to learn the process of replacing cards or disk drives to alleviate a computer problem. Much more detailed knowledge of digital circuitry is necessary if the technician is expected to troubleshoot to the component level. In the usual case, where sufficient replacement circuits and disk drives are available, the technician seldom needs this level of troubleshooting expertise. When component-level troubleshooting is necessary, it is sometimes possible to use a replacement circuit to return the computer to service while the technician takes the defective circuit back to the shop, where it can be worked on at more leisure. Once back at the shop, the technician can install the defective circuit in an otherwise working system and commence troubleshooting procedures there. Troubleshooting to the component level requires a thorough knowledge of digital circuitry, detailed circuit information, and the use of digital test instruments.

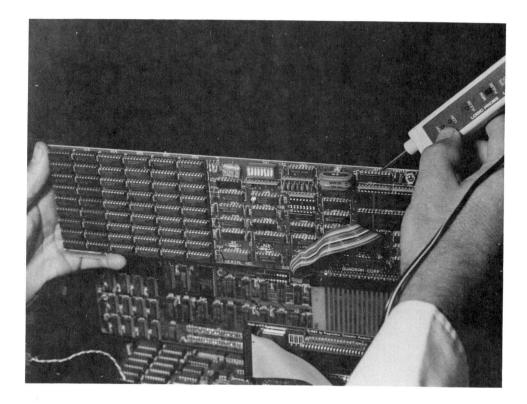

Figure 3.2 Troubleshooting to the component level requires additional electronic knowledge and detailed circuit information, including a block diagram and schematic of the board. (Abbey Enterprises)

ELECTROSTATIC DISCHARGE AND OTHER CAUTIONS

When a computer is received for repair, the technician must make sure that no further problems are introduced into the equipment through carelessness. To this end, observe the following cautions at all times when working:

- Always "park" a hard disk before turning off a microcomputer, and especially before transporting one.
- Never move or jar a microcomputer while the hard disk is running.
- Never close the door of a double-sided disk drive without either a diskette or a dummy cardboard shipping diskette installed in the drive, as shown in Figure 3.3. To close the door with nothing in the drive invites chipping of either or both of the glasslike read/write heads. A chipped drive head can ruin any other diskettes inserted and rotated in that drive.

Figure 3.3 Be sure to install the shipping cardboard or an old diskette when transporting diskette drives. (Abbey Enterprises)

Figure 3.4 Don't leave unprotected diskettes lying about when working. (Abbey Enterprises)

- Always take special care of floppy drive diskettes, keeping them in a protective jacket when not installed in a diskette drive. Don't leave unprotected diskettes lying about the work area (Figure 3.4). They are sure to be contaminated with dust, dirt, or physically damaged by tools or other objects. Use only felt-tipped pens to write on diskette jackets; ballpoint pens can easily put a dimple in a diskette, ruining it.
- Never remove or attach connectors, or remove or insert any option card or integrated circuit (IC) into the computer while power is on (Figure 3.5).
- Likewise, never touch any internal portion of a computer's power supply while it is attached to the power source (Figure 3.6). If voltage measurements are necessary, exercise extreme care to prevent shock hazards and/or damage to the power supply. Certain circuits within monitors also contain dangerous voltages, a subject discussed further in Chapter 9.
- Always observe the static electricity safety measures for ICs. Keep the new components in their static-free packaging until ready for installation

Figure 3.5 Always turn the power off when working inside the computer, for your safety and to prevent damage to the computer. (Abbey Enterprises)

Figure 3.6 Keep your fingers and tools out of the power supply when the power is connected, whether or not the power switch is on. (Abbey Enterprises)

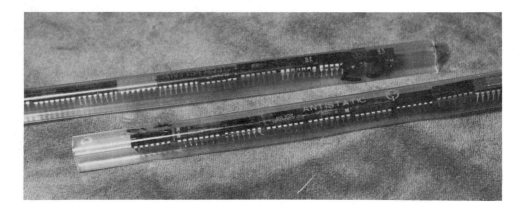

Figure 3.7 Leave good ICs in their original packaging until actually needed. (Abbey Enterprises)

(Figure 3.7). Ground your body to the equipment under test before installing a new chip into the board. If possible, work at a static-free workstation that includes grounded metal surfaces and an antistatic floormat.

- Whenever the computer boards are removed or replaced, be certain that the power to the computer is OFF. This is a fundamental rule that MUST be observed by all servicing technicians, one that cannot be overemphasized (Figure 3.8).
- Whenever ICs are passed from one person to another, the persons should be touching each other first, before they both contact the IC at the same time. In other words, reach out and touch the other person, and while still touching, transfer the IC (Figure 3.9).

These rules should be followed at all times, until they become second nature.

Figure 3.8 ALWAYS turn off the power before removing or installing circuitry in a computer. (Tom Carney)

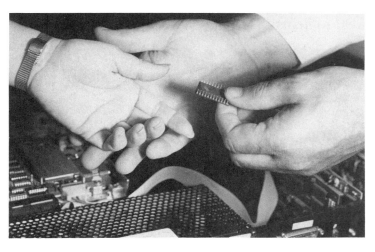

Figure 3.9 Touch the other person to discharge possible static charges between you before reaching for an offered IC. (Abbey Enterprises)

TYPICAL COMPUTER PROBLEMS

Complete Failures

The complete failure is the easiest microcomputer problem to identify. Everything is inoperative: The monitor screen is blank and the computer cooling fan is silent. Almost anyone could begin to troubleshoot this problem. Be sure the plug is in the wall, the fuses are good, and the circuit breakers are closed! Checking the availability of proper voltage is important. Substitute a lamp or other electrical load to see if the outlet is supplying power.

Then check the power cord, substituting another cord if one is available. Check the fuse, which is sometimes accessible on the rear panel of the computer. Then remove the cover of the computer and check the power supply within the computer. (Chapter 7 deals with troubleshooting the power supply circuits.)

Tampered Equipment

Some people are naturally curious and like to look inside their computers. There is no problem with that. The trouble starts when people begin to tinker inside with a screwdriver, particularly with the disk drives. The chances are very good that such efforts will be rewarded with the opposite of the desired effect, and by the time a technician gets the equipment, it may be inoperative. The servicing technician should watch for such telltale signs of tampering as screwheads torn up by a poorly fitting screwdriver or missing screws, nuts, or other parts.

Intermittent Problems

The key to repairing any kind of intermittent problem is to make the equipment stay inoperative long enough to pinpoint the cause. Nothing is to be gained by working on an intermittent problem when the failed symptoms will not appear.

The Mechanical Intermittent. A mechanical intermittent problem responds to a physical thump or pressure applied to a circuit board or connector. By very carefully noting the area of the equipment or the printed circuit board that is most sensitive to mechanical stress, it is possible in many cases to narrow down the problem to the defective component. Take special note of the direction of flexing and the amount of force required to make the computer fail when tracing a mechanical intermittent. As you get nearer to the source of the problem, the amount of force necessary to cause the symptoms will decrease.

The Thermal Intermittent. The typical symptom of a thermal intermittent problem is occurrence of the problem after the equipment is operated for some time.

If the computer is turned off for a time, the problem is often gone when the power is applied again. This thermal cycling can be simulated by the application of heat and/or cold in an effort to duplicate the problem. By selectively directing the heat or cold to smaller and smaller areas of the equipment, it should eventually be possible to isolate the defective component. Wide-area cooling and heating is best done with a commercial freon-based aerosol product specifically manufactured for this purpose and the use of a heat gun or possibly a hair dryer.

The Erratic Intermittent. The erratic intermittent problem is perhaps the most difficult problem to repair: The symptoms seem to magically disappear when the technician appears. The erratic intermittent is also the source of many customer disputes. The customer may assume that the technician can't find the problem through incompetence, and the technician wonders if there really *is* a problem because no unusual symptoms appear when the computer is in the repair shop. Even if the technician believes the diagnosis of the customer, all he or she can do with this kind of intermittent is make an educated guess, replace a suspect card within the equipment, or replace a likely cause of the problem as the operator describes it. The erratic equipment will not respond to changes in heat or cold or to thumping. The problem is just there at some times and not at others.

One of the first things to question is the quality of power available to the computer on-site. Low line voltage or such other disturbances as nearby heavy electrical load changes can cause computer failures that will not occur while the technician is working on the computer in the shop. Field service technicians should be especially alert for erratic problems from these causes.

Suggestions for curing the erratic intermittent include operating the equipment for long periods while running a looped diagnostic program. Diagnostic programs will probably give an audio indication of a failure, a beep or series of beeps to alert the technician, who can be working on other equipment without having to continually watch the suspected computer.

The erratic intermittent may respond to twisting of circuit boards, pulling and pushing of wiring as it enters plugs and jacks, or the cleaning of plug contacts. Some plugs are prone to breaking contact between mating connectors. These contacts can sometimes be resprung so that their mating surfaces again fit tightly together. Methods of bending to restore normal tension in the contacts are left to your ingenuity since there are many different types of connectors. Once a means is found to make the equipment inoperative, normal troubleshooting can commence.

Hint: The common pencil eraser makes a very good abrasive to clean contacts, especially the edge connectors of printed circuit boards. Printed circuit boards are subject to mechanical stresses where long connector posts go through the board. Pushing and pulling on the wires that connect to these posts can easily cause a hairline break in the circuit underneath where it *should* attach to the post. Inspect such post and wire arrangements very carefully, using a magnifying glass if available. An example of this sort of problem is often found where the keyboard connector is soldered to the system board of the computer. These connectors are often not mounted in any other way, depending on the bond between the circuit wiring and the board to absorb all of the stress of plugging and unplugging the keyboard cable to the connector. Stressing the connector back and forth *gently* can sometimes reveal a break from this cause.

Field-effect transistor (FET) gates and digital complementary metal oxide semiconductor (CMOS) ICs behave very erratically if an input is disconnected for any reason. Be aware of this unique possibility when dealing with erratic intermittents in circuits with FETs and CMOS ICs. In digital circuits, a voltage level between the acceptable high and low logic levels can cause erratic intermittent symptoms. Such levels can be detected with an oscilloscope or a logic probe. If any intermittent is general (that is, everything seems to be affected), the power supply is a likely suspect (see Chapter 8).

Application of Voltage in the Wrong Place

A technician using a probe or any metal tool within equipment while it is in operation runs a very definite risk of shorting a pair of IC pins or printed circuit traces together. Often this does no damage, but once in a while the wrong combination comes up and in a few milliseconds a great deal of damage is done. As a simple precautionary measure, do not use anything to probe into live circuitry other than a test probe designed for the job. A good probe like the one in Figure 3.10 is needle-sharp at the tip and very small in diameter. Ideally, it should be small enough not to short IC pins together if placed between them.

If the computer suddenly emits a beep or strange noise, or smokes or otherwise ceases operation when the technician "slips," there is a very good chance that a big job lies ahead just to get back to the original problem. A slip of a tool like this can cause a string of many circuits to die an instant death. Transistor-transistor logic (TTL) ICs, for instance, do not tolerate 12VDC applied to them without permanent damage; a slip from input to output pins of a regulator could accomplish this in the twinkling of an eye. Be careful! Investigation into the problems caused by such an accident should begin by noting exactly where the improper voltage was applied. Carefully note where those points are on the schematic diagram and what components would most likely be damaged. These components include ICs, regulators, transistors, and electrolytic capacitors. Other components are more tolerant of such accidents. Troubleshooting should then proceed to replace or verify as good those components that could have been damaged by the accident. This may require stage-by-stage signal tracing.

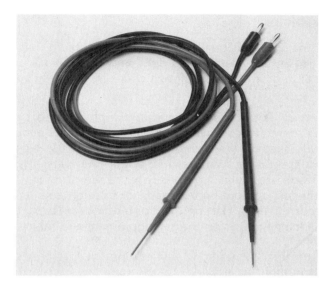

Figure 3.10 Only very sharp, small-diameter test probes should be used to test computer circuits. (Courtesy of Huntron Instruments, Inc.)

Multiple Problems

Once a problem is identified and repaired, it is reasonable to expect that the equipment will work properly when assembled into its cabinet. This is, sadly, not always the case. Once in a while the technician may introduce further problems in the course of finding and curing another. The most common second problem is probably the broken wire. When equipment is opened and circuit boards are dismantled from the chassis, the wiring takes some punishment. Watch for this to happen when dismantling and reassembling computers. It is a sure indication of a technician-induced problem when the equipment was working fine after the repair but ceased operation when inserted into the cabinet. Watch also for pinched wiring, which could cause a short to ground.

Multiple problems may be indicated if a definitely defective component is discovered and replaced, and yet the equipment does not work properly. Perhaps the technician has replaced a failed component that was a secondary failure and neglected to find the principal cause of the problem. Troubleshooting must continue to find the second problem. If the second problem found bears no relationship to the first failure and there is little, if any, chance the technician somehow caused the second failure during the troubleshooting procedure, the technician should suspect a possible voltage transient as the source of this problem and perhaps additional failures, too.

The Tough Problems

Every technician occasionally encounters a problem that defies all identification efforts. Nothing seems to go right, and all the usual procedures don't help at all. What to do then? Consult this checklist carefully, and you may find the problem:

1. Be sure there is no operator or software problem that could make the hardware seem defective when it really isn't. Suspect people and software before you suspect the computer. Over half of the reported computer problems are not hardware related; power line transients, operator error, and software are much more likely to be the problem.
2. Check the test equipment test leads for intermittents or opens that may have occurred since starting the troubleshooting procedure.
3. Did you change ranges on the test equipment and forget to change them back?
4. Try substituting known good test equipment for the test equipment in use, which might have failed. Try the same with the board or computer under test. Remove the suspected unit and substitute a known good piece of equipment to verify the symptoms you are getting.
5. If you have access to a good computer of the same type as the defective one, try comparing readings from the two units to help isolate the problem in the bad. This procedure involves applying power to both units and taking voltage readings back and forth between them. If you are making dead-circuit checks, you would, of course, not apply power to either unit.
6. Get away from the problem for a while. It is possible to get too involved and begin making silly mistakes.
7. When you go back to the job, make notes on paper as you go to keep the facts straight. This is of particular help when you are taking many readings.
8. Get the help of another technician. No one, no matter how experienced, has all the answers all the time. You could be overlooking something very simple that another technician might be able to point out.
9. Start your troubleshooting all over again and take all your readings again. Something may have changed as you were working that could scramble any logical approach you are trying to maintain.
10. Are you sure there was a problem to start with? Some microcomputer boards are turned in for repair when there is nothing at all wrong with them.
11. Consider that the documentation you are using might be in error. Be sure you are working on *exactly* the same model as your documentation, particularly when it comes to schematics. Production changes are very often made to hardware without updating the documentation.

12. Consider the possibility that the instruction manual might be wrong. Inaccurate documentation can indicate symptoms that are extremely confusing.

13. It is not unusual to have more than one problem in a piece of equipment. Remember that the symptoms of two different failures may together cause symptoms that cannot be explained by a single failure.

Overheated Parts Failures

Resistors are made to throw off heat. The bigger they are, the more heat they can safely get rid of without burning up. If hot resistors are mounted directly on a circuit board, they may discolor the board, and in severe cases burn or char it. Small resistors should not get hot. Smaller resistors are used when the wattage ratings are less than a watt, not enough heat to cause any problems with a printed circuit board or nearby wiring. Burning of any small resistor is almost always a result of the failure of another component, usually a transistor or electrolytic capacitor. Capacitors should not feel hot. If a hot capacitor is not being overheated by nearby components, it is probably very leaky. When replacing a capacitor, be sure that no associated failure is causing too much voltage to be applied to the capacitor.

If you suspect a component is overheating, you can obviously get a good idea of gross overheating by holding your finger on the component for a few moments. If your finger is not sensitive enough to feel a merely overwarm component, immediately put that finger to your upper lip, just below your nose. The upper lip is extremely sensitive to minute temperature changes.

CHECK THE SIMPLE THINGS FIRST

Before assuming that the computer is at fault, check out the simple possibilities first:

1. Be sure the power plug is inserted into an energized outlet. Remember that some outlets can be switched off at a wall switch. If possible, change the power cord to the computer to be sure that the cord isn't open.

2. A proper operating system program must be inserted into the booting-up diskette drive. Without the proper programs on the diskette (covered in detail in Chapter 12), the computer cannot be put into full operation. Try other diskettes with the operating system installed. If that is not practical, use a fresh copy of the backup diskettes to see if that cures the problem.

3. Be sure that operator error is not the cause of the problem. Operate the computer yourself, using software with which you are familiar, to eliminate this possibility.

4. If the computer has recently been opened and changes made within it, there is an excellent chance that these changes are the cause of the problem. For instance, if an option card has just been installed and the computer then refuses to work properly, it is a good bet that something involving this installation is now causing the problem. Think over what has been done and retrace the steps to the point where the computer was working properly before the changes were made. For instance, an option card often requires that the system board option switches be changed. If they are changed to a wrong combination, the computer may not work at all. For this reason, it is always a good idea to write down switch settings *before* any changes are made so that this step can be retraced with minimum effort.

5. If the keyboard of the computer does not respond, be sure the operator has not somehow switched the keyboard to the "lock" position. This is a key switch on the front of the computer.

6. The AT computer does not have internal switches for setting initial defaults. This is provided by a battery backup portion of RAM memory for these parameters. The parameters in this area of RAM are set by using a special program for the purpose. This can be a separate setup program run from a diskette, or it may be a program stored in the ROM of the computer, where it is invoked with a special key combination. One make of computer uses the combination of the Alternate/Control/Escape keys to run the setup program.

   It is a good idea for the servicing technician to check the current settings of these parameters before delving into a strange computer. This also orients the technician to the new system.

7. Be sure you have checked all of the external connections to and from the computer for obvious cable problems.

WHICH PART OF THE COMPUTER IS AT FAULT?

Troubleshooting the Power Supply and Fan

Chapter 8 deals with problem diagnosis and repairs to the computer power supply. The symptoms of a defective power supply include blowing of the computer fuse (normally on the rear panel of the computer) and complete inoperation of the computer. A computer in which the power supply is completely dead will have no LEDs lighting anywhere, including the floppy diskette or hard drives. The hard disk, if any, will not be rotating. The cooling fan may be working, however, since it may operate from the input power and not from a power supply output voltage. If these symptoms are noted, refer to Chapter 8 for more information.

Once the "simple things" and the power supply are eliminated as the causes of the problem, the next step is to see which of the following major computer units is at fault:

Printer and monitor cables

Printers

Disk drives

Monitors

Keyboards

System unit (the computer itself)

These items are listed in the approximate order of their likelihood of causing a problem. Since the printer is a mechanical device and it goes through a great many motions in doing its job, it is probably the most troublesome component of a computer system. At the other extreme, the computer circuits themselves are very seldom the cause of a problem. Not mentioned in this list are two major causes of computer problems: operator error and software problems. Eliminate these two common causes of problems, using Chapter 2 as a guide. Specific problems with software are covered in Chapter 12.

Printer and Monitor Cable Problems

The cables between a computer and peripherals such as monitors, printers, and modems are subject to a considerable amount of mechanical damage. They can be caught between desks and the wall or other furniture, burned by cigarettes, or crushed by the weight of heavy computers and printers. Perhaps the greatest stress is placed on a cable by pulling on the cable harness instead of directly on the connectors at either end. Some connectors are securely fastened to the computer or the peripheral equipment by a couple of small bolts. Since the plug cannot come loose, the cable takes any pulling stress directly on the wires at the point they enter the connector. This is the most frequent cause of cable failure. Some plugs can be repaired, while others are meant for a one-time permanent attachment to the cable. A defective cable of the latter type must be replaced as a unit. See Figure 3.11.

Printer Problems

Printer problems can be localized to the printer itself by invoking the self-test found in many printers. The method of starting the self-test routine varies in detail, but often consists of turning on the 120V power while holding down

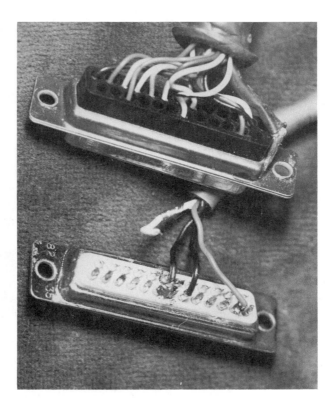

Figure 3.11 Nonrepairable and repairable connectors. (Abbey Enterprises)

a specified key. The self-test consists of having the printer print each of the characters that it is capable of printing, over and over (Figure 3.12). Turning off the printer will stop the routine. The self-test should be run *without* the cable connected to the computer, and it is preferable to disconnect the cable at the printer so problems in the cable cannot affect the printer.

A second test is to substitute another printer into the computer system for the suspected one. If the second printer runs without error, the first printer obviously was defective. Be sure to check the cable to the printer for problems such as broken or stressed connections where the wiring goes into the connectors at both ends.

If two printers of identical manufacture are compared and only one works, be sure to check any internal setup switches that may be inside the printer to be sure the settings are the same.

For further printer troubleshooting refer to Chapter 10.

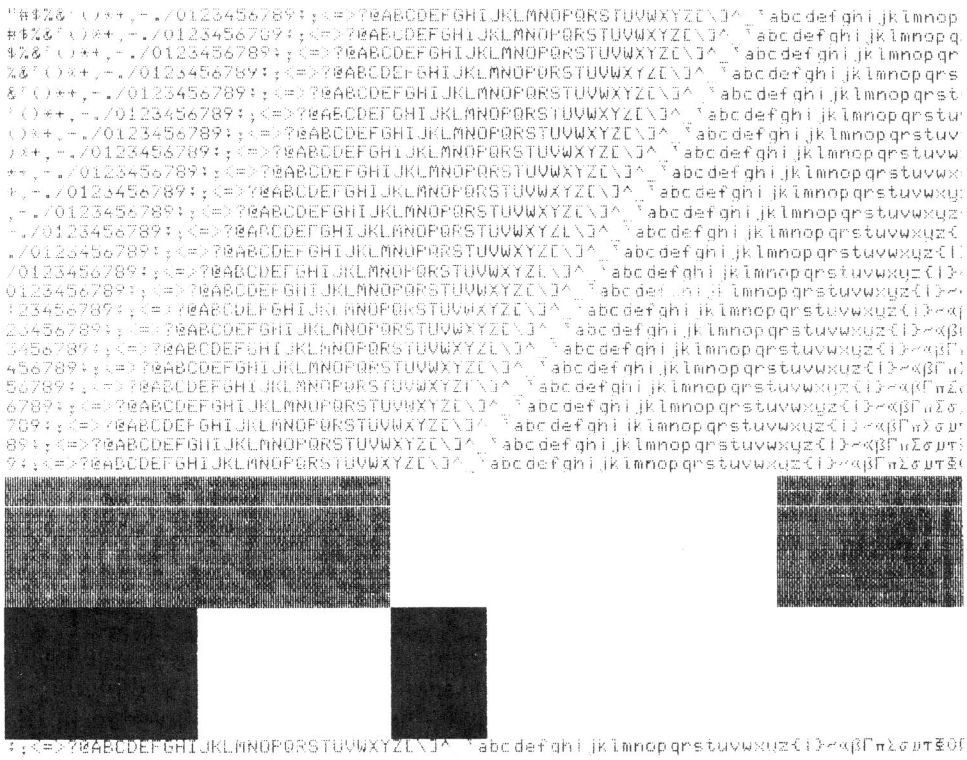

Figure 3.12 Typical result of a printer's built-in self-test. (Courtesy of Mannesmann Tally)

Monitor Problems

Accidental movement of the brightness or contrast controls of a monitor may make it seem dead when there is no problem other than operator error (Figure 3.13). Be sure to check the settings of these controls *first* when a monitor problem occurs.

Monitor problems can best be localized to the monitor unit itself by substituting another monitor known to be in proper working order. A similar monitor *must* be used, monochrome for monochrome or color for color. If possible, the good monitor should get its signals from the same connector on the computer that the original used. It is possible that the good monitor may still malfunction, indicating a problem in the monitor adapter within the computer. This will necessitate the removal of the computer case to get inside the computer. The monitor adapter should be changed with a known good monitor

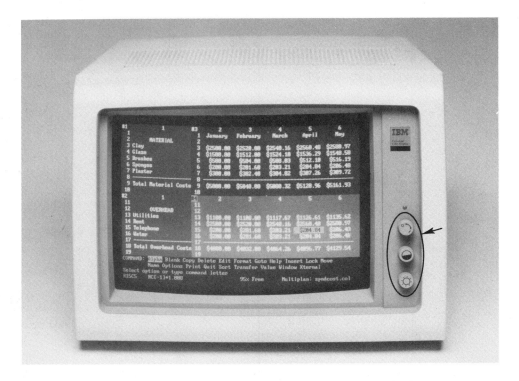

Figure 3.13 Be sure that the operator hasn't accidentally turned down the brightness or contrast controls of the monitor and then reported that the monitor has failed. (Courtesy of IBM)

Figure 3.14 The keyboard may be integrated into a CRT cabinet or it can be a separate unit. (Courtesy of the Keytronic Corp.)

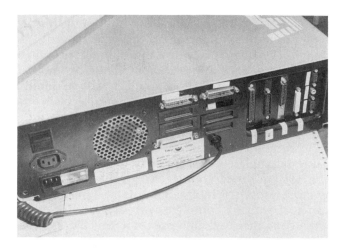

Figure 3.15 Stress on the keyboard cable connector at the back of the computer makes this a common trouble spot. (Abbey Enterprises)

card to localize the problem to the old card. Few computers use a TV screen for a monitor, but those installations that do will have an extra RF modulator unit that may also be causing video problems.

If the monitor has a removable cable, the cable can be changed to eliminate it as a possible problem. Often, however, the monitor has a permanently connected cable, which requires that the cable be considered part of the monitor. Chapter 9 gives more details on monitor troubleshooting.

Keyboard Problems

Keyboard problems can be most easily verified by connecting a different keyboard to the computer. Problems in the keyboard are most often one of two types: The cord is apparently intermittent, or one or more keys are stuck or don't seem to make contact reliably. While some keyboards are part of a computer or monitor cabinet, most are separate units (see Figure 3.14).

Intermittent keyboard cables are a common problem. The cable to the keyboard is constantly being stretched. The wires to the components at the keyboard end of the cable are not often a problem because the cable is usually firmly attached to the keyboard and there is no stress on the individual wires where they attach. The computer end of the cable is where most problems occur. Here is where a connector is often used on the cable. Normal pulling on the keyboard subjects the wires inside to a 90-degree stress from the connector. Many intermittent connections are found inside the wiring where the cable goes into the plug at this point. See Figure 3.15.

Replacement of the cable to the keyboard is a possibility. Before assuming that the cable is defective, however, use an ohmmeter and check the lead from where it contacts the circuitry inside the bottom of the keyboard out to the corresponding pin at the connector on the other end.

Another common keyboard problem is the intermittent connector mounted on the system board at the back of the computer. Microcomputers often use a system board-mounted connector whose contacts are soldered to the fragile printed circuit traces. Stressing the keyboard connector back and forth where it enters the rear of the computer is a good way to damage the system board traces. If the intermittent problem depends on the angle at which the connector is pulled against the system board, this specific problem is identified. Repair will probably require complete disassembly of the computer to gain access to the bottom of the system board connector.

One of the most important replacement items a field servicing technician can carry is a spare keyboard complete with a good cable. This allows the customer to get the computer back into operation quickly. Replacements for the cable alone are also good items to carry along.

Figure 3.16 It may be necessary to strip the computer system to the minimum possible configuration. (Abbey Enterprises)

Localizing Problems Within the System Unit

Manipulating Hardware to Localize the Problem. Once such external units as printers, monitors, and keyboards are eliminated as causes of the problem, it becomes necessary to localize problems inside the computer.

Strip to Essentials, Then Add On. The best way to localize problems within the computer is to remove nonessential cards from the computer and attempt to run the computer without them. Whenever cards are to be removed from or installed in a computer, make certain that the power is *off* before handling them! This is absolutely necessary to prevent damage to the boards from minute electrical charges. If the computer has option cards such as additional RAM, clock-setting hardware, hard disk controllers, and game interface cards, these may be removed to eliminate them as possible problem sources. Strip the computer system to the essentials: a monitor, keyboard, and the system unit itself (Figure 3.16).

Once the nonessential cards are removed from the computer, *write down* the settings of the system board selector switches before changing them. These switches are "read" by the computer during power-up to tell it whether or not certain options are present, such as the number of disk drives installed, kind of video monitor installed, and the amount of RAM memory provided. Changing the installed options requires careful checking and probable resetting of the system board switches (see Figure 3.17).

Figure 3.17 The system board switch settings must be checked and possibly reset when option cards are removed. (Abbey Enterprises)

Understand the switch settings thoroughly before changing them. Documentation on the specific computer should give all the information required to set the switches to new values as the option cards are removed. Here is an example of setting the system switches to a minimum configuration. Before any cards were removed from our sample computer, it had the switch settings for S1 and S2 as shown in Figure 3.18. After removing all cards except the video card and the floppy disk drive controller card, the switch settings would need to be changed to those of Figure 3.19.

After all the nonessential option cards are removed, attempt to operate the computer. If the computer operates properly, the original problem was likely to have been caused by one of the cards removed. Continue to run the computer for some time to be certain that the problem is now gone. After convincing yourself that the computer is still operating normally, turn it off and reinstall *one* of the cards you have removed. Be sure to reset the appropriate system board switches so the computer will know of the presence of the new option board. Run the computer again. If it fails now, the card you just installed is causing the problem. If it does not fail, run the computer for a while to be certain that there is still no problem, then shut it down and install another card. Repeat this process until the problem appears after installing a particular card.

If the computer refuses to operate after the removal of the nonessential cards, one of the necessary option cards may be causing the problem. If this is the case, it will be necessary to borrow or otherwise obtain substitute, known good cards to insert and test. When installing a new board, be sure that it is compatible with your system (an identical replacement if at all possible) and that the switches on the board are properly set as was the original board. Installation of a board that is not compatible with your computer can easily cause extensive and expensive damage. Installation of a good board and the resulting proper operation of the computer confirms that the original was indeed defective.

If the computer will not operate properly after substituting the essential cards, it is likely that the problem is within the system board. This is the most complex, most difficult board of all to repair.

Memory Problems. Programs are retrieved from storage on diskettes, tapes, or hard disks and copied into RAM, where they are then executed. If there is a failure of any bit within the RAM (and there could be millions of bits in a computer with a lot of RAM memory installed), the missing bit could easily cause a computer crash.

The ROM diagnostics program may tell which specific RAM chip is defective out of all of the installed chips. It might do this by flashing a numerical code on the screen for a *brief moment*, then showing

PARITY ERROR

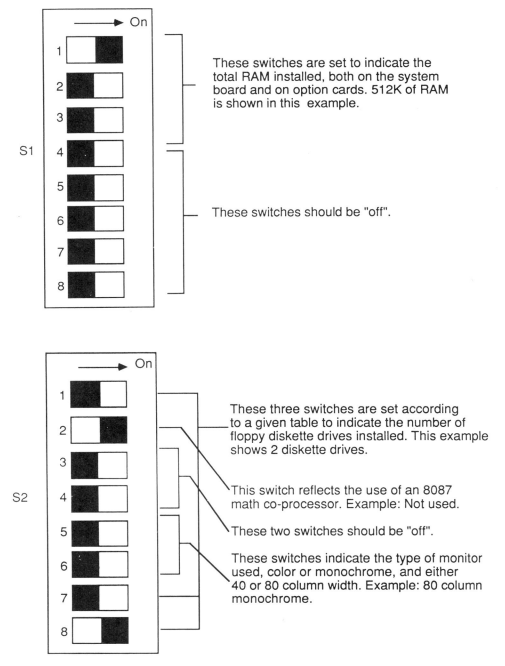

Figure 3.18 Representative example of system switch settings before changing them to the simplest configuration possible.

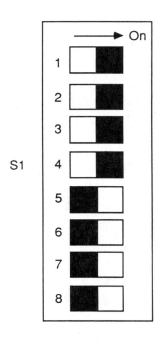

System switches after changing them to show a minimal system. Example: 64K of RAM memory now shown.

These switches still "off".

Note: This switch may be omitted on some later model PC/XT computers.

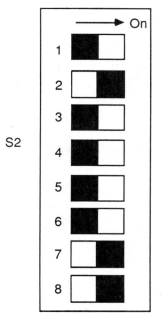

Still no co-processor:
These switches still "off".

Changing one of these three switches reduces the diskette count to only one.

Note: The use of "negative logic" in these representative system board switch settings. When a switch is in the "on" position, that function is "off". This is common practice in system switching.

Figure 3.19 New switch settings show only 64K of memory, one diskette drive, and a monochrome monitor. These switches apply only to PC and XT computers.

It is necessary to note the brief numerical code, if given, to help identify the bad chip. If you miss getting it, the computer must be turned off and restarted again to reset the system. When performing this check, leave the computer off for about 10 seconds to help reduce the electrical stresses of rapid off-on switching of the power.

If the ROM diagnostics give a coded location for the bad IC, the documentation for the specific computer will further assist in decoding to identify the specific chip. Once the defective chip has been identified, it should be removed and a good chip installed with care. If you are fortunate, the IC will be installed in a socket. If not, it will be soldered into the board and must be unsoldered to be removed. Be sure that the new chip is properly oriented before inserting it into the board or the socket.

Memory problems that are not evident during the power-up diagnostics may present a particularly difficult problem to troubleshoot because they are intermittent. These problems may be evident to the computer operator by an unexpected message during normal operation such as

PARITY CHECK ONE

or

PARITY CHECK TWO

or a complete computer crash. Parity check one means that there was an error in recalling information stored in the system board RAM. Parity check two points to a similar memory error in the RAM installed on an option board.

The most efficient way to troubleshoot intermittent memory problems is to run a diskette diagnostic memory test program for as long as it may take to identify the bad memory chip. There are many different ways to test memory chips. One method is to put alternating 1 and 0 patterns into the RAM chips, then go back to verify that all of the bits read back as they should. Then, alternate the pattern with a 0 and 1 pattern and again recheck it. Other patterns can also be used, such as all 1's and all 0's, rechecking results as above. Each pattern is written to memory in 1-byte units (8 bits). Most microcomputers use 9 bits for each byte, the ninth bit being used to keep track of the even or odd status of the other 8 bits written into memory (Figure 3.20). The ninth bit is set or cleared to make the sum of the bits always come out to be the same, always even or always odd, depending on how the parity was set up originally. If the read value including the ninth bit is not consistently even or odd as determined by the software, there must be an error between what was written and what was later read from a specified location.

System board RAM has a single line that, if pulled up, causes an interrupt routine to place the PARITY CHECK ONE message on the screen and halt the processor. Any data that was held in RAM will be lost, since the computer must

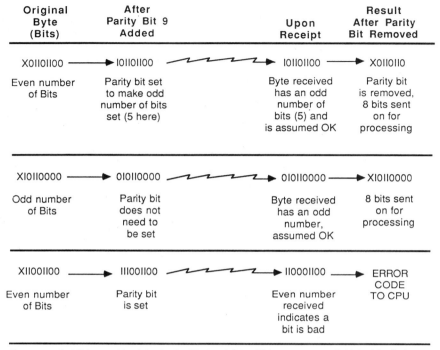

Original Byte (Bits)	After Parity Bit 9 Added	Upon Receipt	Result After Parity Bit Removed
XOIIOIIOO ➝ IOIIOIIOO ⤳		IOIIOIIOO ➝	XOIIOIIO
Even number of Bits	Parity bit set to make odd number of bits set (5 here)	Byte received has an odd number of bits (5) and is assumed OK	Parity bit is removed, 8 bits sent on for processing
XIOIIOOOO ➝ OIOIIOOOO ⤳		OIOIIOOOO ➝	XIOIIOOOO
Odd number of Bits	Parity bit does not need to be set	Byte received has an odd number, assumed OK	8 bits sent on for processing
XIIOOIIOO ➝ IIIOOIIOO ⤳		IIOOOIIOO ➝	ERROR CODE TO CPU
Even number of Bits	Parity bit is set	Even number received indicates a bit is bad	

How a parity bit is used to detect a bad byte of data. This system was initiated for 8 data bits and odd parity checking.

Figure 3.20 The use of a ninth memory bit with each 8-bit byte is an effective means of detecting single-bit errors between write and read operations of the memory within a microcomputer.

be restarted from a cold reboot, which does not allow continuing from where the program left off when the error occurred. This kind of failure is very frustrating to a computer operator. The RAM expansion cards have a similar separate line that causes a PARITY CHECK TWO message to appear before halting the processor. There is no practical way to identify a specific defective chip during program execution. Only an indication that there is a problem is possible; this is where the diagnostic program proves invaluable. The diagnostic program can be left running for days, if necessary, to identify a defective chip. There are many free or shareware RAM diagnostic programs available.

TO REPAIR OR NOT TO REPAIR?

It is often cost-effective to troubleshoot computer problems only to the board level. Once a card is determined to be causing a problem, several choices are available:

1. A defective board may still be under the manufacturer's warranty and should be sent to the factory for repair.
2. Return the card to the factory to have it repaired. This is often a wise move, and the factory can often repair a card at less expense than a technician's time would involve. Or, if the card is not too expensive, it may be cost-effective simply to replace it and discard the old card.
3. If the bad card is not absolutely necessary for a specific computer application, perhaps it could be eliminated from the system without severely limiting the use of the computer until the card can either be repaired or replaced.

LEARNING AND LOADING THE DIAGNOSTIC PROGRAM

A Word to the Wise

When first learning to use a diagnostic program, learn it on a computer in good operating condition. Note the various prompts and the options available along the way. It is much easier to interpret the program in a real troubleshooting situation if you recognize the normal responses.

A Summary of Diagnostic Programs

The diagnostic program is used to locate a problem in a computer. These programs are more detailed than the ROM diagnostics that are executed during power-up. The computer is used to troubleshoot itself at high speed rather than requiring a technician to attach oscilloscopes, logic analyzers, or other test instruments, and then to interpret the instrumentation results.

If the computer is *not* operational to where the DOS prompt appears (signifying satisfactory loading of the operating system), a different approach must be used. See Chapter 6.

If the computer *is* operational enough to load the diagnostic program from a floppy disk drive, the following items can be analyzed with software to find specific problems:

The system board (the main computer printed circuit board)

System RAM memory

The monitor

Parallel or serial ports

The keyboard

The game port

Floppy disk drives (see Chapter 6)

Hard disk drives (see Chapter 7)

Note that diagnostic programs generally have no provision for testing printers or modems. Printers and modems should have their own internal diagnostics that can be executed independently of the computer.

There are many diagnostic programs available today. Some equipment-specific programs are written by computer manufacturers, while other generic programs may be shareware, freeware, or copyrighted, written by programmers having no direct ties with any particular computer manufacturer. Computer bulletin boards are a good source of diagnostic software, particularly small programs that test only one part of the computer.

Equipment-specific diagnostic programs are developed by computer manufacturers and are intended to be used only on their computers. While these programs perform very well on the intended computers, their use on other computers may be totally unsatisfactory, calling out problems that are not really there, failing to recognize actual problems, or simply crashing the computer. While these programs might be used in some cases, interpretation may be a problem. Equipment-specific software may be available from the manufacturer of the computer, if it is assembled by a single company. Modular computers built of parts from many sources have no such software available.

Generic diagnostic programs are not equipment-specific. These programs are usable on the majority of microcomputers that run the MS-DOS or PC-DOS operating systems. These programs are said to be written by "third-party" programmers. They cannot, however, be expected to run with 100% satisfaction on all computers, as computer hardware is not exactly the same from one brand of microcomputer to the next. Thus, it is a good idea to run the diagnostics program first on a good computer that is exactly like the one having a problem. Third-party diagnostic programs are often quite small programs, written to test only one part of the computer, such as the communications ports. A collection of these programs can be as effective as a large, complete diagnostic program.

Loading the Diagnostic Program

Running a diagnostic program involves having the program available in either a floppy drive or on a hard disk. Get a directory of the programs available, watching for the extension of the file names. A program is begun by typing the name of the file on the disk that has an extension of *.exe or *.com. An example is a program listed in the directory as DIAGS.COM. Only the DIAGS part of the file name need be typed.

While some diagnostic programs test only one part of the computer, others may test various parts. In the latter case, there should be a menu from which to select that portion of the computer in question. Just follow the prompts to get the results of the software testing.

COMPLETING THE SERVICE CALL

Reassembling the Equipment

There isn't much to putting things back together if you're the person who took them apart. If someone else took the equipment apart some time ago, don't be surprised if the bolts are not there or other small hardware is missing. It often happens that way.

Beware of putting long bolts into holes not intended for them. This can sometimes cause problems if the bolt is long enough to contact parts of the circuit board. Also beware of pinching wiring when tightening cover screws.

Another professional touch that can impress the customer very favorably is to give the cabinet a bath. When equipment is returned looking cleaner than when it came into the shop, it helps customer relations immensely. Common household cleaners will work fine, a favorite being "Formula 409." Be sure to use only a little, and only on the outside of the cabinet.

When a computer has been repaired, it must be operated to be certain that the repair is effective. It is not unusual to find that another problem has arisen, a problem that may or may not be directly related to the original. Just working on the ICs of a computer may have stressed one or more of the ICs with a static discharge, or a break may have been caused in the circuit board by the process of replacing a part.

Once the computer cabinet is reinstalled, it is a very good idea to run the diagnostic program or other appropriate software to be sure that the computer does work as it should. It is not unheard of that the replacement of the cabinet has resulted in a broken or pinched wire that now prevents it from working normally. The usual ways to test a computer are to either run the software that originally gave the problems symptoms or by running a diagnostic program to ensure that the computer is again in normal operation.

Necessary Paperwork

Although not required by most employers, it is a good idea for the technician to keep a personal log of equipment worked on. These logs can come in very handy when questions arise weeks later in reference to a specific job. Minimum information is all that is needed, such as the date, the equipment type, the problem, and the serial number, Since it is a personal log, it might also be a good place to make other notes, such as symptoms and cures.

Shop policies should be established that indicate how the customer is to be billed. The time spent on the repair and the part numbers of the parts used should be noted at the completion of each job. Perhaps a piece of paper with this information is handed to the company clerk who handles it from this point. In some cases, the technician makes out a job order sheet with this information and this document is used to bill the customer. Ask your shop supervisor how the paper work for billing is handled.

Packing for Shipment

Pack electronic equipment for shipment with care. Almost any packing that will cushion the equipment can be used. One exception is the use of any of the styrofoam packing materials that are now in common use. These produce static and should not be used. This is especially important to note when packing bare printed circuit cards. These cards have many input and output leads coming to the edge of the card without special protection.

Wrap the equipment and tape the wrapping in place. Put the bundle into a suitable cardboard box along with any paper work required to be inside the box, and seal it with nylon tape. Attach the mailing label and any shipping documents to the outside of the box as indicated by shop policy. Don't forget to record the shipment in case there are inquiries as to the date and place shipped.

CHAPTER SUMMARY

TROUBLESHOOTING TO THE UNIT AND BOARD LEVEL indicates that complete failures are the easiest problems to find. Check the simple things first. There are three kinds of intermittent problems: mechanical, thermal, and erratic. Memory problems are often shown as parity errors. If a problem is determined to be within the computer, strip the system to the minimum essential cards, reset the system switches if necessary, and attempt to reboot. Due to the usual unavailability of circuit schematics, it is generally not cost-effective to attempt repair of a computer's printed circuit boards; instead, they are returned to the manufacturer for replacement or simply discarded.

The best way to test peripheral equipment and cables is by substitution. Printers often have internal diagnostic routines for test purposes. Diagnostic software is a major tool to localize problems in computer systems, but it should be learned on a good system before being used on defective equipment.

When repairing a computer, try to avoid introducing new problems. Be aware of and guard against possible damage due to electrostatic discharge. Never move or jar a computer while the hard disk is operating. Park the hard disk before turning off the computer, especially before transporting one. An accidental slip with dull test probes can cause major damage.

REVIEW QUESTIONS

1. What is the easiest problem to repair in a computer system?
2. Is there any danger in replacing printed circuit cards with the power applied?

3. Where should new IC chips be stored before use?
4. If you are required to work on equipment with ICs installed without the proper antistatic products, what is the absolute minimum precaution that should be observed while servicing within the equipment?
5. Which family of ICs is more sensitive to electrostatic discharge damage, TTL or CMOS?
6. When handing a "naked," unpackaged IC chip from one person to another, what precaution should be observed?
7. Name some of the safety precautions necessary to prevent damage to microcomputers during servicing.
8. Name some of the items that could be checked when encountering a particularly tough microcomputer troubleshooting problem.
9. Name the three kinds of intermittents.
10. Why should only sharp, small-tipped test probes be used in microcomputer circuits?
11. Name some of the "simple things" that should be checked before removing the cover of a microcomputer system and troubleshooting within it.
12. What do most printers have that will help the technician identify a problem within the printer?
13. Name a common "simple thing" that can cause a monitor to appear defective.
14. Name a "simple thing" that might make a keyboard seem defective.
15. What is the first general approach in determining where a problem lies within a computer?
16. What is a common indication of a memory problem?
17. Why does RAM memory use nine bits for memory if only eight bits are necessary for memory functions?
18. What options are available once a particular card is determined to be the problem?
19. What is the quickest way to localize a problem within a computer without removing the covers?

part three

Assembling and Adding Options to a Microcomputer

chapter four

Assembling a Microcomputer from Modules

CHAPTER OBJECTIVE

ASSEMBLING A MICROCOMPUTER FROM MODULES gives the technician the necessary background to understand the relative merits of the individual components of a microcomputer system. The decisions as to what to buy, based on individual needs, for a minimum operational system can be made based on information given in this chapter. This information is particularly beneficial when a technician is asked, "What should I buy?" The relative merits of various kinds of diskette drives, whether to buy an AT computer or a PC/XT, and the kind of video display to choose are some of the many tips offered. The advantages of additional options are also covered, such as more memory, a math coprocessor chip, and more ports. The technician is advised on how to assemble a microcomputer system from modular components, including the use of DIP switches. Tips on setting up (configuring) a computer are also given.

MICROCOMPUTERS ARE MODULAR

The microcomputer industry has achieved a workable set of standards for the connectors used and the signals passed between computer modules, the main system printed circuit board, and the **option** cards that plug into it. These standards began when IBM (International Business Machines) produced the first personal computers. Other companies immediately scrambled to get a share of the profits and began marketing plug-in cards for such functions as video processing, additional memory, and floppy diskette controllers. Each was claimed to be "IBM-compatible." This term has now been shortened so that a "compatible" computer is one that works just like an IBM microcomputer. The internal cards are interchangeable.

Eventually, complete computers became available in modular form. At first these boards were very expensive, but demand and competition have greatly reduced the price. Sources for these boards are local distributors and mail-order companies. An assemble-it-yourself market has developed. Considerable savings can be realized by shopping for the best board at the best price, then assembling the computer yourself. Local distributors of "generic" computers do just this—they order boards, assemble them, then sell the completed computer with their own brand-name sticker on the front.

The microcomputer technician might find a job assembling computers from generic modules at a microcomputer company. Many computers must be assembled and tested each day before release to the public in order for a generic computer company such as this to survive. It is a good idea for the technician to have a personal computer at home on which programs can be learned during leisure time.

Assembling a computer from modules takes only a few hours. The chances of getting a bad board out of the box are very small. Installation of these boards, however, leaves room for the possibility of many small yet incapacitating errors. Although a small error, such as not having a jumper on a printed circuit board in the right place, is not hazardous to the board, the board may not work properly, if at all. The results can be mystifying.

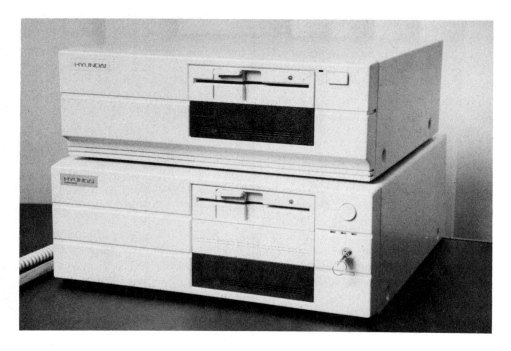

Figure 4.1 The two general types of microcomputer cases, the two-high and three-high styles. (Tom Carney)

AN OVERVIEW OF MINIMUM HARDWARE REQUIRED

Case

Two popular sizes of cases are available for generic microcomputers, the "two-high" and the "three high" cases (Figure 4.1).

For the following discussion, floppy diskette drives and hard disk drives are assumed to be the "half-height" size, approximately 1¼ inches high. Older drives are sometimes twice this height, taking up twice the space in the computer. Half-height drives are recommended for the simple reason that more of them can be installed in a given computer. One possible exception is the hard drive of substantially more than 30 megabytes. These drives must be taller than a half-height drive.

While the 5¼ inch, 360 kilobyte floppy diskette drive seems to be the current "standard" for microcomputers, other sizes and capacities of diskettes and drives are also available. See Chapter 6 for details on the kinds of drives and their storage capacities. At present, a pair of 360 kilobyte floppy diskettes will ensure compatibility with most applications. The current trend for original software distribution seems to be toward the use of the 720 kilobytes or 1.44 megabytes, 3½ inch drive.

The two-high case can accommodate up to four drives, mixtures of floppy diskette and hard drives. All are visible from the front panel. The three-high case can hold three drives of any type visible from the front, and another two drives hidden behind the front panel of the cabinet. Of course, only a hard disk drive should be installed behind the front panel because other drives need to be "fed" diskettes from the front during operation.

The most popular configuration for a microcomputer is probably to have a hard disk and two 360 kilobyte floppy diskette drives. The pair of floppy diskette drives makes copying files from one to the other much easier than using a single drive. The hard disk is used for the (considerably) increased speed and convenience of operation. With a hard disk, only seldom will it be necessary to use the diskette drives.

Control Panel

While not necessary for the computer to operate, some cases come with a small control panel, mounted on and visible from the front of the computer. This panel may feature a key-operated switch that disables the keyboard. This is a nice feature if you wish to keep others from tampering with the computer. Although this switch can be bypassed by removing the cover of the computer, it offers some security for computer information. Its best use is to prevent idle tampering with the computer or hit-and-run data theft.

One of the best features offered on a control panel is a pushbutton, often red in color, that is used to restart the computer from "ground zero" again.

Figure 4.2 This control panel of a microcomputer offers a keyboard lock, master reset switch, and LED indicators for power, turbo mode, and hard disk drive access. (Tom Carney)

Hitting this switch is the same as turning off the computer and turning it back on again. It is the ultimate "panic button," to be used only rarely and with great care. Any information in the computers' RAM memory will be lost if this button is hit. Hours of computer work can be lost in this manner. It is provided to accomplish the same result within the computer as the turn-off, turn-on operation, but avoiding the unnecessary power surges within the equipment that are caused by manipulating the power switch. Generally speaking, use this master reset button *only* when the "warm boot" key combination of Control-Alternate-Delete has lost control and will not reset the computer.

Speaker

There is a small speaker to be installed within the computer. This speaker normally functions as a "beeper" to warn the operator of an invalid keystroke or other problem, but can be programmed through appropriate software to sound various tones or rudimentary music and even to "speak" to some extent (Figure 4.3).

Figure 4.3 The computer internal speaker can be mounted anywhere inside the computer, often in the front left corner. (Tom Carney)

System Board

The system board, sometimes called the "mother" board because of its expansion slots, is the main board of the computer. It holds the central processor unit (CPU) and the support chips directly involved with it. Both PC/XT and AT system boards measure about 8½ × 12 inches and are multilayer boards. Other specialized functions such as the handling of digital information to and from the disk drives and the video section are handled by additional specialized processors, which are mounted on separate boards that plug into the typically eight expansion slots of the system board (Figure 4.4).

The PC and XT system boards use the 8088 CPU chip. This chip passes information back and forth in 8-bit chunks called a byte. An improved version of this processor is the direct replacement V-20 CPU chip. The V-20 chip provides two internal paths for data rather than the single internal path of the 8088. An overall improvement of about 30% in speed can be expected when replacing an 8088 with a V-20 chip.

The 8086 chip is very close to an 8088 chip, except that data can be handled outside the chip in 16-bit chunks, 2 bytes. This results in improved speed over

Figure 4.4 Photo of microcomputer system boards for a PC and an AT. Note the additional expansion slot connectors and the square CPU chip of the AT board. (Abbey Enterprises)

the 8088. As might be expected, a V-30 chip is available as a direct replacement for the 8086, again providing a substantial increase in computer speed over that of the 8086.

The AT computer uses an 80286 CPU chip, a major improvement in performance and capability over the 8088, the 8086, or the V-20 series. Operating at about twice the speed of a PC or XT, the 80286 offers additional new advanced modes of operation.

The system board of a microcomputer may be provided with several sets of jumpers, all of which should be checked by the installing technician. Failure to have any of the jumpers in the proper positions can cause the system board to appear defective.

Before going any further, please take special note of the following: BEFORE CHANGING ANY JUMPERS OR SWITCH SETTINGS ON ANY COMPUTER BOARD, WRITE DOWN THE INITIAL SETTINGS! This will make it possible to go back to where you started if need be.

The final word on the setting of jumpers should come from the documentation provided with the system board or from the vendor of the board. Without proper information, setting jumpers is a lengthy, hit-or-miss procedure involving repeated attempts to operate the computer. The following is a *representative* list of some of the jumpers that might be provided on the system board and recommendations for each.

ROM Size. The ROM chip of a computer can have different capacities. ROM chips of 64, 128, and 256 kilobit capacity are commonly used in microcomputers. The chances are very great that the initial settings from the manufacturer are correct. The only reason this jumper might not be correct is if someone has accidentally or foolishly changed it.

Wait States. While a PC or XT will run at the maximum clock speeds of the 8088 or 8086 CPU, there is a speed bottleneck in AT computers when dealing with RAM. Time is required for the memory chips of the computer to return the information requested by the CPU. Faster RAM chips return the information in less time than slower RAMs. To accommodate slower RAM chip *access times*, provision is sometimes made via a jumper to effectively slow down the 80286 of the AT computer or the 80386 CPU in a "386" machine when accessing the RAM. This is an overall slowdown of the computer, but may be necessary with a given set of RAM chips. Initially, use the jumper setting recommended by the manufacturer or the slowest setting if a recommendation is not available. You may wish to experiment later to see if the computer will run reliably with fewer or no wait states as set by this jumper.

Turbo Mode. Some PC or XT computer system boards are capable of running on either of two speeds: normal (4.77 MHz) or "turbo mode" (6 or 8 MHz). An AT may be operable on any pair of speeds, selected from 6, 10, or 12 MHz, depending on the capabilities of the system board and the specifications of the 80286 CPU being used. The newest 80386 computers can operate as high as 25 MHz. The only reason to run such a board on the "normal" speed is when the software in use requires it. Some software can either crash the computer or run unacceptably fast (such as some games) in the turbo mode, requiring switching to a slower CPU speed. Generally speaking, the turbo mode should be jumper selected on the system board. Any slowdown should then be done with the special keyboard keystroke combination provided if and when the need arises. A common keystroke combination, determined by the BIOS ROM of the computer, is pressing the Alt (Alternate), Ctrl (Control) and " – " (minus) keys together.

An IBM System Board Note. When selecting an expansion slot on the mother board, keep in mind that IBM (only) made the last slot (the one closest to the power supply) slightly different from the other slots, which were simply wired in parallel with each other. This eighth slot on an IBM board will probably require that a serial interface card, such as one used for a mouse interface, be specially jumpered for operation in this particular socket.

Video Adapter and Monitor

Chapter 9 gives full information on the kinds of monitors that might be installed.

Monochrome and color graphics adapters (CGAs) generally do not have jumpers to set. There may be jumpers if there are additional functions on the card other than the handling of the video signals. Sometimes a parallel port is provided along with a monochrome video adapter, for instance. Setting of the jumpers for an I/O port is covered later in this chapter.

Complex video boards are usually used with enhanced graphics adapter (EGA) and video graphics adapter (VGA) monitors. They can automatically operate a specified monitor with any kind of software, providing the best video output possible under the given conditions. Such a card has to be "told" what kind of a monitor is being used. This is usually accomplished by a set of dual in-line plastic (DIP) switches. The settings of this switch must be correct for the kind of monitor in use. Only the information provided with these boards can give the proper switch settings. If offered, the switch setting for automatic video output optimization should be selected. See Figure 4.5.

Figure 4.5 This complex video adapter board can provide the best possible video output with any given monitor, and with any software. (Tom Carney)

Keyboard

Keyboards come in a variety of layouts. See Figure 4.6. Selection of a keyboard is largely a matter of preference, often based on the layout of the keyboard the operator used when first operating a computer. There is a difference in the codes generated between a PC/XT and an AT keyboard. A PC keyboard cannot be used on an AT. A generic keyboard may be switchable between PC/XT and AT computers. Look for this switch on the bottom of the

Figure 4.6 Two different styles of keyboards. Note the location of the function keys in particular. (Courtesy of Keytronic Corp.)

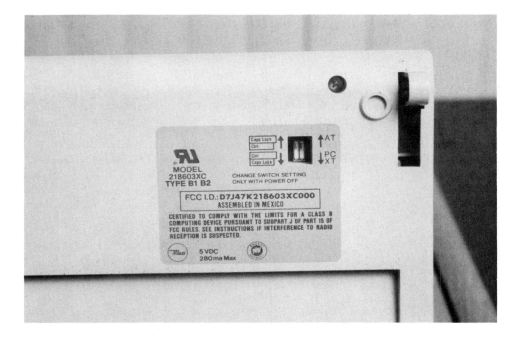

Figure 4.7 Keyboard switch on the bottom of a generic PC/XT or AT switchable keyboard. (Tom Carney)

keyboard. It may be recessed so that a sharp-pointed tool must be used to change the settings. See Figure 4.7.

A keyboard will require 5VDC at about 250 milliamperes from the computer power supply. Appendix A gives the keyboard connector pinout.

Power Supply

Power supplies come in various power output capabilities. The original IBM PC was provided with a 63.5 watt power supply. With the addition of more and more option cards, this power supply sometimes proved inadequate. Power supplies are now available with 150 and 200 watt capability. Either of these supplies should be more than adequate.

Floppy Diskette Controller/Diskette Drive(s)

5¼ Inch, 360 Kilobyte Drives. These drives are the most popular floppy disk drives. They are plentiful and reasonable enough in cost that repair, if required, suggests a new drive rather than attempting to fix the old one.

Figure 4.8 Integral floppy diskette drive motor. These motors provide reliable, precise rotation of the diskette. (Tom Carney)

Older diskette drives used a belt and pulley arrangement to rotate the diskette inside its envelope. This left the way open for failures of the belt, such as slipping or coming off the pulleys. Today's improved drives use a specially made motor that directly drives the diskette, turning it at a precise 300 rpm without the use of any gear or belt speed reduction. See Figure 4.8.

While these motors are extremely precise in their speed and are very reliable, they can be easily damaged by careless handling. Be particularly careful not to handle a diskette drive with this integrated motor by squeezing the edge of the rotating armature, on the bottom of the drive. Handle the drive by its edges, using two hands.

5¼ Inch, 1.2 Megabyte Drives. The 1.2 megabyte drives are built with more precision than the 360 kilobyte drives and have four times the storage capability since they have twice the number of tracks (80) and they place data on the surface of the media almost twice as densely. The physical appearance and installation of the 1.2 megabyte drives is identical to that of the 360 kilobyte drives.

3½ Inch, 720 Kilobyte Drives. These drives occupy the same front panel area as a 360 kilobyte drive, but the medium is a smaller, fully enclosed, removable package when out of the drive. See Figure 4.9.

The 3½ inch drive uses 80 tracks and 9 sectors to obtain the specified storage capability of 720 kilobytes. Although the 3½ inch drive offers twice the storage capacity of the 360 kilobyte floppy drives, the diskettes themselves are more expensive. Partially because of this, these diskettes are not as popular as the 360 kilobyte diskettes. On the other hand, a big advantage of 3½ inch diskettes is that they are better protected from dust and accidental contamination of the recording surface. Add to this the smaller physical size of the medium, and it becomes an attractive alternative for use in some computer applications.

A denser 3½ inch drive, the 1.44 megabyte floppy diskette, is also becoming available. This is basically the same drive, recording 18 sectors

A full discussion of floppy diskette drives and their installation is in Chapter 6.

ADDITIONAL HARDWARE OPTIONS

Additional Memory

PC/XT Memory Notes. The first personal computers introduced in the mid-1970s came with only 64K of memory installed on the system board. Programs, according to Parkinson's law, quickly expanded to fill this amount of available memory.

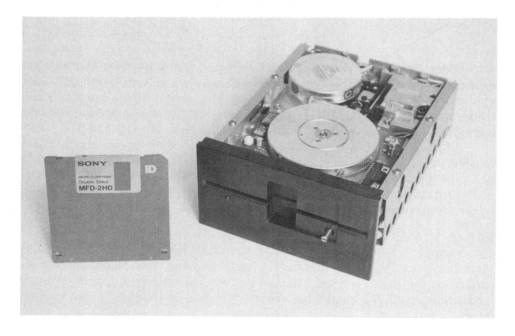

Figure 4.9 3½ inch diskette drive and diskette. (Tom Carney)

It became necessary to add more banks of memory. At first, chips of 64 kilobit capacity were used. Each chip held 64 kilobits of information. Since the memory scheme of the computer was based on bytes of 8 bits each, it was necessary to install eight of these chips for each new 64K bank of memory. A ninth chip was also needed to keep track of the accuracy of the other 8 chips. This chip was used to parity check the data. The end result was that for each 64K of memory expansion desired, nine chips were needed. The number on these chips was usually 4164, although chip manufacturers sometimes used unique numbering systems.

Technology continued to make memory chips denser after the 4164 was in common use. Chips with a capability of 256 kilobits became available and the price was attractive. A single 256 kilobit chip could replace four 64 kilobit chips, so the manufacturers began designing system boards that could hold an entire 640K of memory. Two banks of 256 kilobit chips and two of the 4164 chips were all that was required. One megabit chips may be the memory chips of the future.

The 64 and 256 kilobit chips must be installed in the socket locations intended for their use. Do not install a 256 kilobit chip in a 64 kilobit socket or vice versa. Look for appropriate socket markings on the system board before installing more memory chips.

A popular scheme for 64 kilobit memory chips was to provide for up to 256K of memory (4 banks) on the system board, expandable by an additional 384K on a plug-in memory expansion board. The availability of 256 kilobit chips then made possible the installation of the full 640K on the system board.

A typical microcomputer memory map is shown in Table 4.1. The physical limit on the amount of memory that can be installed in a PC or XT was the addressing capability of the original microprocessor chip, the 8088. This chip and its cousin, the 8086, were designed to have a memory space of up to 1 MB. Part of this memory space was used for the system BIOS ROM, video memory space, and space reserved for accessing an optional hard disk drive. Only 640K was actually available for RAM use.

Since 640K was the upper limit of RAM access capability for the 8088, only ten banks of 64K could be installed before the system was "fully populated" with memory chips. This amount of memory is called *base memory*.

Application programs again expanded to fill the available memory. The limit of 640K was quickly reached and a way was found to get around it. Up to an additional 8 MB of memory could be used with special software support. This additional memory was called *expanded memory*. It consisted of memory chips installed on printed circuit boards that plugged into the system expansion slots. Special software was required to access this additional memory.

Software schemes were also developed to put additional RAM memory chips into a relatively small 128K "hole" that existed in the original 1 MB of memory space. This hole was located at memory locations D0000H through E0000H. This space was originally left to support a cartridge data storage scheme,

Table 4.1 Typical Microcomputer Memory Map

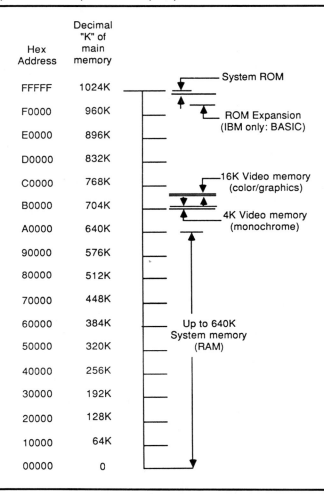

Hex Address	Decimal "K" of main memory	
FFFFF	1024K	System ROM
F0000	960K	ROM Expansion (IBM only: BASIC)
E0000	896K	
D0000	832K	
C0000	768K	16K Video memory (color/graphics)
B0000	704K	
A0000	640K	4K Video memory (monochrome)
90000	576K	
80000	512K	
70000	448K	
60000	384K	Up to 640K System memory (RAM)
50000	320K	
40000	256K	
30000	192K	
20000	128K	
10000	64K	
00000	0	

an original provision that never really developed for PC users. This block of memory was convenient for use as a RAM disk, since it was not available for programs because it was isolated from the normal RAM memory. A RAM disk is used as though it were an additional floppy disk drive, but programs and data stored on a RAM disk are accessed much, much more quickly than those that must be retrieved from an actual floppy disk. A 10:1 improvement in speed can be expected. The disadvantage, however, is that information on the RAM disk is lost when the computer is turned off. ALL DATA STORED ON A RAM DISK MUST BE WRITTEN TO AN ACTUAL DISK DRIVE BEFORE TURNING OFF THE

Table 4.2 AT Memory Mapping

Hex Address		
000000 to 09FFFF	640K	Base memory
0A0000 to 0BFFFF	128K	Video display buffer
0C0000 to 0DFFFF	128K	Reserved, ROM on I/O adapters
0E0000 to 0EFFFF	64K	Duplicated code, FE0000
0F0000 to 0FFFFF	64K	ROM, main board, duplicated code at FF0000
100000 to FDFFFF	Maximum memory to 15 MB	I/O channel or onboard

COMPUTER! Programs on a RAM disk, if also present on an actual floppy disk, need not be copied each time. Only new data needs to be copied to a floppy disk.

RAM disks are installed by inclusion of the proper software, usually by means of the CONFIG.SYS file. The documentation supplied with the software should give the details of how to institute a RAM disk.

Memory chips can be installed in the system board or on option cards for memory expansion. Older PCs and XTs did not have sufficient room on the system board for the 640K, using only 4164 chips. Additional memory had to be installed by using a plug-in option board. In this case, the system board memory sockets had to be filled before adding memory on an option card. Memory chips must be installed next to existing RAM memory so that no "holes" are left between memory banks.

The system board of the PCs and XTs usually had a bank of DIP switches to indicate how much base memory was installed on the system board. These switches had to be reset after changing the amount of memory available on the system board. Memory that was physically added would not be used unless these switches were correctly set for the new memory. The instruction manual for the system board must be consulted to set the switches correctly.

AT Memory Notes. The 80286 processor is used in the AT computer. This processor is much more advanced than its predecessor, the 8088. It is faster and incorporates some major improvements. It allows the use of virtual memory, where the processor uses disk storage space in lieu of actual RAM memory, thus enabling the use of larger programs and data than would otherwise be possible. The 80286 has the same 640K base memory as the PC/XT computers. See Table 4.2.

The use of memory can be extended beyond this 640K base memory using software routines already built into the 80286 processor, a special capability called the *protected mode*. AT memory beyond the base memory of 640K is called *extended memory*, which is not to be confused with the expanded memory scheme used in the PC/XT computers.

The 640K of base memory is usually entirely on the system board of an AT computer. Both 256K and 64K memory chips are used, two banks of each, in appropriately marked sockets on the board. Memory beyond 640K must be installed with special option cards that plug into the system expansion slots. The memory of the system boards must be filled before using extended memory.

Application programs that are memory-hungry, such as large data base programs, can use this extended memory through configuration of the program. The AT must also be "told" how much extended memory is available. This is done with the AT's *setup* program.

A computer's central processor reads and writes to RAM memory in the blind. The only way to verify whether the data was correctly stored is to write the data, recall it, and compare the data read to what was originally written. Since writing and reading of memory data is blind, sufficient time must be allowed for relatively slow memory to react. To write data, for instance, the data are made available, the memory cells are selected, and the command to memorize the data is given. Since memory chips vary in the time required to actually carry out the task of writing the information internally, sufficient time must be allowed for the memory chips to respond. If the memory chips are fast and the processor is relatively slow, proper timing results without special consideration. But if the processor is faster than the memory chips, the processor must allow additional time for the memory to respond. This is accomplished by inserting *wait states* on each memory access, thus allowing the necessary additional time when dealing with memory. Selecting the wait states is most often done by placing a jumper in the appropriate position on the system board of the computer.

Math Coprocessors

The math coprocessor is an additional IC that is an option for the PC/XT, AT, or "386" computers. Math coprocessors are relatively expensive. A math coprocessor chip is not normally needed for programs such as word processing and data bases. It may offer a substantial increase in speed for data base programs and computer-aided design programs. The screen regeneration time for a large drawing can be reduced from minutes to seconds using such a chip. The application and relative time spent waiting for the computer to do its work will determine whether the investment in these expensive chips is worthwhile.

Clock

The computer uses an internal clock to keep track of when files were last changed. When DIR is typed at the system prompt, the directory entries are shown with their dates and times of the last change. This is a valuable feature, since two diskettes with files of the same name can be analyzed to see which of the two files is the latest one. In addition, many software applications programs use the clock. For example, word processors can use it to place the current date in documents, and communications programs can use it to automatically send information over the telephone network at predetermined times.

It is possible to manually set the time and date of a PC/XT computer each time it is booted up. If there is no AUTOEXEC.BAT file in the root directory of the boot-up drive, the operator must respond to the time and date prompts. The presence of an AUTOEXEC.BAT file eliminates this automatic prompting. In this case, the operator must remember to set the time and the date with the two commands, TIME and DATE.

The automatic setting of the internal clock in a PC/XT is a worthwhile convenience, which eliminates the possibility of forgetting or setting the wrong date. Automatic setting of the internal clock requires a means by which the computer can somehow keep track of time, even when power is turned off or the computer is unplugged. A battery-operated clock is the answer. This clock, once set to the correct time, runs continually inside the computer. Even if power is turned off, the clock continues to keep track of time.

The PC and XT computers require an option card to have a battery-operated clock. Additional software is also necessary to set the internal clock of the computer from the battery-operated clock. The AT computer has a battery-operated clock on the system board, so no extra hardware is required. The AT will also set the internal clock from the battery-operated clock without special consideration.

I/O Ports

There are two kinds of ports through which most peripheral equipment can be connected to the computer: serial and parallel ports. There are a few special-purpose connectors for such options as the video monitor and joystick, but the serial and parallel ports account for most of the connections to options such as printers, plotters, and modems.

Parallel ports are labeled LPT1, LPT2, or LPT3. THE CONNECTOR FOR A PARALLEL PORT IS USUALLY A 25-PIN "D" CONNECTOR OF THE FEMALE VARIETY. Parallel ports are usually used only for printers. Printers, like the parallel ports themselves, are principally a write-only device. Only handshaking is needed; no actual data need flow back to the computer. Parallel cables are limited in length to about 50 feet due to the TTL data levels used. The maximum voltages encountered on a parallel cable are 0 and 5 V. At present, only three parallel ports are supported by DOS. The installation of more than three parallel ports must rely on special software support from the program using the additional ports.

DOS makes a very basic assumption in regard to a printer. Unless directed otherwise, the LPT1 port is where all printer information is sent. In other words, LPT1 IS THE DEFAULT PRINTER PORT. This point should be kept in mind when installing printers.

DOS 3.3 currently supports only two serial ports, COM1 and COM2. Serial ports are used when data must pass both to and from the computer. THE

CONNECTOR FOR A SERIAL PORT IS USUALLY A 25-PIN "D" CONNECTOR OF THE MALE VARIETY. Serial data transmission is also used when data must be sent more than about 50 feet. The voltage levels on a serial cable are about +12V and −12V, making cable length less of a problem than when using a parallel port. Again, special software is necessary to make use of additional ports beyond these two. Even at that, not all of the capabilities of the computer are available when using ports greater than #2.

Wiring of cables to use serial and parallel ports is covered in Appendix A.

The choice of whether to install serial or parallel ports is determined by the equipment to be connected to the computer. A parallel printer requires a parallel port. A serial printer requires a serial port. Some printers and other peripheral equipment can be set to accept either kind of data communication, as they are provided with all kinds of input hardware. In the absence of all interfacing information, the serial port can handle all forms of data communication and is therefore the best choice when in doubt.

Multifunction Cards

It is common for a parallel port circuit to be included on a monochrome video adapter board. Additional parallel or serial ports require more cards. A multifunction card (one with several separate features) may incorporate one or more additional ports and takes up less space in the computer. These cards commonly include various combinations of ports (including a joystick/game port), a clock, and one or more parallel or serial ports.

Although it is possible to operate more than one peripheral equipment from a single port by using an external switch, it is more convenient to have a separate port for each peripheral. This way, the output is automatically switched according to the program in use by the program running on the computer, and there is nothing for the operator to remember.

Additional Monitors

A few software applications such as computer-aided drafting programs can make use of both a CGA and a text monitor at the same time. Since video memory is located separately for each of these monitors, all that is needed as far as the hardware is concerned is to install the two video adapters within the computer and to connect the proper monitors to the adapters. Note that the computer must be "told" which monitor to use as a default. This is accomplished by appropriate setting of switches or jumpers on the video adapters and/or the DIP switches on the system board.

Printers

The installation and operation of printers is covered fully in Chapter 10.

Hard Disk Controller/Hard Disk

A full discussion of hard disk drives and their installation is in Chapter 7.

Modems

Chapter 11 covers the installation and operation of both internal and external modems.

PUTTING IT ALL TOGETHER

BE CAREFUL OF ELECTROSTATIC DISCHARGE! If you have access to static discharge prevention products, use them. Some of the more important products are the antistatic mat and the grounding wrist-strap (Figure 4.10). If these products are not available, use other methods to make sure that there is no buildup of static electricity. This can be done by leaving the computer plugged

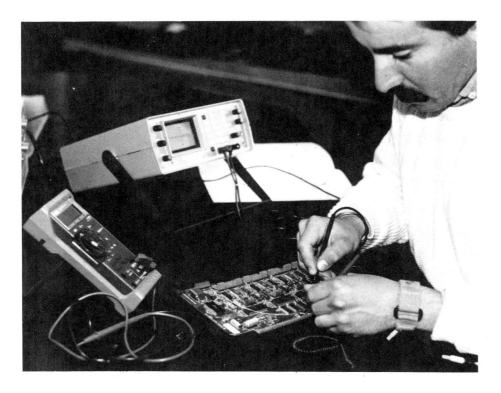

Figure 4.10 Use a static mat and a grounding wrist-strap to prevent the buildup of static electricity. (Abbey Enterprises)

in (providing a good path to earth ground through the third wire of the power cord) but TURNED OFF at the power switch. Touching, and preferably keeping contact with the computer case, will ensure minimal buildup of static charges.

Installing the System Board

The system board jumpers should now be set for the various functions as explained earlier. The system board is typically mounted by the use of eight insulating, snap-in standoff bushings. The location for each of the snap-ins is identified by looking at the holes into which each fits, on the bottom of the computer case. Snap-ins are installed only into those system board holes that are mated over teardrop-shaped holes in the case. One or two of the holes in the system board are intended to be mounted to the case using metal bushings. These metal bushings prevent the board from sliding back and forth once the system board is installed. IT IS VERY IMPORTANT TO USE INSULATING WASH-ERS ON THE TOP AND BOTTOM OF THE SYSTEM BOARD OVER THESE METAL BUSHINGS. Failure to use insulating washers may short circuit the DC power supply output, causing the power supply to malfunction due to the overload. Mount the metal bushings on the case bottom, slide the system board into place by inserting the snap-in feet into the teardrop holes, then insert the screws through the insulating washers into the metal bushings to hold the board fast.

After the system board is mounted, the system board DIP switch should be set. The DIP switches inform the computer system of options and, in the case of the PC/XT, the amount of memory installed on the system board. Switches should be set according to the manufacturer's settings or the following chart, which is *representative* of most system switches:

SW1: Normally off, not used.
SW-2: Is 8087 coprocessor present?
  On = none; off = 8087 is present
SW-3 and 4: Amount of system memory installed
  With only 256K sockets provided
    3 off, 4 on = 128K installed
    3 on, 4 off = 192K memory installed
    3 off, 4 off = 256K memory installed
  With full 640K sockets provided
    3 off, 4 on = 512K installed
    3 on, 4 off = 576K memory installed
    3 off, 4 off = 640K memory installed
SW-5 and 6: Type of default memory display
  5 on, 6 on = No display at all
  5 off, 6 on = CGA (40 × 20 mode)
  5 on, 6 off = CGA (80 × 25 mode)

5 off, 6 off = monochrome or both monochrome and CGA displays
SW-7 and 8: Number of diskette drives installed
  7 on, 8 on = 1 drive
  7 off, 8 on = 2 drives
  7 on, 8 off = 3 drives
  7 off, 8 off = 4 drives

The wait state jumper of an AT computer should be placed in the position that allows the processor to run with the least amount of wasted time. In other words, if the computer will run reliably with 0 wait states, then that setting should be used. If the computer crashes or acts "flaky," then more wait states should be tried in an effort to cure the problem. The initial setting should be the maximum wait states.

Installing the Power Supply

The power supply is most easily installed if it is plugged into the system board before mounting the power supply to the computer case. There are usually two connectors to be mated to the system board. THE TWO POWER SUPPLY CONNECTORS CAN BE INADVERTENTLY PLUGGED INTO THE WRONG CONNECTORS ON THE SYSTEM BOARD. This can cause major damage to the system board. These two plugs are usually called P8 and P9. They can be identified by the color of the wires used with them. The connector with three red wires and two black is the P9 plug. This plug has only +5VDC (the red wires) and ground (the black wires). It usually mates with the connector FARTHEST from the rear panel of the computer, (Figure 4.11).

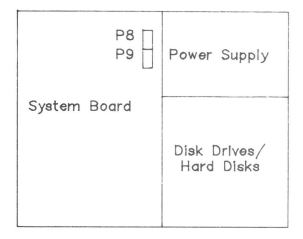

Figure 4.11 Locations of P8 and P9, the power supply connections to the system board.

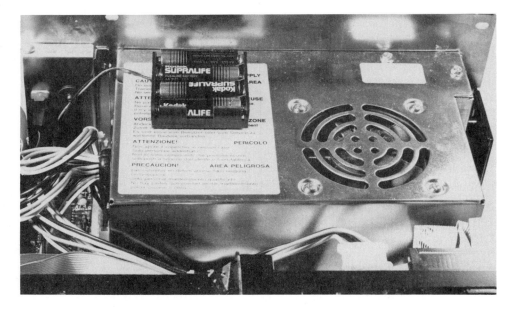

Figure 4.12 Separate battery holder used for the AT clock and for setup memory. (Abbey Enterprises)

Installing the AT Clock and Setup Memory Battery

The AT is different from the PC or XT computers in that the clock is battery powered during periods of shutdown and power disconnection. The battery might be installed on the system board (a quarter-sized silver button) or possibly through the use of a separate battery holder for larger size AA alkaline batteries. Alkaline batteries are preferred over the less expensive carbon-zinc batteries because they last longer and are less apt to leak corrosive electrolyte into the computer interior. The separate battery holder is often connected to the system board through a two-wire cable and connector (Figure 4.12). The battery holder can be mounted with double-backed tape in a convenient location, often on top of the power supply enclosure.

Installing a PC/XT Clock Card

Installing a battery-operated clock in a PC or XT computer is mostly a matter of physically installing the clock circuit, usually one of several features of a multifunction card. Once the card is inserted into the system board, two things remain to be done. Using the software that must be provided with the card, set the battery-operated clock to the proper time. Each time the computer is booted up, the battery-operated clock must be used, again via software, to set the system clock. The system clock is the clock that is actually used to date-stamp documents, etc. The only function of the battery-operated card is to supply the correct time to the system clock, preferably automatically by using an entry in the AUTOEXEC.BAT file to invoke the appropriate program for this purpose.

Installing the Control Panel

Installation of the control panel is simple, if one remembers to connect the various LEDs properly before mounting the panel. In some cases, mounting the panel prevents connecting the LEDs afterward due to the spacing behind the panel. Once the LED wiring is completed, the panel is screwed to the frame of the computer.

Installing the Video Card and Monitor

The first four switches of EGA video adapters tell the adapter what kind of monitor will be attached. A typical set of switch settings for these first four switches are given here:

	SW-1	SW-2	SW-3	SW-4
Monochrome	OFF	OFF	ON	OFF
CGA 40 × 25	ON	OFF	OFF	ON
CGA 80 × 25	OFF	OFF	OFF	ON
EGA Normal*	ON	ON	ON	OFF
EGA Enhanced	OFF	ON	ON	OFF

Note that switch settings may not be as normally assumed—DOWN could be ON, and UP would be OFF. This would apparently reverse all of the settings of this table.

BE SURE THAT THE SWITCHES HAVE BEEN SET FOR THE CORRECT TYPE OF MONITOR TO BE USED! It is possible to damage the monitor if the wrong combination is selected.

Video hardware installation is simple: Once the video display switch settings or jumpers have been set correctly on the adapter card and/or the system board, just insert the video adapter printed circuit board into a convenient slot in the system board. One of the slots farthest away from the power supply is usually used, because this card seldom has any additional cables or other special considerations. The card slots nearest the power supply are usually used for the storage media cards. The video monitor is then plugged into the appropriate connector on the rear of the card.

Installing a Floppy Diskette Drive and Adapter

Installing the floppy drives into the computer case is done by mounting the drives, then installing the floppy diskette controller card. See Chapter 6 for installation details.

Installing a Hard Disk Drive and Controller

The details of hardware and software installation of a hard drive are thoroughly covered in Chapter 7. One caution bears repeating here. Handle the drive more carefully than eggs! These units are made with extreme precision and are very fragile.

General Notes on Installing Option Cards

The installation of cards within a computer may mean that there is not enough room on the narrow back panel of the card for all of the connectors that may be necessary to support the functions of the card. Multifunction cards, particularly, may require as many as four connectors to make all of the features of the card available. For instance, if the card provides a parallel port, two serial ports, and a game port, four connectors are required. This is too many connectors to place on the tiny rear panel of a card. Additional small rear-mounted cover plates may be provided with the additional connectors that are necessary. This means that the multifunction card of our example may take up the rear panel area for two cards instead of one.

Installing additional rear panel connectors means that another of the original blank panels must be removed and replaced with a panel with one or two connectors. These connectors are connected in turn to the appropriate card by a ribbon cable, terminating in a special connector there. The technician must be certain to connect the ribbon cables to the proper connectors on the card concerned and that the connector is not reversed by plugging it in upside down. The kind of connector used between the card and the ribbon cable will often plug in upside down just as easily as it will connect properly. The trick to connecting these ribbon cables properly is to match up the indicated pin #1 on the card with the ribbon cable's edge marking for pin one, usually a red or blue stripe down one edge of the ribbon cable.

Installing a Modem

The installation and configuring of a modem is covered in detail in Chapter 11. Installation of any modem requires the use of a serial port, COM1 or COM2. An internal model uses the address of either COM1 or COM2, even though a serial port is not physically installed as separate hardware. An external modem requires the installation of the hardware for one of the ports and an extension cable to interface to the modem.

Installing Additional I/O Ports

Additional I/O ports must be properly configured before installation, usually by the proper selection of jumpers on the printed circuit card. The accidental programming of a pair of ports at a single address via these jumpers results in a "port collision," which causes both ports to malfunction. It is important to designate the installation of the ports so that each port hardware is assigned a different addresss. The selection of an interrupt line is also important. These items are explained in Chapter 5.

CHECKING OUT THE FINAL ASSEMBLY

When all of the cards and drives are installed into the computer, the cables should be checked to be sure they are not likely to be snagged by the opening or closing of the computer cabinet. Ribbon cables can be made to look neater if installed with 90-degree bends, actually folding them to form the corners. Take a last look to be sure that the connectors are all seated properly, particulary the connectors that can be installed incorrectly. These are the multi-pin connectors used to attach ribbon cables to the cards within the computer, and the power connectors to the system board. Ribbon cables are identified with pin #1 having a red or blue stripe down one entire length of the ribbon cable. Connectors on the ends of these cables should also be identified with pin #1 (or the last pin) being printed on the circuit card. BE SURE THESE RIBBON CABLES ARE CONNECTED PROPERLY BEFORE APPLYING POWER!

Configuring a PC or XT Computer

Remember that additional software may be required for the following devices commonly used in a microcomputer:

Battery-operated clocks (PC/XT only)

Data storage devices other than the "standard" 360K floppy drives and hard disk drives of more than 64 MB capacity. See Chapter 7 for more details on hard disk drives and Chapter 6 for more information on floppy drives.

A mouse or other digitizer

Configuring an AT Computer

An AT computer has a battery-operated clock on the system board, so no additional software is required to use the clock.

Data storage devices other than the "standard" 360K floppy drives and hard disk drives of more than 64 MB capacity may or may not require additional software, depending on the capabilities written into the computer system ROM, the BIOS software. Again, see Chapter 7 for more details on hard disk drives and Chapter 6 for more information on floppy drives.

Configuring an AT computer requires a small program. This program may be in the system ROM, where it can be invoked by a special keyboard combination (Control/Alternate/Escape is an example) or it may be part of the software that came on a floppy with the computer's system board. IBM used a special program within the diagnostic file to configure their computers.

If an AT computer continues to run well, the number of wait states can be reduced or eliminated by selecting the proper jumper combination on the system board. This requires running the computer with all of the anticipated software programs to be used, noting any errors that may be caused by operating the memory too fast. Operate the computer at the fastest speed it is capable of handling.

CHAPTER SUMMARY

ASSEMBLING A MICROCOMPUTER FROM MODULES shows that certain items are necessary to set up a microcomputer system, while others are optional. The minimum equipment includes a case for the system, a power supply, a system board, a keyboard, a video adapter and monitor, a floppy diskette adapter, and at least one floppy diskette drive. Other options can be added as needed, such as more or different diskette drives, a hard disk, a modem, a math coprocessor, and more memory. Certain jumpers may have to be set according to the installed hardware and other parameters of the system to be built. The 5¼ inch, 360K floppy diskette drive is currently the most popular kind of diskette drive. The PC/XT requires a separate option card to have an internal battery-operated clock, while the AT has one on the system board. The serial I/O port is more versatile than the parallel port.

REVIEW QUESTIONS

1. What is a "compatible" microcomputer?
2. Name the minimum equipment necessary to have a working microcomputer.
3. What is the fundamental difference between a PC and an XT computer?
4. What is the fundamental difference between an XT and an AT?
5. You decide to change the settings of the system DIP switches. What is a good thing to remember before changing them?
6. What are wait states?
7. What is the basic idea of a "turbo mode" on a computer?

8. Can an XT keyboard be used on an AT computer?
9. What is a good capacity for a microcomputer power supply, in view of possible future additions, thus more load?
10. What is currently the most popular diskette drive and size?
11. What is additional RAM memory beyond 640K called in an XT? An AT?
12. When is a math coprocessor a good investment?
13. Where is the clock of an AT located?
14. A clock is desired on an XT computer. How is it installed and operated?
15. A customer wishes to have three serial ports. What limitations should be remembered?

chapter five

Adding Options to an Existing Microcomputer

CHAPTER OBJECTIVE

ADDING OPTIONS TO AN EXISTING MICROCOMPUTER gives the technician information on the pros and cons of adding hardware to the basic computer, thereby improving its performance. More memory, I/O ports, and a clock are possibilities. Installing a faster "turbo" board in a PC/XT computer will improve the speed of the computer. Making a major upgrade from an XT to an AT, using all the possible hardware from the old system is covered. Improving performance with a math coprocessor and changing to a better video display is considered. Installation of a larger power supply, light pen, mouse, digitizer pad, and joystick is discussed.

A CAUTION TO OBSERVE

Before opening a computer for internal work, be sure to review the electrostatic discharge precautions in Chapter 3. Don't introduce more problems when all you want to do is to improve the situation!

ADDING MORE MEMORY

Many of the more popular programs for microcomputers call for a lot of memory. Programs for computer-aided drafting (CAD), electronic spreadsheets (like LOTUS 1-2-3), and even some word processors may require the addition of more RAM memory. Besides these main programs, each resident program used concurrently with them requires additional memory. Programs like SIDEKICK and many public domain programs fall into this category. The usual amount of memory to have installed is 640K. This is called the base memory of the computer.

Additional memory beyond this base 640K is called *expanded memory* in a PC or XT computer, and *extended memory* in an AT computer. The need for additional memory is evident if the operator is getting occasional error messages such as "insufficient memory," and the computer refuses to execute the previous command. Before rushing out to purchase more memory, however, be sure that your software is able to take advantage of it. Chapter 4 reviews some of the requirements that must be met in order for newly installed memory to be recognized. In particular, look at the possible resetting of the system DIP switches in a PC/XT computer.

Additional memory consists of banks of nine 64-kilobit memory chips for each 64K bank of memory desired, or possibly banks of nine 256 kilobit chips for an additional 256K of memory, depending on what the chip sockets can accept. The 64 kilobit chips are often marked "4164," and the 256 kilobit chips are marked "41256." These chips, if possible, should be made by the same manufacturer as those currently in the computer. RAM chips made by different manufacturers are sometimes incompatible, and this may result in RAM error messages (parity errors).

Another thing to watch for is the speed of the RAM chips. Many manufacturers add a dash and a pair of numbers to the RAM chip designation to indicate the speed of the chips. A chip marked "4164–12" is a 64 kilobit chip with a 120-nanosecond access time. Installing chips that are slower than those already in the computer may also cause RAM errors. Chip access speeds are critical in an AT or a faster computer, such as one using the 80386 microprocessor. In these computers, do not use chips slower than those installed and already operating. Memory slower than 120 nanoseconds can sometimes be used in an AT computer, if absolutely necessary, by changing the system board jumper that selects the use of wait states. Introducing wait states allows the use of the slower chips at the expense of an overall slowing of the computer.

ADDING ADDITIONAL I/O PORTS

Additional ports may be necessary if more external peripherals are added to the computer. Another printer, for instance, may require the installation of another parallel port.

DOS 3.3 will recognize only two serial ports, COM1 and COM2. While some software may routinely recognize and use additional ports, not all of the facilities of the DOS operating system may be available through them. As an example, the popular communications program PCPLUS operates through serial ports as high as COM8. When operating in the host mode (where the computer answers the telephone ring and responds to commands from a remote location), some of the DOS commands will not work unless the modem is connected to either of the first two ports. Other programs may not recognize the installation of additional ports, simply because they "see" the ports only through the DOS facilities.

The bottom line when installing additional ports is to be sure that the added ports can be used by the software in question. It is sometimes possible to switch the addresses of the ports around so that port addresses between applications programs beyond these DOS limitations are not a problem. For instance, if a serial mouse and printer must be used along with a new modem in the host mode, perhaps the three serial ports could all be used properly if the host is assigned the first port, the mouse the second, and the printer the third. Whether this combination will work depends on the programs using the individual peripherals.

Each port, serial or parallel, has a specific hardware address within the computer through which it is accessed via DOS. Along with each address, there is a "standard" interrupt line that the CPU uses to service that port when necessary. The port addresses and interrupt lines for the first two serial ports are

COM1:	3F8 to 3FFH	IRQ 4
COM2:	2F8 to 2FFH	IRQ 3

Two more addresses may tentatively be used for two more ports:

COM3:	3E8 to 3EFH	IRQ Not yet specified
COM4:	2E8 to 2EFH	IRQ Not yet specified

Before these two new ports can be used, however, the software used must be written and/or configured to "catch" the interrupts at the proper line. Interrupt 5 is used for the hard drive on an XT computer, for instance, and thus cannot be used for a serial port interrupt. Interrupt 5 can be used for parallel port #2 on an AT, however.

The port addresses and interrupt lines for the first three parallel ports are

LPT1:	378 to 37FH	IRQ 7
LPT2:	278 to 27FH	IRQ 5
LPT3:	Not yet specified	Not yet specified

ADDING A MULTIFUNCTION CARD

In many cases, the basic microcomputer does not include serial or parallel ports. These must be added, usually in the form of an extra card inserted into an expansion socket on the system board. Another desirable item is the internal clock for a PC or XT computer (the AT has a built-in internal clock). Other extras that might be required include a game port for a joystick or sockets for additional RAM memory, if they are not already provided on the system board. Cards are available that provide these options in various combinations. These cards are usually called *option* or *multifunction cards*.

A multifunction card almost always has switches or jumpers that must be set. The following are some of the options that might be selected with these switches or jumpers:

- **Internal clock:** Provision may be made to enable or disable the internal battery-operated clock. This would be necessary if, by some chance, another circuit clock is also available within the computer.
- **Game port:** An enable/disable selection, for the same reasons as just given.
- **Serial port address:** An additional serial port must not conflict with any port already installed. Each port must be assigned a different address within the memory space of the computer. Having two ports at the same address results in neither of them working, even though the hardware is in perfect working order. The address selected for the serial port determines whether it will be addressed as COM1 or COM2. The address for COM1 is usually given in the accompanying information sheet as 3F8 and that of COM2 as 2F8. The proper interrupt for COM1 is IRQ4, and IRQ3 for COM2.

A serial port may be provided a jumper or switch setting that will disable the port if desired.

Additional serial ports beyond COM2 and the interrupt lines to be used are determined by the specific software being used, as their existence is not acknowledged by DOS. As an indication, COM3 may use an address of 3E8, and COM4 an address of 2E8. The interrupts used with these addresses are open to discussion and determined by the software used.

UPGRADING AN XT TO AN AT

The AT computer offers a very substantial improvement in operation speed compared to a PC or XT. The AT handles 16 bits of data at a time rather than the 8 bits at a time of the PC/XT computers. This advantage alone means a doubling of speed. The 80286 CPU of the AT runs at higher clock speeds of up to 12 MHz compared to the 4.77 MHz of the basic PC and a speed advantage of 2.5 times over the PC. These two factors result in a fundamental speed advantage of about 5:1 over the PC/XT computer.

The speed of an AT computer may not be important to some relatively simple software. Word processors work quite well at slower speeds. However, running large spreadsheets and CAD programs at much more efficient speeds saves expensive operator time. The specific use of the computer determines whether or not it is worthwhile to upgrade to an AT just for the speed advantage.

The AT system board is often the same size as the original PC or XT system board, making it possible to use the same computer case. The same disk drives and hard disks can also be used, but new floppy and hard disk controller cards are necessary to take advantage of the wider data bus. A new keyboard is usually required for a new AT system board. Some keyboards are generic, and are switchable between the PC/XT and AT computers.

Chapter 4 lists the steps necessary to install the new system board and to set the various switches and/or jumpers on the system board.

UPGRADING AN XT WITH A TURBO BOARD

A partial solution to the speed problem sometimes encountered by operators is to install a "turbo" board. A turbo board is often basically the same as the original system board, but the CPU is selected to operate faster than the normal 4.77 MHz clock speed. Since operation at turbo speeds could cause problems with some software, the turbo board can be changed from the faster speed to the usual 4.77 MHz speed by hitting a specified keyboard combination, such as the "Ctrl-Alt-Minus" keys.

The turbo board should fit the same case as the original PC/XT system board and be easily installed since it is basically the same board, except that it has a second crystal clock for the CPU.

Installation information for the turbo system boards is covered in detail in Chapter 4.

INSTALLING A MATH COPROCESSOR

Installation of a math coprocessor can make a very definite improvement in the speed of operation of *some* software. The math coprocessor handles floating-point arithmetic up to ten times faster than the basic CPU chip. The speed advantage of using a coprocessor depends on how much a program uses this kind of math. A word processor uses it very little, if at all. A spreadsheet program might use it somewhat, while a CAD program will benefit the most. While they are expensive, these chips can be a good investment for those whose time is valuable and if they use programs that will benefit from the added speed.

The PC/XT CPU is an 8086 or a V-20 chip. The math coprocessor used with these CPUs is the 8087. On the other hand, the 80286 CPU uses an 80287, and the 80386 and 80387 are similarly matched.

The PC and XT computers require that one of the DIP switches, usually switch #2, be changed to the OFF position to indiciate the presence of the new coprocessor. The ON position, contrary to logic, means that no coprocessor is installed.

INSTALLING A BETTER MONITOR

If you are operating with a monochrome or CGA monitor, there is good reason to upgrade to an EGA monitor. The addition of color makes long hours at the computer much more enjoyable, and, in some cases, allows software to present more easily understood displays. There is no good reason to change from a monochrome to a CGA monitor because of the gigantic leap backward to poorer resolution.

The new monitor will probably require the purchase of a new compatible video adapter. While some EGA video adapters can operate virtually any kind of monitor, upgrading usually means that the existing video adapter will be unable to support the high requirements of the new monitor.

Chapter 8 of this book deals more deeply with the installation of video adapters and monitors.

INSTALLING AN ADDITIONAL FLOPPY DRIVE OR HARD DISK

An additional floppy disk drive is an option to be considered, especially if one wishes to have the advantages of the new high-capacity drives. This is particularly important when passing files between a microcomputer and a laptop computer, which usually uses a 3½ inch drive.

The installation and software cautions of installing additional drives are covered in Chapter 7.

INSTALLING A LARGER POWER SUPPLY

The only reasons to install a larger power supply in a microcomputer is because the old one failed or because additional option cards and/or drives make it advisable or necessary because of an increase in the power consumed. See Chapter 8.

INSTALLING A LIGHT PEN

A light pen is a small, pencil-like device used to select menu items and interact with the video display. It operates by sensing the passage of the CRT light trace past the photosensitive element imbedded in its tip. The light pen can only be used with software written to use it. Be sure that the software under consideration will work with your display.

The light pen simply plugs into the light pen connector on the video board. The video board detects the passage of the trace under the pen tip, then generates an interrupt that the software uses to make the selection.

INSTALLING A MOUSE

A mouse is a digitizer, a device to convert linear movement of the operator's hand across the desk surface into a string of information used to locate the position of a cursor on the monitor screen. It is used, like the light pen, to interact with the video display. It is commonly used to select menu items anywhere on the screen and is sometimes used in graphics programs to draw objects on the monitor screen.

A mouse must have a *driver* to properly interact with the computer, and the software in use must be designed to use a mouse. The driver for the mouse

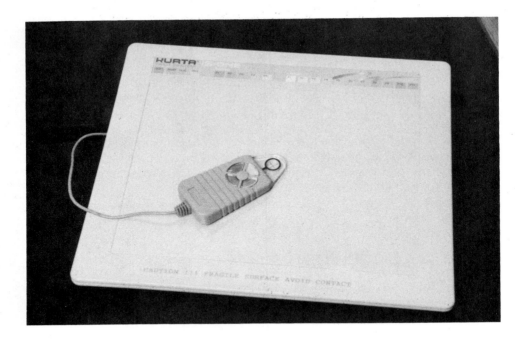

Figure 5.1 A digitizer pad. (Tom Carney)

is a file with a name something like MOUSE.SYS (always ending in .SYS) that is placed into RAM memory for use when needed by an applications program. All that is needed is to place the file name in the CONFIG.SYS file on a separate line like this:

DEVICE=MOUSE.SYS

INSTALLING A DIGITIZER PAD

A digitizer pad is a rectangular electronically scanned drawing area that responds to the position of a puck or stylus near its surface (Figure 5.1). The digitizer pad is usually supported by a driver that is part of the applications program. This makes it unnecessary to have a device driver within CONFIG.SYS. The digitizer pad is faster than the mouse and can be customized for the commands most often used by the operator, including chained commands that require such movement of a mouse.

INSTALLING A JOYSTICK

The joystick is especially popular for use with games. It is installed by plugging it into the game port. No additional software is required, since the program or game will ask whether or not a joystick is present during configuring of the software.

CHAPTER SUMMARY

ADDING OPTIONS TO AN EXISTING MICROCOMPUTER justifies and directs the technician in choosing options that may be suggested for a given system. Adding options to a computer can extend its usefulness and improve its speed of operation. A better video monitor is more pleasant to use and can provide finer detail than the original in some cases. Digitizing devices such as a mouse, joystick, light pen, or digitizer pad provide quick, easy entry of position information into the computer. More memory may be required by some memory-hungry programs. Memory chips come in different speeds, with memory with a speed of at least 120 nanoseconds required for most AT computers. Upgrading a PC or XT with a new turbo system board can result in a significant improvement in speed, and all of the old plug-in cards should work without change. Upgrading from an XT to an AT, however, requires a new keyboard, floppy diskette, and hard disk drive adapters. Other plug-in cards should work in the AT system board without change.

REVIEW QUESTIONS

1. What is the basic 640K of memory of an AT or a PC/XT called?
2. What are two most common capacities of RAM memory chips presently in use?
3. How many chips must be purchased to increase memory by one bank?
4. What is the significance of a "−15" behind the identification number on a RAM memory chip?
5. Will changing from a monochrome monitor to a color graphics monitor improve the detail of the display?
6. When installing a mouse, what must be done besides connecting the hardware?

chapter six

Installing and Troubleshooting Floppy Diskette Drives

CHAPTER OBJECTIVE

INSTALLING AND TROUBLESHOOTING FLOPPY DISKETTE DRIVES gives the technician the information necessary to understand the operation of the diskette drive and the medium it uses to store information, the floppy diskette. The special terms used in describing and operating diskettes are explained. The differences in diskette drives using quad-density and the newer 3½ inch drives are covered. The method of writing and reading data is explained. Hardware installation is explained in detail along with the symptoms of a failing drive. Tips are given to help localize problems within the drive or the controller. Figure 6.1 shows a block diagram of a typical floppy diskette drive and controller.

FLOPPY DISKETTE DRIVE MECHANICS AND TERMS

For all the electronic complexity of the diskette drive, the mechanical portion of the drive is not complicated. It consists of a motor drive to rotate the spindle at a precise rate of speed, the read/write heads sliding along a radial track, and detectors to read the passage of the index hole and one to read the status of the write-protect notch in the diskette jacket (see Figure 6.2). Each time the drive is accessed by the computer, the motor for the drive is turned on and the read/write head is moved along a radial path until the appropriate track is encountered. The data is then read by the computer.

The use of floppy diskettes has given rise to some special terms:

- **Centering.** Centering of a diskette on the drive spindle is critical. Any off-centering causes all of the tracks to wander in radial alignment—much like trying to play an old 45 rpm record (with its large center hole) on a standard small-spindle turntable. Where the turntable arm might follow the grooves of a record, the read/write head of the diskette drive is fixed in one position and the tracks would wander back and forth past them.

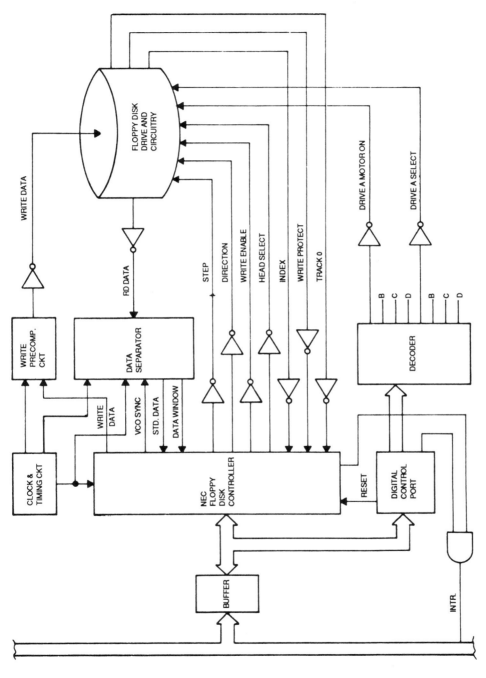

Figure 6.1 Block diagram of a typical floppy diskette drive and controller. (Courtesy of IBM)

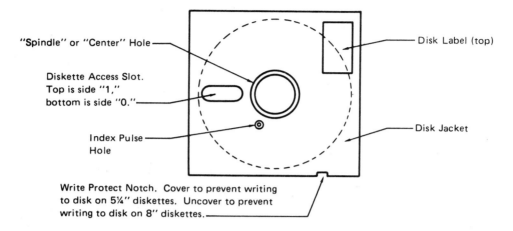

"Spindle" or "Center" Hole

Diskette Access Slot.
Top is side "1,"
bottom is side "0."

Index Pulse
Hole

Disk Label (top)

Disk Jacket

Write Protect Notch. Cover to prevent writing
to disk on 5¼" diskettes. Uncover to prevent
writing to disk on 8" diskettes.

Figure 6.2 The parts of a floppy diskette.

- **Rotational Speed.** The 5¼ inch floppy diskette turns at precisely 300 rpm: exactly 200.0 milliseconds per revolution. Software that checks for rotational speed often reads out the period of the speed rather than the rpm, 2000 rather than the proper 200.0.
- **Index Width.** The most popular diskette is the soft-sectored diskette, which has a single index hole. The hard-sectored diskette has multiple index holes. The index hole is visible through the diskette jacket, near the center; see Figure 6.2. The signal derived from the index hole is used to indicate to the computer that there is a diskette in the drive and that the drive is turning. The index hole is about 4000 microseconds wide at the proper rotational speed of 300 rpm. The exact width of the electronic index pulse derived from the index hole of a rotating disk may be anywhere from 2000 to 5000 microseconds.
- **Radial Alignment.** The tracks on a diskette, 40 on each side of a 5¼ inch diskette, are concentric. These tracks begin at the outside of the diskette with track 0 and number inward toward track 39, near the center hole (see Figure 6.3).

    The read/write heads of a disk drive are usually moved from track to track by a stepper motor. The stepper motor moves a precise distance at each phase increase of the electronic circuits that drive it. From the home position, track 0, the stepper moves a precise distance to each given track. There is no means on the standard floppy drive to lock onto a track: The stepper motor is "blind" and steps out a certain distance. If the track is where it is supposed to be on the diskette and the head moves the right distance, the two coincide and everything works well. But sometimes the stepper motor puts the read/write heads slightly off the centerline of a track. Once out of true alignment position on a track, the drive has no way

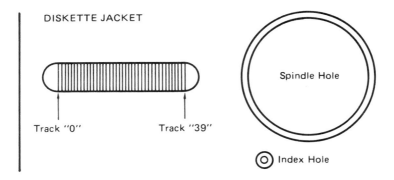

Figure 6.3 Floppy diskette tracks begin from the outside with track 0.

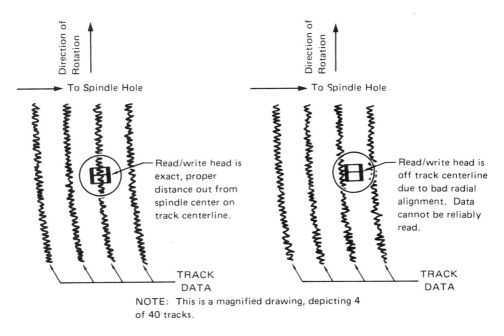

Figure 6.4 If the read/write head is not exactly on track center, data may be inaccessible.

of finding it again. This can happen, for instance, if the head mechanism is friction-clamped to the stepper motor shaft by a coupling that can loosen and slip. See Figure 6.4.

- **Azimuth Checks.** The heads of a diskette drive must meet the data at precisely a 90-degree angle. Looking directly down on a drive, any rotation of the head about its center is a misalignment of that head's azimuth (see

Figure 6.5). The bottom head of a double-sided drive (or the only head of a single-sided drive) cannot be changed in azimuth because these heads are usually set into epoxy and are therefore not adjustable.

- **Index-to-Data Timing Check (Skew).** Skew is a measure of the amount by which the head, in moving from the outside to the inside of the diskette, departs from a true radial course straight to the center of the diskette (Figure 6.6). Skew can be measured by noting the time between the beginning of the index pulse and the first reading of data from an alignment diskette. If there is no skew, the time between these two events is the same whether the drive is reading track 0 or track 34 (Figure 6.7).

DATA STORAGE ON THE FLOPPY DISKETTE

Some years ago, the single-sided diskette was used in microcomputers. Today, the double-sided, double-density diskette is the standard. Diskettes sold as single-sided are often those that had one side fail the manufacturer's stringent quality testing. These diskettes are inserted into their jackets with the good side down, on the opposite side from the diskette label. Many of these diskettes can be used in a double-sided drive without noticeable problems. The FORMAT program will mark any really bad areas and they will not be used for future data storage.

The operating system used in microcomputers requires that the data on the diskettes be placed in very well-defined areas on the diskette surface, exactly the same for all drives and diskettes. To maintain *interchangeability* of floppy diskettes between diskette drives, each drive must move the read/write head

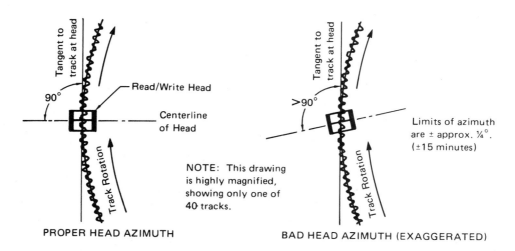

Figure 6.5 Data must come into the read/write head at 90 degrees, ±15 minutes.

blindly, to exactly the same position on any given diskette. If a drive places its read/write head improperly, it may not be able to read information written to by a good drive. Such a drive is *out of alignment*.

KINDS OF FLOPPY DISKETTE DRIVES

The "Standard" 360K Floppy Drive

Early versions of DOS recorded less data on the same diskette that is today's "standard" diskette, the 360K, 5¼ inch floppy diskette. Data is placed on

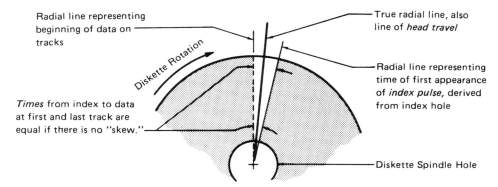

REPRESENTATION OF A GOOD, "NO-SKEW" CONDITION

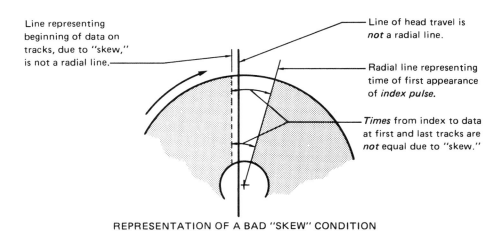

REPRESENTATION OF A BAD "SKEW" CONDITION

Figure 6.6 Skew is a measure of how far the read/write heads depart from a true radial line to the center of the diskette.

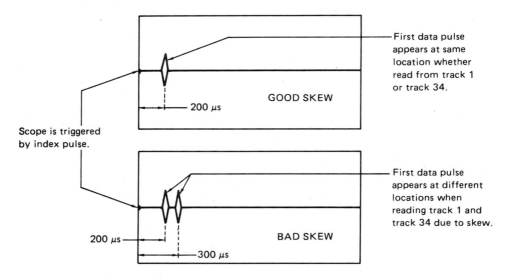

Figure 6.7 Oscilloscope patterns showing different skew conditions.

a diskette by magnetically recording sectors on the diskette, usually 9 on each of the 40 tracks (spaced at 48 tracks per inch) of a double-sided, double-density 360K diskette. Each sector can store 512 bytes of data storage. With two recording sides, this adds up to 512 × 9 × 40 × 2 = 368K of storage, part of which is used for directories and the file allocation table. The end result is that about 360K is left for actual data storage. The tracks, sectors, and other initialization required for a new diskette is done by using the FORMAT program, part of DOS. At as low as $0.25 per diskette in quantity, these diskettes are currently the most popular portable recording medium. Up to 112 different files can be kept on a single 360K diskette. A standard floppy diskette controller is all that is necessary for these drives. See Figure 6.8.

The Quad-Density Floppy Drive

A quad-density diskette drive can access 80 tracks on a diskette instead of the 40 of a double-sided, double-density diskette (96 TPI). The quad-density diskette can store twice as much data as the standard floppy diskette, or about 720K. This format has however, not been popular.

The High-Density Floppy Drive

A high-density 5¼ inch drive will result when a basic quad-density drive is improved to record 15 sectors on each of the 80 tracks rather than 9. This

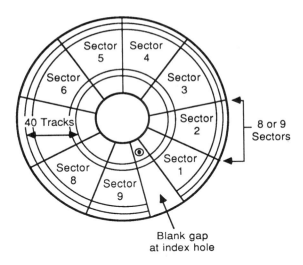

Figure 6.8 Each sector of a diskette has its own code for positive identification.

increases the data storage of the diskette to about 1.2 MB for the diskette. Up to 224 files can be stored on such a disk. High-density diskettes appear to be the same as a standard diskette, but they are not. High-density operation requires that the diskette have a thinner, denser recording surface; thus, standard diskettes will not work reliably, if at all. The quad-density, high-capacity drive also requires a special floppy diskette drive controller. The computer may also require special software, called a driver, in order to use the high-capacity drive.

All 5¼ inch diskettes can be protected from being written to by covering the notch provided for this purpose, cut into the edge of the jacket.

The 3½ Inch Floppy Drive

The 3½ inch drive originally placed data on its smaller, enclosed diskette just like the 5¼ inch diskette, double-sided and 40 tracks, with a resulting 360K of storage. This was quickly doubled to a 720K capacity by recording 80 tracks on the diskette. Up to 112 files could be placed on a 720K, 3½ inch diskette. The 3½ inch, 720K diskettes can be identified by a single write protection hole through the cartridge. Further increase of data density is possible by increasing the number of sectors to 18. With this format, these tiny diskettes can store 1.44 MB and up to 224 files. These high density 3½ inch diskettes can be identified by a hole through the cartridge opposite the write protection slide.

Older microcomputers may have problems using 5¼ and 3½ inch, high-density drives because their system ROM BIOS may not recognize the new devices. Software patches may be necessary.

To write-protect a 3½ inch diskette, open the small slide provided for this purpose.

WRITING DATA ON A FLOPPY DISKETTE

The bottom side of the diskette is called side 0, and the top, the label side, is side 1. Data is recorded on the diskette in a manner similar to that used to record audio on magnetic tape. A tiny electromagnet with a microscopic gap in the head magnetizes the part of the diskette that is in direct contact with the head. See Figure 6.9.

A diskette can be read without modifying the data on the diskette. Writing, on the other hand, destroys all data previously written by the recording head. See Figure 6.10.

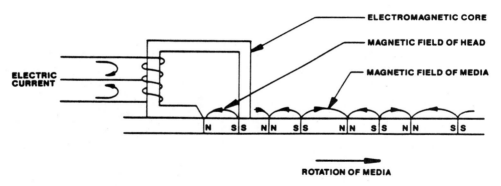

Figure 6.9 A tiny coil produces a magnetic field that is concentrated into a microscopic gap that magnetizes a spot on the diskette. (Courtesy of the Tandon Corp.)

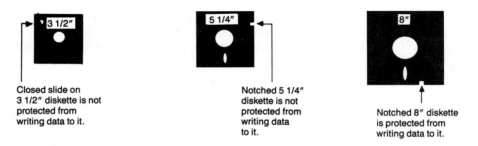

Closed slide on
3 1/2" diskette is not
protected from
writing data to it.

Notched 5 1/4"
diskette is not
protected from
writing data
to it.

Notched 8" diskette
is protected from
writing data to it.

Figure 6.10 The write-protect notch on a diskette prevents accidental writing on a protected diskette by disabling the writing circuitry of the diskette drive at the hardware level.

THE FLOPPY DRIVE CONTROLLER

The electronic circuits necessary for the operation of the floppy diskette drives are split between two boards. The more complex operations are carried out within the floppy drive controller, a card that is usually installed in one of the expansion slots. Both the card and the major controller chip on it are sometimes called the *floppy drive controller.*

Block diagrams show the circuits involved in a read/write operation of the disk drive electronics board. (Figures 6.11 and 6.12).

The floppy drive controller is a complex chip that generates the necessary drive signals and processing data streams to read and write to the diskette. The signals generated by the floppy drive controller card then drive the interface board, which is attached to the diskette drive itself.

CAUTIONS FOR HANDLING FLOPPY DISKETTES

Chapter 2 of this book covers the cautions to be observed when using and handling floppy diskettes. That material should be reviewed at this time, if necessary.

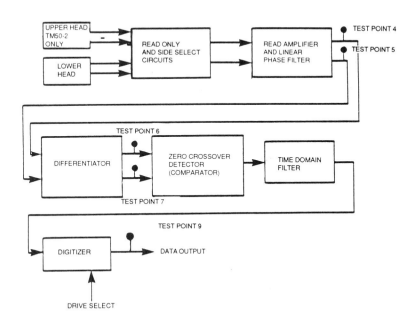

Figure 6.11 These blocks of the floppy diskette system are involved in a read operation. (Courtesy of Tandon Corp.)

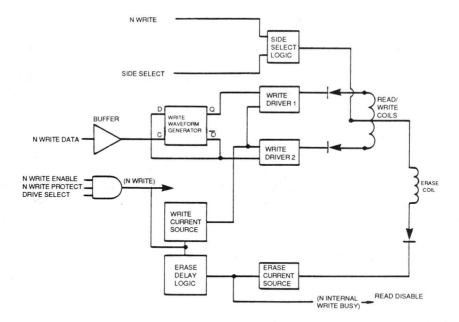

Figure 6.12 These blocks of the floppy diskette system are involved in a write operation. (Courtesy of Tandon Corp.)

CAUTIONS FOR HANDLING A FLOPPY DRIVE

Some cautions are in order here to help the technician prevent further damage to the drives and the diskettes used in them.

1. Never close the door on a double-sided diskette drive without a diskette in the drive. To do so puts the ceramic heads on the top and bottom sides of the diskette in direct contact with each other, which invites chipping. A chipped head can instantly ruin a diskette rotated in the drive. Transporting a drive without the protection of a diskette or a cardboard protector is especially dangerous because of the vibration and bumping of normal transportation.

2. When inserting diskettes into the drives, insert the diskette slowly and carefully, all the way in. Close the drive latch or door carefully, too. Inserting the diskette and clamping it when the drive motor is running will assist greatly in properly seating the drive spindle into the hole with less stress on the edges of the diskette hole. Some drives are designed to rotate while the diskette is being clamped.

CAUTIONS FOR HANDLING A FLOPPY DRIVE CONTROLLER

The floppy drive controller is sensitive, as is any computer circuit board, to electrostatic discharge. All electrostatic discharge prevention methods should be used, particularly when handling the board outside of its antistatic bag. The use of antistatic work mats and with a wrist-strap is highly recommended. Be careful not to touch the card on its edge connector. This is a particularly vulnerable area of the board. Handle it by the edges only.

WHAT A FLOPPY DRIVE FORMAT DOES

The DOS FORMAT program does different things to a floppy diskette than it does when used on a hard disk. The program prepares a floppy diskette for use by setting up all of the required tracks and sectors, laying out and identifying each, and setting up the file allocation table and directory areas. Always remember that FORMATTING A DISKETTE ENTIRELY DESTROYS ANY DATA that may have been on it. Formatting a diskette, in other words, is a start-from-scratch operation.

FLOPPY DRIVE HARDWARE INSTALLATION

The floppy drive controller is a card that processes the commands from the system board to the diskette drive and passes appropriate bytes back to the system board from the recording medium. The controller can be installed in any system board slot, but it is recommended that the card be placed as close to the drives as possible because of the short interunit cabling. Short cards rather than the long, full-length controller cards take up less room inside the case.

The floppy diskette drives themselves are usually installed one on top of the other on the right side of the computer as viewed from the front. Half-height drives are assumed. A pair of older, full-height drives will require the full height of both the right and left sides of the computer. When placed one above the other, the top drive is usually assumed to be the A drive, and the bottom is the B drive. When two drives are installed horizontally, the left drive is usually the "A", the right the "B" drive. Installation of more than two drives seldom has any distinct advantage, although some controllers can handle four drives. A possible exception is the installation of several drives, each of a different capacity.

The floppy diskette drives may be bolted directly to the frame of the computer, or they may be mounted by rails bolted to the sides of the drives. See Figure 6.13. Before tightening the screws holding the rails to the drives, try both drives in the computer to be sure that the proper holes were used on the rails. Also, be sure that the drives come out to the front of the computer and are not recessed too far or too little. The exact rail holes to use are dictated by the specific computer case.

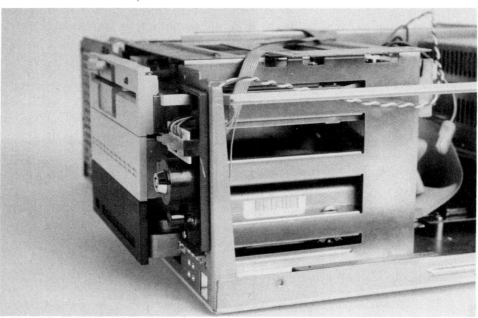

Figure 6.13 The direct mount and rail mount methods of installing floppy diskette and hard drives. Note the use of a hold-in clip on the rail-mounted drive. (Tom Carney)

The signal and control cable is a ribbon cable with 32 wires. It is important to note that the #1 wire is marked along one edge of the ribbon cable. One edge of the cable might be colored red, blue, or black, which indicates the #1 wire. On the controller, pin #1 of the proper plug, usually marked J2 must be on the same end as the #1 cable wire. At the drive, the #1 wire should be matched with the edge connector end that is nearest the small notch cut into the circuit board edge connector.

If two drives are to be installed, the signal control cable will have two connectors for the floppy drives. *The last drive connector on the cable is for the A drive.* The middle connector, of course, is for the B drive.

The power cable from the power supply is also keyed, but cannot be accidentally connected backward since it has a unique keying mechanism. Any of the usual four power connectors that are provided from the power supply will run the drives.

SYMPTOMS OF A BAD FLOPPY DISKETTE DRIVE

A diskette drive that is slightly out of mechanical alignment may very well read a diskette it has itself written on. The written path and the reading path are the same, so the signal is retrieved without problems. Such a drive, however, could be totally unable to read diskettes written on by other drives that *are* in proper alignment. In other words, inability to use a disk from one drive in another drive is a good indication of alignment problems. This problem can be localized to one drive if a known good diskette will not read properly on that drive. A known good diskette is one that has been written by a drive known to be in good condition.

If the drive door of the booting drive is left open or the drive is not providing normal reading of data from the diskette during booting up, the computer will do one of three things: (1) show only a blinking cursor on an otherwise blank screen; (2) in the case of IBM computers, BASIC will load from the IBM ROMs in the computer and the prompt will be the standard BASIC logging-on information and the BASIC prompt OK; or (3) an appropriate "use a system diskette" message appears on the monitor. If the drive access light of the booting drive comes on for a few moments, then goes off without providing the normal data required to boot the computer, a problem is certainly indicated.

LOCALIZING A PROBLEM TO A FLOPPY DISKETTE DRIVE

The following items indicate a probable diskette drive problem:

1. Frequent error messages appear on a specific drive, such as CANNOT OPEN FILE.
2. Diskettes written by one drive cannot be read by another drive.

3. The operating system will not consistently load, if at all, from a particular drive. (Be sure you have a good system diskette for this test.)
4. There is no LED activity indication and files on a drive cannot be accessed.
5. IBM PC computers only: If an IBM PC's A drive is the drive used to load the operating system, a bad drive there will cause the computer to miss loading the system, of course, but the computer will then default to loading BASIC from the ROM chips within the IBM. Only the IBM PC has these ROM chips.

The appearance of

```
The IBM Personal Computer BASIC
Version XXXX Copyright IBM Corp 198X
XXXX Bytes free
Ok
```

is a sure indication of an A drive problem or a floppy diskette problem in that drive.

Either mechanical or electronic problems will cause malfunctions. To verify whether a drive is defective, be sure that the drive motor is operating when the drive is accessed for data and the diskette is revolving within its envelope. See that the activity LED is lighting at the same time. There are two common ways of confirming the condition of a suspected drive. The first method is to substitute a known good drive (if one is available) for the suspected drive; the other is to switch between drives A and B to see if the problem also switches location.

CHECK THE SIMPLE THINGS

Be sure you are using a good diskette before judging that the diskette drive is bad. Try the suspect diskette in another computer if possible. Remember that a drive that is out of alignment may be able to write to and to read its own diskettes just fine, but it won't reliably read a diskette written to by a drive in proper alignment.

Another item that may cause problems is the intercard wiring or the cables. Substitution is the best method to prove the worth of suspect cables.

TROUBLESHOOTING THE FLOPPY DRIVE CONTROLLER

The floppy drive controller can best be eliminated as the source of a problem by substitution. The problem can be localized quickly by taking a suspect controller and trying it in a good machine, or by substituting a known good controller into a malfunctioning computer.

Another option that is a bit easier to do is to swap the controlling and signal cables to the two diskette drives, if so provided. This indicates whether or not the problem is in a single disk drive. With a good drive and a bad drive, the problem should continue with the new control cable.

The first step in isolating a problem within the diskette drives is to eliminate the drive and the interface electronics mounted to it. Since the failure is most likely a mechanical one, substitute another drive. Often, simply switching control cabling with another drive connected to the same computer is the best step to take. Switching drives is a matter of exchanging the control line plugs between the two units. The old A drive becomes the new B drive and vice versa. If this procedure is used, the computer will boot up on the opposite drive from normal. If the problem switches *with* the drive, the problem is probably in the floppy drive controller card, although, of course, a bad diskette can also cause these symptoms. Substitution of another controller card can verify that the old card was causing the problem.

If exchanging the drive control cables shows that the problem remains with the originally suspected drive, that drive should be examined further to see if the cure is a simple one. It is possible that the electronics mounted to the diskette drive are causing the problem. Some diskette drives allow easy removal of the boards, in which case a known good board on the drive can be substituted. Other drives have more complicated connections between the mechanical and electronic units, and substitution of another board may not be as attractive an option (see Figure 6.14).

Figure 6.14 Circuit boards on some drives are easily substituted and can thereby be eliminated as the possible cause of a problem. (Abbey Enterprises)

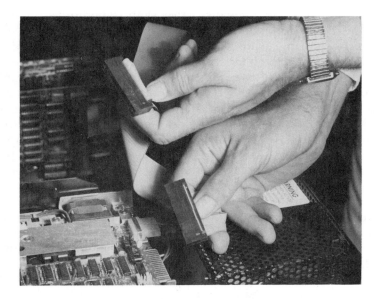

Figure 6.15 Exchanging the A and B drives is a quick way to determine where a floppy diskette drive problem lies. (Abbey Enterprises)

Figure 6.16 Make note of the jumper positions before changing them. (Abbey Enterprises)

Switching Diskette Drives to Verify a Suspected Bad Drive. The technician may decide that it would be a good idea to substitute the normal B drive of the computer for the normal A drive. If the software is then readable in the new A drive, it can be assumed that the original drive A was indeed defective.

To temporarily change the B drive to act as the A drive, you must turn off the computer and remove its cover. When the cover is off, the signal plugs to the A and B drives are removed (see Figure 6.15).

The cable that originally went to the A drive is then placed on the PC connector of the B drive.

The two drives may have a set of jumpers that must be examined before the drive can operate properly (Figure 6.16). These jumpers may be exactly the same on the two drives, the original A and B drives. If so, they may be ignored. If they are different, write down exactly how they differ before you make any changes. Then change the original B drive jumpers to match those of the A drive. The jumpers of a Tandon™ drive are explained in Figure 6.17.

The final item to check in swapping the drives is the terminating resistor, which is installed only on the last drive on a control cable string. In most cases, the cabling comes from the floppy drive controller card to the B drive first, then the A drive. Thus, the A drive will have a terminating resistor installed. This resistor often resembles an ordinary IC (see Figure 6.18).

Although resistors may be installed into a circuit either way, the terminating resistor array in an IC is not necessarily reversible. Note any markings indicating

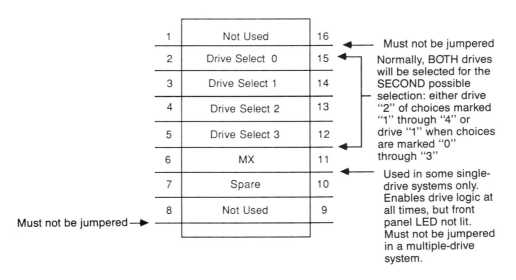

Figure 6.17 Jumpers on the diskette drive enable the drive to be customized to a specific installation.

Figure 6.18 The terminating resistor should be installed on the last drive of the connecting cable. (Abbey Enterprises)

pin #1 of the IC and place it into the socket correctly. Now that the original B drive has the terminating resistor and its jumpers are the same as the original A drive, it should perform as the booting drive. Place an appropriate bootable diskette in the drive, apply power, and see if the computer now loads the program properly. If it does, the original A drive is probably out of alignment or otherwise defective and should be further repaired or discarded.

Keep in mind that there is a small possibility that either the power cable or the signal and control ribbon cable to the drive might be defective. From the center two wires of the power cable to either outside wire should show +12V on one side, +5V on the other. See Appendix A for details of the power plug.

FLOPPY DISKETTE DRIVE PREVENTIVE MAINTENANCE

Preventive maintenance of floppy diskette drives is very easy. Contrary to some thinking on the subject, it is the author's opinion that cleaning a diskette drive read/write head is not particularly beneficial. Floppy disk drives serve for years without giving trouble. By the time the drive might need service, the computer may be out of date and the whole machine may be due for upgrading to something better and faster.

Probably the most beneficial preventive maintenance for a floppy drive is a test run of a special program and diskette available from Xidex. The Investigator™ diskette is a very friendly program that comes with its own specially recorded data. Data is deliberately twisted and made to wander off track to measure the ability of a drive to follow the errant data. Since the data is deliberately off-track, the diskette cannot be effectively copied. See Figure 6.19.

REPAIRING FLOPPY DISKETTE DRIVES

Some years ago, a floppy diskette drive cost more than $300. Now they are available for less than $100. At this price, it is not economical to repair a drive. It is usually easier and less costly to simply discard a proven bad drive and install a new drive. However, as a word of caution, it is a good idea to keep the old drive until the new drive proves to be the solution to the problem. It would be very embarrassing to destroy an old drive thinking it had to be the problem, only to find that a bad cable or the floppy drive controller was the real problem!

CHAPTER SUMMARY

INSTALLING AND TROUBLESHOOTING FLOPPY DISKETTE DRIVES provides information on installing and using this popular means of transferring data from one machine to another. A floppy diskette drive installation consists of one diskette drive adapter card that plugs into the system board and at least one, but up to four, diskette drive units. Some of the terms explained are centering, rotational speed, index width, radial alignment, azimuth, and skew. All drives

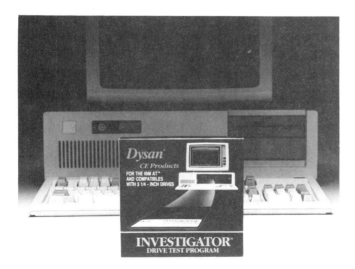

Figure 6.19 The Investigator software, with its specially recorded data, provides an easy, fast way of monitoring floppy drive performance and possible long-term deterioration. (Courtesy of Xidex Corporation)

must go blindly to the same identical position on a diskette in order for the drives to be considered to be "in alignment," thus making it possible for diskettes to be interchangeable between drives. The popular 360K drive uses 40 data tracks with 9 sectors, and 2 sides. Quad-density 5¼ inch drives use 80 tracks and 9 sectors, increasing storage to about 720K. A high-density 5¼ inch drive records 15 sectors rather than 9, storing 1.2 MB of data on special diskettes. A basic 3½ inch drive records 80 tracks of data in 9 sectors, or 720K of storage. Special diskettes and an increase to 18 sectors result in 1.44 MB of storage. Data can be repeatedly read without changing the information on the diskette. Writing, however, destroys all data previously stored on the medium. Formatting a floppy diskette destroys all information previously recorded. The two drives of the average computer installation are designated A and B, with the A drive on the top or the left. An early indication of a diskette drive going out of alignment is failure of the diskettes to interchange between one drive and another. Preventive maintenance is best accomplished by periodic analysis of the drive with the diagnostic diskette available from Dysan, the INVESTIGATOR. Interchanging drives A and B is a good way to determine if one of the drives is defective or if the controller is at fault. Substitution of the controller is the easiest, most conclusive test of the card. A terminating resistor pack should be installed only on the last drive of a daisy-chained set of drives.

REVIEW QUESTIONS

1. What are the two major components of a floppy drive installation?
2. Why would a diskette written on by one drive be unreadable by another drive?
3. How many different files can be kept in the root directory of a 360K floppy diskette?
4. How many files can be kept in the root directory of a high-density floppy diskette? How many files can be kept in the root directory of a 3½ inch, high-density floppy diskette?
5. Which side of the floppy diskette is the "0" side?
6. What caution should be observed in closing the door of a double-sided diskette drive?
7. What is dangerous about the FORMAT command?
8. What are the two cables connected to the diskette drive?
9. You suspect that a particular drive is defective. How can you easily determine whether the problem is caused by the controller or the drive?
10. A drive is definitely determined to be defective. What is the probable course of action?
11. How should the drive selector option on a diskette drive be configured to use the drive?
12. Name one effective, detailed diagnostic program for floppy diskette drive analysis and failure prediction.

chapter seven

Installing and Troubleshooting Hard Disk Drives

CHAPTER OBJECTIVE

INSTALLING AND TROUBLESHOOTING HARD DISK DRIVES explains how to install the hardware of a hard disk system. It also contains hard-to-find information on the configuration methods that can be used. Do's and don'ts of handling hard disk drives and their unique terminology are explained. The internal construction of a typical drive is briefly discussed along with how to calculate the capacity of a hard disk drive. Limitations of the disk operating systems versions 3.3 and 4.0 are pointed out as they relate to the use of a hard disk. Tips are given to take advantage of a new hard disk, things that need to be done with the CONFIG.SYS and AUTOEXEC.BAT files. Finally, the loading and configuration of applications programs is discussed in a generic format.

CAUTIONS FOR HANDLING HARD DRIVES

Both the hard drive and the hard drive controller have plug-in connectors on the edges of the printed circuit boards. These connectors lead directly into the internal workings of some of the ICs mounted on the boards. These ICs do not tolerate the stresses of electrostatic discharge. A pulse of static discharge of as little as 50V can immediately ruin an IC, or it can contribute to future failures. Therefore, handle the controller by the insulated edges of the card, and handle the drive unit by its frame.

The hard drive is an extremely precise mechanical device. Dropping a drive onto a hard surface from as little as half an inch can damage it. In other words, handle like eggs, a warning that at least one hard drive manufacturer puts right on the packing material.

Keep the controller and the drive in their original packaging until the last moment, just before actually installing them. When working with a hard drive for which no packaging is available, store the drive temporarily on padded material such as foam rubber.

When a computer is operating, the read/write heads of a hard drive are "flying" on a cushion of fast-moving air, just above the surface of the rotating disk. The air carried along with the rotating disk causes the heads to rise slightly. The heads are riding a microscopic distance above the medium, 14 microinches near the center of the disk and 19 microinches at the outer edge, according to one manufacturer. If the heads should ever strike the medium while the disk is rotating at its normal 3600 rpm, the heads can damage the coating on the disks and cause catastropic failure of the drive. This is called a "head crash." For this reason, NEVER MOVE OR JAR A COMPUTER WHILE IT IS IN OPERATION if it has a hard drive installed. Immediate failure of the hard drive can occur.

A hard drive can be operated in a horizontal position, as they are usually seen. They can, however, be operated standing on either side, as when the computer is placed on end on a desk, for instance. Some hard drive manufacturers state that their drives should not be operated tilted more than 5 degrees from these positions. In other words, it is not a good idea to block the front end of a computer to tilt it back if there is a hard drive installed.

When a computer is turned off, the heads gradually and gently descend to the surface of the disks as the disks slow down. The heads then contact the medium, right on top of the recorded data. Normally, one can get away with this treatment for a long time before data failures occur. The heads come down at random places on the disk, but always on the data tracks. Transporting a hard disk while the heads are in contact with the data areas of the disk is a poor idea. The heads, through rough handling, can damage the fragile coating on the disks. The heads can be placed in a safer area, however, by running a short PARK program. This puts the heads in a nondata area of the disk, one of the inner tracks not normally used. Thus, you should PARK THE HEADS OF A HARD DISK PRIOR TO TRANSPORTATION, and preferably before turning off the computer after each use. This will bring the heads down in the landing zone, away from the data portions of the disk. An added advantage of parking the heads after each use is that the heads, being on the inner tracks, have less ability to act as a brake when the disk is started up again.

POWER REQUIRED FOR A HARD DRIVE

Adding a hard disk to a computer places an additional load on the computer's power supply. While earlier computers had power supplies of marginal capability, a modern computer should have plenty of reserve for this purpose. Original power supplies had as little as 63 watts of capability, while modern supplies produce as much as 200 watts of power from an enclosure of the same size.

The best way to determine whether the power supply is sufficient to drive a hard disk is to simply install the hard drive and try it. An overloaded switching power supply, the kind usually used in computers, simply refuses to operate if it is overloaded. No fuses will blow and no damage will be done. If the hard drive operates and comes up to normal speed, the power supply is doing its job, at least that far. A final test should be made: Run the diskette drives while the hard drive is also running. This can be done by invoking the DISKCOPY program and attempting to copy from one diskette drive to the other while the hard drive is running. If the DISKCOPY program runs without data read or write problems, then the power supply will do. If, however, the computer stops cold, then reboots itself, the power supply is not sufficient for the job. A power supply of greater capability must be installed to allow reliable operation.

It is interesting to note that the latest hard drive models require less power than earlier models. If you are replacing an old drive with a new one, there is little reason to think that the power supply will not perform adequately.

Appendix A provides the power supply pinouts for connecting power to the hard drives via a 4-pin AMP connector.

HARD DRIVE CONSTRUCTION

Hard Drive Capacity

The capacity of a hard drive is determined by the number of cylinders used, the number of read/write heads (the sides of the platters actually used), the number of sectors within each cylinder, and the number of bytes written into each sector. To find the unformatted capacity of a hard disk knowing these factors, simply multiply them:

Cylinders × Heads × Sectors × Bytes/Sector = Unformatted Capacity.

Example: A hard disk with 615 tracks, 4 read/write heads, and 26 sectors per track puts 512 bytes of data into each sector. What is the unformatted capacity?

615 × 4 × 26 × 512 = 32,694,272 bytes.

A considerable amount of the recording area of the disk is used in writing overhead information such as the identification of each track and sector, the boot record, the file allocation tables, and the hard disk directory. After all this is recorded on the disk, the remaining area is available for the recording of data. Approximately ten percent of a hard disk is used for the recording of overhead data.

Hard Drives Are Sealed Units

Hard disk drives are sealed units. This is necessary because of the microscopic spacing of the heads over the rotating medium, as explained earlier. A piece of dust, a cigarette smoke particle, or a hair can look like a boulder to the flying heads.

Because the units are sealed, A HARD DRIVE SHOULD NEVER BE OPENED unless the drive is ruined and will not be repaired. Special "clean rooms," costing thousands of dollars to build and maintain, are required to safely open a hard drive for repair.

The Drive Number

A hard drive installed into a computer has a number that is used to identify which of a possible two drives it is. DOS 3.3 supports only two hard disk drives. There is a lack of standardization in the numbering of hard drives. Some manufacturers start counting with 1. Others start with 0. Either method can be used for hard drives, and the servicing technician should be constantly aware of the possible confusion that could result. Thus, a drive can be called 0 or 1 if it is the first drive in the computer, making the second drive the 1 or 2 drive, depending on the numbering system used.

Another term sometimes encountered during a formatting session is relative drive. This is nothing more than referring to the two possible drives as drives 0 and 1.

A typical hard disk controller for use in a microcomputer can handle one or two separate hard disks. The first drive is always called the C drive, and the second, if any, is called the D drive.

Tracks or Cylinders

Figure 7.1 shows the concept of cylinders. Cylinders of data recording, sometimes called tracks, are concentric paths under the read/write heads on which the data are recorded. The tracks are concentric, not spiral like the grooves of a record. Using tracks makes it possible to go quickly to a specified location to get data rather than having to run through the long distance of a spiral to find it. The tracks of a hard disk are always numbered beginning with 0. There may be 305 to more than 1224 tracks on a hard disk. The number of tracks is set at the time of manufacture. This is determined by the ability of the read/write heads to record in a small area and the number of steps available from the stepper motor that moves them from track to track.

Sectors

The sectors of a hard disk are arcs along each of the cylinders. The path of the read/write heads on a given cylinder is divided by software into 17, 26, or 34 sectors. Each sector has within it an area into which the data is recorded. The sectors are always numbered beginning with sector 1. Each sector usually has space for 512 bytes of data storage.

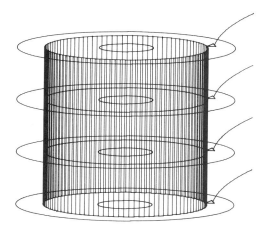

The four heads shown move in or out together. At any given location, the accessed tracks can be visualized as a cylinder.

Figure 7.1 The concept of cylinders within a hard disk drive.

Platters

A hard disk drive will have two or more disks that rotate together at 3600 rpm. Each side of a disk can have a red/write head. A hard drive with three disks could have either five or six heads, for instance. Not all sides of the platters need to be used; thus, a drive can have an odd number of heads.

Number of Heads

There are one or two read/write heads per platter. Drives are available that have from 2 to 30 heads. Heads are always numbered beginning with 0.

Data Recording Methods

There are two methods of recording hard drive data in common use: modified frequency modulation (MFM) and run length limited (RLL). In the MFM system of data recording, data is stored and retrieved at a data rate of 5 megabits per second. The platters are coated with an oxide material that is used as the data storage medium.

In the RLL system of data recording, the rate of data storage and retrieval is 7.5 megabits per second. This requires read/write heads of greater frequency capability than those used in the MFM drive. Platters for RLL operation are generally thin film-plated or sputtered media. Where MFM drives usually use 17 sectors per track, the RLL drive can record 26 sectors per track.

The controller and the drive must both be of the same type, either MFM or RLL. An RLL drive, however, can be operated with an MFM controller, but the drive must be used as an MFM drive. In other words, it must be used with 17 sectors.

Hardcards

A hardcard is an integrated unit consisting of the controller and the hard drive in one package. This card is larger than normal. The hardcard is installed by simply plugging it into a system expansion slot.

INTERNAL OPERATION OF A HARD DRIVE

The controller takes care of the interfacing between the computer, which operates in terms of reading or writing files, and the hard drive itself, which operates on commands such as READ or WRITE to a specified cylinder head and sector.

Besides knowing something about the internal construction of a hard drive, there are some additional software criteria and definitions that the technician should know.

Write Precompensation

Precompensation is used to prevent data errors when reading and writing on the inner cylinders of a hard disk. Certain bit patterns actually migrate slightly on the data surface, producing timing errors upon reading data or the clocking signal. Data can be required to be written either slightly earlier or later than normal by a few nanoseconds (perhaps 12), depending on the previous bit pattern. The use of precompensation is not required on the outer cylinders, but it is instituted beginning with a specified cylinder as the heads move in toward the center of the disks. The cylinder at which the precompensation is to begin is specified by the drive manufacturer for a particular make and model of hard drive. The drive tables in Appendix E show examples of precompensation.

The use of precompensation is begun at a specified track. If track 0 is specified as the beginning track, the entire disk will use precompensation. If precompensation is not used, the last track available plus one should be selected.

A sample of the bit pattern arrangement follows:

Previous Bits		Sending Now	Next Bit	Timing Used
X	0	1	1	Write data late
X	1	1	0	Write data early
1	0	0	0	Write clock late
0	0	0	1	Write clock early

Failure to use precompensation when required will probably result in soft errors in data retrieval. Soft errors occur intermittently, not consistently on each access of the disk. Hard errors, on the other hand, cannot be corrected by repeatedly rereading the information.

Reduced Write Current

Earlier disk drives required reduced write current. Due to decreasing track circumference on the inner tracks, the spacing of the bits becomes more crowded. The current used to write data on the medium surface can be decreased to prevent pulse crowding. As noted, the cylinder where this process of reduced write current begins must be specified. Choosing 0 results in the entire disk being written with reduced current, possibly causing soft errors. If reduced write is not needed, the last track plus one should be specified.

Error Correction Code

The hard disk controller has its own sophisticated microprocessor, dedicated to handling the interfacing of the DOS system requirements to the hardware and software requirements of the hard disk drive. In the process of handling the high-speed transfer of data, error detection and correction software is used to ensure the accuracy of data storage and retrieval. The controller uses the specified error correction byte in its internal programming. A value of 8 or 11 is common.

CCB Option Byte (Step Pulse Rate)

A definite amount of time is required for the heads to move to a new track. The speed at which the step pulses are sent to the hard disk drive is called the *step rate*. This is not the same as the track-to-track seek time, the time required to actually move the heads from one track to another. Track-to-track seek time varies from one drive make and model to another. Typical track-to-track seek time is about 20 milliseconds. When step pulses can be sent to a hard drive at a faster rate than the heads can move, the drive uses a *buffered step* mode. The number of steps is accumulated in a counter, then the heads step at their own slower rate until all of the accumulated count is accomplished. A modern 30 MB drive, for example, will probably use a step rate of about 13 microseconds per step pulse.

Landing Zone—The PARK Program

During formatting, the technician may be required to specify the cylinder to be used for a landing zone. Some programs ask for an offset value to be used from the last cylinder, rather than a cylinder number. This offset value may be a value from 0 to 16. The landing zone is that track used only for the storage of the heads during power down. No data are recorded in the landing zone. Specifications for a particular drive should include the cylinder to be used as the landing zone. The PARK program uses the landing zone track for head storage and moves all the heads there when invoked.

Interleaf

Data are copied from a hard disk into a temporary memory storage area called a *buffer*. The data is then taken out of the buffer for use elsewhere in the computer. This writing and reading takes time. During this time, the disk continues to rotate beyond the end of the sector just read into the following sector. By the time another read is accomplished from the disk, the next sector will have passed beneath the heads, too. How far the disk has progressed is a function of the speed of the computer CPU. In view of the timing involved, it is best to place data into the sectors of the disk in an interleaf fashion. Continuous sectors of data are found, in an interleaf of three, for example, in every third sector. Placing data this way allows faster access. If data were placed consecutively, the disk would have to rotate 26 times to read all the data on a 26-sector cylinder. Using interleaf, however, may allow only three rotations to accomplish the same data transfer. In this case, nine sectors would be read every revolution.

A hard disk can be customized for a particular computer by selecting the interleaf factor that gives the fastest data transfer. An AT will run reliably with an interleaf factor of three, whereas an XT may require an interleaf of four to six. Smaller interleaf factors can be chosen to substantially speed up the operation of a hard disk.

THINGS TO KNOW ABOUT A PARTICULAR DRIVE TO INSTALL IT

Bad Tracks on the Hard Drive

Each hard disk should come from the manufacturer with a record of the defects of the recording medium. Small blemishes may make tiny portions of the disk surface unusable. The manufacturer determines bad areas by rigorous analog and temperature testing. A few blemishes are acceptable, since the software using the disk drive automatically goes to alternative areas of the disk instead of the bad areas. This results in what appears to be a "perfect" drive.

The primary format, sometimes called a low-level format, begins preparation of the disk surface and identifies bad areas on the disks. Entering the manufacturer's bad track data is usually not necessary. The DOS FORMAT utility also identifies and locks out any bad areas of the disk.

If you want to enter bad track data for permanent lockout of the tracks, it can be done in two ways: manually during the primary format in response to the prompts or by using a text editor or the COPY CON: command to enter the defects into an ASCII (simple character) file. Such a file may look similar to the following:

(File name: DRIVE.DEF)

```
; Defect list for Drive serial _____
; Data entry cylinder/head/byte offset
;
32/3/3211
201/1/2118
456/3/3245

>Z
```

(This file must end with a blank line and a carriage return to work properly)

Inspection of the above entries shows that the first of the numbers is the cylinder number, the second is the head number. The last number is called a *byte offset*. This offset is a number provided by the manufacturer to identify the exact area of the medium along a given cylinder that has a problem. This byte offset can be expressed in an MFM format or in an RLL format. The RLL format is 1.5 times the MFM location.

Data entry via the keyboard follows a similar format. Note that the cylinder number and the head numbers may need to be reversed from the previous example.

Using Commercial Primary Formatting Programs

The use of a primary formatting program simplifies and speeds up hard drive installation. This is probably the best and easiest way to install a hard drive. A primary formatting program is recommended when many hard drives must be installed; for example, at a computer distributorship. All that needs to be known is the make and model of the hard drive to be installed, or the standard drive type. Standard drive types are listed in Appendix E.

An example of a commercial primary formatting program is SPEEDSTOR. This program is available through distributors or from Storage Dimensions, 2145 Hamilton Ave., San Jose, CA 95125.

Using the Controller Primary Formatting Program

Hard disk controllers may have the necessary primary formatting programming within their ROM BIOS chips, located on the controller card. With this program, there are two ways to enter primary formatting drive data:

1. Using the controller's built-in installation default tables (jumper-selected tables)
2. Manual or "dynamic" entry of data entry.

Using Built-In Installation Defaults. Using the tables provided within the controller's ROM requires that the documentation for the controller be available. The drive make and model are matched with one of the tables in the controller instructions. If a match is found, the jumpers on the controller are changed accordingly. For instance, the author's controller has built-in tables containing information as follows:

65 MB capacity, 5 heads, 26 cylinders, no Precomp
92 MB capacity, 7 heads, 26 cylinders, no Precomp
33 MB capacity, 4 heads, 26 cylinders, Precomp @ 300
33 MB capacity, 4 heads, 26 cylinders, Precomp @ 128

Tandon model TM755 and Vertex model V150 both have 65 MB capacity, 26 sectors per cylinder, 981 tracks, and 5 heads. These drives would both use the default parameters for the first entry of the table listed. All that the technician would have to do to call up these defaults during the formatting process is to place a jumper on the controller in the proper position and proceed with the manual formatting procedure. Tandon, Vertex, Priam, Microscience, Miniscribe, and Seagate all have drives that fall into one of these four categories. Other drives with requirements identical to those in the tables can also be formatted using these tables.

Two different drives can be formatted using the tables. Two jumpers may be provided to select different default tables for each of the two drives. The instruction manual for the controller will give details on using the default tables.

In applications where many similar hard drives must be installed with the same kind of controller, jumper selection of the default values is a good way to format the hard disks. For instance, this might be the best way for a computer distributor to install hard drives in 100 machines, if commercial formatting software is not chosen.

If a match is not found between the default values provided in the controller jumper-selected tables and the requirements of the drive to be installed, the manual method must be used.

Manual or Dynamic Method of Data Entry. Without commercial formatting software or information on the jumper table defaults provided on a controller, a hard drive can still be formatted using the software included in the controller's ROM. Besides the basic information on cylinders, number of heads, formatted capacity, and sectors, there are a few more things that must be known to properly respond to prompts during the manual formatting process.

Step rates for sending stepping pulses to the new drive should be known. Most hard drives use a buffer to keep track of how many steps to go. This buffer is filled at a high rate of speed, called the step rate, from the controller to the drive. It is best to use a longer step rate than a shorter one when in doubt.

Step rates are usually coded into a single number. While step rate codes may vary from one brand of controller chip to another, the following codes might be used in the absence of exact information, but without any guarantee of their accuracy.

Code	Step Pulse
0	3.0 milliseconds (unbuffered)
1	46.5 microseconds
2	30 microseconds
3	13 microseconds
4	200 microseconds
5	70 microseconds
6	28.5 microseconds
7	10.5 microseconds

HARD DRIVE HARDWARE INSTALLATION

One or two hard drives are installed and cabled similar to Figure 7.2. The best source of information for the installation of a hard drive and a controller is, of course, the documentation that comes with them. Lacking this information, the following methods may be used with a high degree of confidence.

Configure the Controller Jumpers

The controller card may have several jumpers, the locations of which should be verified with the documentation received with the controller to be sure that the factory default settings are intact. Occasionally, a jumper gets moved by "no one" and causes all sorts of problems during installation. Verify. Be sure. In the absence of instructions to the contrary DON'T CHANGE ANYTHING ON THE BOARD FROM THE FACTORY SETTINGS. In the unlikely event that it is necessary to change a setting, WRITE DOWN THE INITIAL JUMPER SETTINGS before changing any of them. This way, you can always backtrack to the beginning. If worst comes to worst, perhaps the controller card vendor can assist in getting the jumpers correct for your hard drive application. Jumpers may be provided for such things as enabling internal controller diagnostics, jumper-selecting the step rate to be used, the size of the controller ROM chip installed, various factory testing jumpers, and the digital address of the controller.

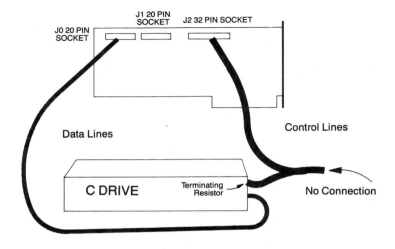

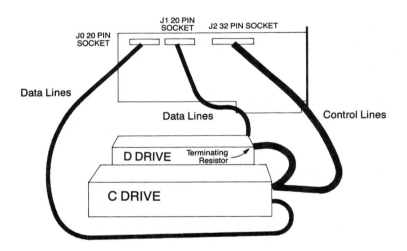

Figure 7.2 Block diagram of hard drives and the cabling used.

Configure the Hard Drive Hardware

Again, it is best to have the proper documentation for the hard drive in question. Vendor help may also be available.

Hard Drive Jumpers. The main selection to be made on a hard drive is the drive select jumper. This setting determines whether the drive responds as the first or the second of up to two drives. The first drive must be jumpered to respond as the first drive. The second drive, if any, must be jumpered to respond as the second drive. This is the case unless the data cable (the wide one) has a twist at the last of the connectors. In this case, *both* drives should be jumpered as the second drive.

One of the jumper choices is whether or not to operate the drive in a radial configuration. A radial configuration would have a 20-pin and a 34-pin cable to each of the drives. This configuration is not used in microcomputers; the daisy-chain method is used instead. Therefore, DO NOT select the radial option on the drive. To do so would cause software failure in operating the drive, and all output signals would be forced active. (The drive LED would be on all the time.)

The Terminator Resistor (Resistor Pack). The hard drive is controlled through flat ribbon cables. Because of the high-frequency signals passing back and forth within the cables, reflections can become a problem. The controller and the drive are engineered to terminate cables on both ends in their characteristic impedance, thus eliminating reflections that would cause data errors. This termination takes the form of a resistor pack of 220 to 330 ohms. Since the installation of a hard drive involves the cables, the termination varies with the system. The end result is that the last hard drive in a system with two hard drives should have the terminator resistor in place. It should be removed in the first drive. If a single drive is installed, the terminator resistor should be installed in the drive.

Mount the Hard Drive

If the front of the hard drive is to be visible when the case cover is installed, the LED in the front of the drive is easily seen lighting when the drive is accessed. If, however, the drive is installed behind the front panel of the computer, this LED is not seen. It is necessary to unplug the LED at the front of the drive. Another LED should be provided on the control panel of the computer for this monitoring purpose. Simply run the wiring from the control panel LED into the drive and connect where the original LED on the drive connected. Remember that the LED is polarity sensitive and must be connected properly to light. If in doubt, connect the LED either way and check its operation during the first power-up. If the LED does not light, try reversing the connections. Accidental reversal of the leads to the LED does not harm it.

Floppy diskettes are usually installed one above the other on the right side of the computer. The hard drive is then installed in one of the slots to the left. An empty space is covered with a blank panel. Two hard drives can be stacked on the left side.

It is possible that the bottom of a hard drive will electronically interfere with the operation of a floppy diskette placed directly beneath it. If a hard drive and a floppy drive are to be stacked together, place the hard disk on the bottom.

The hard drive may be bolted either of two ways, the same as the floppy drives. The first way is to simply bolt it to the inner framework of the computer, and the second is to use the more sophisticated slide rails installed on the side of the drive, slipping it into the slots provided. The installation of the rails can be varied within a half-inch or so to allow proper flush mounting of the front of the drive to the front panel. Before tightening the rail screws, try the front cover in place to be sure the drive extends the right amount.

Before sliding the drive all the way in, connect the two ribbon cable edge connectors to the drive. Remember that the flat cable is marked with a strip of paint down one edge, identifying wire #1. The edge connectors on the drive have a small slot near the #1 end of the connector. Connect the four-wire power connector last. A small bracket and screw is then installed at the front of the rails to hold the drive in place.

Install the Controller

The control and data cables should then be connected to the controller. The connector often used for this purpose can often be connected incorrectly, so BE CAREFUL WHEN ATTACHING THE CABLE. Be sure that pin #1 is identified correctly (sometimes the markings on the board are not clear or can be misleading). Insert the connector carefully, being careful also that both rows of the connector engage and that the connector is not off by one pair of pins. The colored edge of the ribbon cable identifies pin #1 on the cable connector.

If only one drive is to be connected to the controller, connect the 20-pin connector to the controller connector labeled J0. The J1 20-pin connector is used only when two drives are installed. J2 identifies the connector for the control cable. Two different cables are available for this use. If a single hard drive is to be installed, a simple cable is used, connecting the far end to the single drive, drive C. If two drives are to be installed, a different cable is used. This cable plugs into J2 of the controller, but has two printed circuit board edge connectors on the other end. These connectors connect to the two hard drives. Inspection of the cable shows that a few of the wires within the cables are twisted. The connector with the twisted cable is for the second drive, drive D.

The controller can be inserted into any of the system board expansion slots. Because of the broad cables used, the controller is usually installed in one of the first slots, near the power supply. The usual location may have to be changed if the card is too long to fit there. Remove the dust cover over the rear access slot, if any, and gently insert the card into position. Be sure the card's edge connector is lined up with the expansion slot and press firmly on the card, rocking slightly front to back, to work it into the connector. Lock the card into place with a screw at the top of the rear access slot.

The signals passed back and forth between a hard drive and the controller are as follows:

Data Signals. Data signals are passed to and from the drive via a connector on the drive, AMP part number 88373-6:

Signal	Ground	Signal Name
1	2	Drive Selected
3	4	Reserved
5	6	Reserved
7	8	Reserved
9	10	Reserved
	11	Ground
	12	Ground
13		+ Write Data
14		− Write Data
15	16	Ground
17		+ Read Data
18		− Read Data
	19	Ground
	20	Ground

Control Signals. Control signals are passed to the drive via a connector on the drive, AMP part number 88373-3:

Signal	Ground	Signal Name
2	1	Head Select, Binary 3
4	3	Head Select, Binary 2
6	5	Write Gate
8	7	Seek Complete
10	9	Track Zero
12	11	Write Fault
14	13	Head Select, Binary 0
16	15	Recovery Mode
18	17	Head Select, Binary 1
20	19	Index
22	21	Ready
24	23	Step
26	25	Drive Select 1
28	27	Drive Select 2
30	29	Drive Select 3
32	31	Drive Select 4
34	33	Direction In

HARD DRIVE SOFTWARE INSTALLATION

A Little Background Information

While it is not unusual for the hard drive and controller to be made by different manufacturers, the technician should attempt to verify that the controller will operate the specific drive to be installed. Documentation for the controller may help, or the vendor for the controller may verify whether the two are compatible. Lacking such information, it may still be possible to match the controller and driver. If the drive table information for the controller is available, one can determine the default settings thus simplifying the process for multiple hard drive installations. For a single installation, the technician can attempt manual entry of all of the information for the drive during the primary formatting process.

A few definitions are now in order. The software used to install hard drives assumes certain definitions are understood. A *physical drive* is the one that you buy. It is a single hard drive. A *logical drive*, on the other hand, is what the computer *thinks* you bought. If you configure the physical drive accordingly, the computer will think that the single drive is two separate drives, the logical drives. A logical drive is also sometimes called a *virtual drive*.

Another term that can be confusing is *relative drive*. Relative drive 0 simply means drive 0, the first of two possible drives. Relative drive 1, of course, is the second of two drives.

DOS Version 3.3 supports only two hard disk drives, whether they are physical or logical drives. Thus, if two physical drives are installed, the first one should not be split into two logical drives.

Another limitation of DOS 3.3 is that it will not support a logical drive of more than 32 MB. If your hard drive has less than 32 MB, there is no problem. You may, if you wish, divide that drive into two logical drives, C and D, with software. This will probably speed up operation of either logical drive somewhat because the heads do not have to cover all the cylinders while seeking information. This division of the drive into two parts can be done during either the primary format or later with the DOS FDISK program. The FDISK way is the simpler of the two methods. If your hard disk has between 32 and 64 MB, you must divide it so that both logical drives, C and D, are less than 32 MB. DOS 3.3 will support only one of these larger capacity drives.

Hard drives of more than 64 MB capacity, up to a limit of 256 MB, can be used with DOS 3.3, but special partitioning input/output driver software must be used. Such software may be available from ONTRACK COMPUTER SYSTEMS, (612) 941-4504 or CHASE TECHNOLOGIES (202) 894-5544.

DOS version 4.0 does not have the 32 MB limitation, allowing up to 2 gigabytes (GB) on a hard drive.

The Primary (Low-Level) Format

Primary formatting is the most involved part of installing a hard disk. Primary formatting destroys all the data on a hard disk. All new cylinder and sector information is placed on the disk, and all data is written over during a write/verify procedure that is part of the primary format program. NEVER PRIMARY FORMAT A WORKING HARD DISK WITHOUT FIRST BACKING UP ALL DATA! Primary formatting is not something to play with unless you can afford to lose everything from the drive.

Once DOS 4.0 is installed on a computer with a hard disk, booting up on a DOS 3.3 diskette will result in not being able to access the hard disk.

Primary formatting may already have been done by the computer vendor. This is often done when a controller and a drive are purchased together. Remember that the controller and the drive are linked together once a primary format has been done. Trading off the drive or the controller or both means that a new primary format must be done. One way of determining whether the drive has already been primary formatted is to run FDISK and ask for a display of the partition information. The FDISK program will report an error if the primary format has not been done.

If you have purchased two drives, each must be formatted separately. If you have elected to logically partition a drive during primary format, one pass of the primary formatter will do the job for both C and D logical drives. Primary formatting typically takes about 30 seconds per megabyte of storage capacity.

A hard drive should be primary formatted in the orientation of use. In other words, if the drive will be used in a computer that is normally used on its side, then the drive should be formatted while in this position.

What the Primary Format Does. The primary format sets up the cylinders and sectors on the hard disk from scratch. Into each of these are placed their addresses, space for error correction information, and space for the actual data to be stored. As a means of testing the disk surface for defects, all of the data areas are written into with data and then those data are read back. Although a controller is able to correct data that are read incorrectly, this feature is not used during the verification process—the information has to be read back perfectly without any software help. If the correct information comes back, there is no defect on the medium. Some controllers make two passes during primary formatting to write and to verify data to be sure that the surface is free of defects. One manufacturer uses a binary pattern of 11100101 during the write/read verify passes.

If one of the sectors of a cylinder is determined to be bad, the primary formatter may reformat the entire track, adding a single additional sector to that track. The new sector is then substituted for the bad one, and the bad sector is "locked out" and never used. For instance, if an RLL controller finds that 1 of the 26 tracks of a cylinder is bad, the track is formatted again, this time with 27 sectors. The new sector takes the place of the bad one.

If more than one sector of a track is found bad, the entire track is marked bad. One of a few unused inner tracks reserved for this purpose is then substituted for the bad track. This produces a "perfect" hard disk with full capacity. If there are an excessive number of bad tracks, this will reduce the total capacity of the disk.

The formatting information input during the primary format is then written to the disk as part of the primary formatting. The number of cylinders, heads, sectors, and the precomp cylinder are written to the disk where they are used in initializing the hard disk controller each time power is applied to the computer. This information is written on cylinder 0, head 0, sector 1. A bad track table is also written for the use of the controller. All of this information is transparent to the computer user.

The recording of this information links the controller and the drive together. Changing drives or controllers usually makes it necessary to re-do the other primary format on the drive.

DOS Limitations. DOS 3.3 has a space limitation of 32 MB per drive (physical or logical) and a maximum of two hard drives. Thus, DOS 3.3 by itself has a limitation of 64 MB of hard disk storage, regardless of the drive size. Additional drivers are required to handle larger drives with this version of DOS.

DOS version 4.0, on the other hand, has a limitation of 2 GB (2000 MB). The FDISK program provided with version 4.0 makes it easy to divide a large drive into as many as four separate logical drives.

The "Automatic" Method of Primary Formatting. The easiest way to primary format a hard drive is to use commercial software. Answer a few simple questions, and the drive is primary formatted. If no such program is available, proceed to the "manual" method of primary formatting.

Ease of use makes a primary formatting program particularly dangerous to data already recorded on a hard drive—DON'T MESS AROUND WITH PRIMARY FORMATTING PROGRAMS UNLESS YOU DON'T MIND IF ALL OF THE INFORMATION ON THE HARD DISK IS LOST FOREVER! This software is intended to be used on new drives, or when moving hard drives or controllers to new machines. It is not necessary to primary format a hard drive if the controller and the hard drive stay together as a pair.

Another caution is that primary formatting software can change the CMOS setup memory of an AT computer, even without actually invoking the formatter itself. Such a change causes the hard drive to apparently malfunction, making it impossible to read any data from the drive. The cure is simple: Run the SETUP procedure for the computer and reestablish the proper parameters for the drive as prompted. An immediate cure of the problem should result.

When using commercial formatting software, all one needs to do is to boot the computer with a floppy disk, using the latest version of DOS. DOS versions

3.1 or later are recommended. This boot up diskette must include the operating system, which consists of two hidden BIOS and DOS files, and the visible file COMMAND.COM.

The DOS diskette can now be removed and replaced with the commercial primary formatting software diskette. Invoke the program by typing the appropriate command, depending on the software used.

SPEEDSTOR is an example of commercial software used for primary formatting of a hard disk. It also includes some very good diagnostics to analyze the integrity of the hard disk surface. This program is invoked by typing INSTALL and following the simple prompts. The INSTALL.BAT file of SPEEDSTOR contains all the directions necessary to step you through the primary formatting and the preparation of the disk partitions. (Note: DOS 4.0 may not be compatible with the partitioning part of SPEEDSTOR. If this is the case, use only the primary formatting part of SPEEDSTOR, then use the FDISK program provided with DOS 4.0 for the partitioning.)

The program must be told the number of cylinders, number of sectors, number of heads, and whether to use precompensation. There are three ways to do this, in order of ease:

1. Specifying the drive make and model
2. Specifying a standard-type drive
3. Entering each parameter individually.

Commercial software does not use any jumper-selected configuration tables that might be provided on the controller.

The "Manual" Method of Primary Formatting. There is software available within most controller ROMs to accomplish the primary format. This method of formatting can be done one of two ways:

1. Using the jumper-selected configuration tables of the controller
2. Entering cylinder, sectors, head, and precompensation data manually in response to prompts. This method is sometimes called "dynamically" configuring the drive.

If no commercial formatting software is available, it is necessary to use the controller's ROM formatter. The computer must be booted up on a floppy disk using DOS 3.1 or later. This diskette should have the following files on it, to speed things up:

DOS operating system

COMMAND.COM

DEBUG

FDISK

FORMAT

The next step is to direct the computer's CPU to begin a special program within the controller's ROM. The easiest way to do this is to use DOS's DEBUG program. This program is used extensively by programmers because it gives a direct "handle" on the CPU. One of the commands is the "g" command, used to tell the CPU to "go" to a specific location and execute the program there.

At the DOS prompt, type DEBUG and a carriage return. After a few moments, you should see a "-" or dash. This is the DEBUG program's prompt. Type the following information and hit return:

This is a command to the computer's CPU to go to an address in memory of C800 with an offset from there of 5 bytes. This is the exact starting point for the primary formatter program. Alternate starting points are C800:CCC or CC00:5. If the first location of C800:5 crashes the computer, try rebooting one of the remaining alternate addresses. Western Digital, a major manufacturer of hard disk controller cards, sponsors a technical support line that can be reached at 1-800-777-4787. Perhaps this number can be of use to you if you are caught on an important job without information.

Read the prompts very carefully. Pay particular attention to any instructions that may require you to enter formatter data in other than decimal format! Some formatters use hex notation, and all information entered must be converted to that numbering base. Improper conversion to hex causes errors and the primary format will probably fail.

At least one formatter program asks whether you wish to virtually configure the drive. This question might be better termed, "Would you like to make two logical disks out of one physical disk?" If you chose to do so, you need to divide the disk into two parts by cylinder number, adding up to the total number of cylinders available. As an example, you could virtually configure the disk into two drives, C and D, by dividing an available 615 cylinders into two virtual disks of 300 and 315 cylinders. The first number of cylinders are allocated for the C drive, the second for the D drive.

The trick now is to recognize some of the words used in the controller prompts during the installation:

1. Use Default Parameters? This means, "Do you wish to use the jumper-selected tables?" If you do, respond with a "Y." If you wish to bypass the tables and enter data manually as prompted, select "N."
2. Are You Dynamically Configuring the Drive? This means, "Do you wish to enter data manually?" If you do, respond with a "Y" and enter data as prompted. If you respond with an "N," the default values as selected by the jumpers will be used.

When you respond that you wish to use the jumper-selected defaults, you will not be asked for the maximum cylinders, the number of heads or sectors, or where to begin precompensation, if any. The jumpers must have been properly set for these values during the configuration of the jumpers on the controller card.

It is possible that one of the jumpers on the controller is used to prevent the manual entry of data: dynamic configuration of the drive. If you do not get the expected prompts, look for this possibility.

The answers to most of the prompts depends on understanding the terms and explanations covered in this chapter. Basically, this amounts to knowing the following:

Maximum number of cylinders

Number of heads

Number of sectors

Cylinder to begin precompensation

Cylinder to begin reduced write current

Error burst length (ECC Byte)

Step rate

Appendix E or F may help to determine unknown values or verify values in the event of format failure. If you cannot determine all of these criteria, your controller/hard disk vendor should be able to supply the needed information.

When the primary formatting program is done, you must reboot the system, either through a warm boot using the Ctrl-Alt-Del keys or by hitting the reset button on the computer. The power can also be turned off, but this is harder on the power supply than the other methods of rebooting. Rebooting the computer is necessary for the new information to be read from the hard disk. This is part of the normal power-up initializing of the hard disk controller. Without a reboot of the computer, the FDISK program will not run properly.

Failures of the Primary Format. While the normal conclusion of a primary format may vary, its success often informs the user to reboot. If there is a problem in the format, the following suggestions may solve the problem.

1. **Mismatch between drive and controller:** A format will fail if the wrong number of cylinders, sectors, or heads are entered and the drive does not match those criteria. Check the positions of the jumpers on both the controller and the drive. Be very sure that you have not selected radial configuration on the drive. Check the make and model if using the tables in Appendix F to verify the parameters used.
2. **Drive 0 for first drive:** Remember that the drive designations will vary according to the numbering system used: 0,1,2,3 or 1,2,3,4.
3. **Note hex/decimal entry format:** Rerun the formatter again, looking for an entry that may require you to convert decimal values to hex values before entering them. If this is required, recheck your hex values to be certain they are correct.

4. **Read errors. Check write precomp and reduced write values:** If you get many errors in spite of the correct cylinder, head, and sector counts, verify that you are using the proper write precompensation. Not using precomp when it is required will result in soft errors.

5. **Proper cable connectors used:** Be sure you have properly seated the connectors between the controller and the drive and that you have the cable oriented so that pin #1 is where it should be on each end. Be sure you have plugged in J3 on the drive, the DC power input plug.

6. **Swap drive:** If all else fails, change out the drive or the controller with another known good unit, then retry formatting. If substitution of one does not cure the problem, change out the other. This is a sure way of determining whether the controller or the drive has a problem.

7. **Blew it? Must redo primary format:** An error that results in formatter failure makes it necessary to do the primary format all over again. This is necessary because the correct information must be recorded on the hard drive for reading each power-up.

Don't forget that the computer must be rebooted on successful completion of the primary format.

Using FDISK

The FDISK program provided as part of DOS is used to put the boot record on the hard disk in the proper place. The boot record is part of a program used to load the DOS operating system. The FDISK program can also be used to divide a single physical drive into two logical drives, in a manner similar to that of the primary format.

The FDISK program should be used with great caution. DO NOT ATTEMPT TO CHANGE THE PARTITIONING OF A HARD DRIVE WITH DATA ON THE DRIVE! Partitioning should be done once, when the disk is first installed or after all data has been copied off the drive, preparatory to copying it back on later.

The FDISK program of DOS 3.3 will work with only two drives, either logical or physical. It can also be used to divide a physical drive of less than 32 MB into two logical drives (with DOS 3.3) by setting the partition at any point on the drive. A drive of 32 MB, for instance, can be divided into two drives of 20 and 12 MB with this program. DOS 4.0's FDISK will work with up to four logical or physical drives.

Verify with FDISK that the primary format was accomplished properly. Following the prompts, ask for a display of the partition information. This should show the number of available cylinders minus one.

To divide a single physical drive into two or more logical drives (depending on the DOS version in use) with this program, follow the prompts. Specify the size of the desired logical drives. If the entire disk is specified for the partition, the partition is placed at the end, resulting in a single logical drive. If the drive has already been divided using the primary formatting program, each of the drives will require the separate use of FDISK.

If there are problems in running FDISK, it may be necessary to go back to the primary format and check that, possibly redoing the primary format if you find a problem with it.

Using FORMAT

The FORMAT program, one of the DOS utility programs, accomplishes the final tasks in preparing a hard disk for use. When used with a hard disk, FORMAT senses that it is not working with a floppy disk and operates entirely differently. The FORMAT program establishes the file allocation tables. It then sets aside the proper areas for up to 512 directory entries. It then deallocates bad sectors of the hard disk.

The command to format the C drive is

FORMAT C:

The FORMAT program will also, if the proper command is given, install the operating system on the hard disk on drive C. Putting the operating system on the hard disk makes it possible to boot up the computer without having a floppy disk in drive A. The proper command to prepare the hard disk, including the operating system, is

FORMAT C:/S

It is not necessary to put the operating system on the hard disk if data is to be restored from disks that used the BACKUP program to store data on them. The operating system from the original hard disk will be copied onto the new hard disk during the running of the RESTORE program. The FORMAT program must be run on all drives, logical or physical.

It is interesting and important to note that the FORMAT utility does not overwrite the data sectors on a hard drive. Although a new boot record, file allocation table, and directory are made, the old data remains on the hard disk. Special software is available that can retrieve the old data without benefit of the disk areas that were written over. An example of this software is the MACE-Plus software package.

CHECKING THE HARD DRIVE INSTALLATION

If the normal operation of a microcomputer is still new to you, this is a good time to review the information in Chapter 1.

If the hard disk is installed on an AT computer, it is necessary to run the SETUP utility so that the computer will run properly. An XT needs no special setup.

The SETUP utility can be a program on a diskette for some computers. In some cases, a special three-key keyboard combination can be used to invoke similar software located within the computer's ROM. One such combination is Ctrl-Alt-Esc. The SETUP program needs to know the same cylinder, head, sector, and precomp information used during the primary formatting of the hard disk. This information is most often entered by using the standard-type numbers as listed in Appendix E. If you have used commercial primary formatting software, the AT setup may have already been changed by that software.

The computer should now boot up from the operating system installed on drive C. Do a warm boot (Ctrl-Alt-Del) or hit the reset button on the front of the computer. Be sure the A drive door is open so that the computer cannot boot on any floppy diskette that may be there.

Failure to boot from the C drive after a successful primary format and running FDISK is usually caused by not having the operating system installed properly. The operating system must be the FIRST files placed on the C drive. Before copying any other data to a new hard drive, be sure the operating system is there and that the computer will boot up from the hard drive.

If for some reason the computer will not boot up from the hard disk after using the DOS utility FORMAT, the operating system can be manually installed using the SYS command. Put a diskette with the operating system and the SYS.COM file on it into drive A and boot up the computer. Use the SYS command:

SYS C:

The SYS program will transfer the DOS and BIOS files of the operating system to the root directory of the hard disk where they belong. When the SYS program is finished, it is necessary to manually copy one more file to the hard disk before it will be bootable. Copy the program COMMAND.COM onto C drive, then try the boot-up again.

When the computer is booting properly from the hard drive, attempt to copy one diskette to another using both the floppy disk drives. This places the maximum load on the power supply, since the hard disk will also be running all the time. If a successful DISKCOPY can be made, the power supply is sufficiently powerful to handle the added load of the new hard drive.

There is one obscure caution to observe when running IBM Advanced Diagnostics. This program will destroy any data placed on a second virtual drive.

TUNING UP THE COMPUTER FOR HARD DRIVE USE

Merely adding a hard disk to a computer does not automatically take advantage of all of the possible speed available from using a hard disk. A computer with a hard drive can be customized to take advantage of the added capabilities by adding two lines to a special file in the root directory called the CONFIG.SYS file. This file is "looked for" at each power-up (the only time it is ever used). With the added storage capability, it is now advantageous to allow the computer to have several files open at the same time. Besides this, it behooves us to have a "bigger bucket" in which to transfer data from the hard disk to the application programs requesting and writing it back to the hard disk. A file called CONFIG.SYS should contain at least these two lines:

FILES = 20
BUFFERS = 40

The interleaf factor of a hard disk may be changed for optimum speed of hard disk access. Once the hard disk is up and running, even if it has data on its surface, the interleaf factor can be changed. This is rather like making a bed without disturbing the occupant.

A program such as the shareware CORE is an excellent analysis of the performance of a hard disk. Of particular importance is the amount of information that can be transferred in a given amount of time. Using this program as a measure, another program such as SPEEDSTOR can be used to change the interleaf factor without using the primary format. One available option in SPEEDSTOR is to reinitialize the disk, changing the interleaf factor. Here are some results of changing the interleaf factor on the author's AT:

AT with interleaf of 1 =   29.0 KB/sec
                       2 = 274.8 KB/sec
                       3 = 252.7 KB/sec
                       4 = 190.4 KB/sec

The higher the data rate, the faster information is written to and read from the hard disk.

Data fragmentation occurs when files are changed. A written document produced by a word processor, for instance, might have been changed dozens of times. The file as written on the hard disk is not written in consecutive sectors, but, after editing, ends up with pieces scattered in many different tracks and sectors on the surface of the disks. This scattering of the file does not hurt the file at all and is completely transparent to the user.

Excessive scattering, however, slows down the gathering of a large document, requiring the movement of the heads to many different cylinders before the entire file is available. A file that has become scattered is said to be *fragmented*.

Files can be defragmented using software written for this purpose. Such software should be foolproof, not allowing the loss of files in the event of power failure or any external problem. A good program for this purpose is OPTIMIZE. This program will reorganize directory entries and will even test the computer's memory to be sure it is up to par.

Any well-organized hard disk directory should be alphabetized. While some menu programs automatically sort directory entries alphabetically before displaying them, the actual directory is not sorted. The Norton DIRSORT program is exceptionally good at very quickly putting a directory into alphabetical order.

INSTALLING APPLICATIONS AND DATA

When a hard disk is initially loaded with programs, each application program should be put into its own directory. Data files for each should be put under those directories in subdirectories. Only files that are used often should be put on a hard disk. One-time use files such as printer drivers should not occupy space on a hard disk. Keep these on the diskettes where they are available if needed once in a great while.

After a hard disk is in operation for a while, it should be backed up using the DOS BACKUP program. Files are copied from the hard disk onto floppies in a somewhat compressed form, and as such cannot be used directly from these diskettes. The BACKUP program has the distinct advantage that it will split up a large file into smaller portions that can be put on several diskettes.

The DOS RESTORE program is used to copy files from backup diskettes back to the hard disk. RESTORE will put files that have been split up and recorded on separate diskettes back together when placed on the hard drive.

TROUBLESHOOTING HARD DISK DRIVES

A hard disk is a mechanical thing. And because it is mechanical, it will wear, and, with enough hours of operation, eventually fail. Since this is always a possibility, work should be copied from the hard disk whenever it reaches a point where sudden loss of the hard disk would be more than just an inconvenience. Using the BACKUP command with the appropriate options makes this easy.

Before backing up a hard drive, have enough formatted diskettes ready to receive all the files of the hard drive. This will amount to about 3 diskettes (362K size) for each megabyte used on the hard disk. The amount of storage used is the total formatted capacity of the hard disk minus the amount shown whenever a directory command is given. As an example, the author's AT has a 20 MB hard drive, and after running the DIR command, about 8.9 MB remain. Rounding this down to 8 MB to be safe, one calculates that 12 MB have been used to store programs and data. About 36 diskettes should be available to back up all of this hard disk. Since BACKUP will not format a diskette, each of the 36 diskettes must first be formatted using the DOS FORMAT program.

To back up the entire C drive, for instance, have the BACKUP program available (use the PATH command in the AUTOEXEC.BAT file). Be sure you are in the root directory of C as the default directory. Type the following command:

BACKUP C: B:/S

This will back up the entire C drive to diskettes placed in the B drive. Just follow the prompts. This procedure should be done perhaps once a month.

For daily or more frequent backup, the following command will back up only the files that are new or changed since the last BACKUP command. Be sure to be in the C root directory as the default:

BACKUP C: B:/S/M/A

This will back up only the Modified files from all Subdirectories and Append them to the end of the string of floppies originally used to back up the entire C drive. You must place the proper numbered BACKUP diskette in drive B for this to continue properly.

Since it is difficult to remember all of the codes involved, the following batch file, arbitrarily called BU.BAT, is suggested for daily use in backing up all the new files. It is entered directly into a disk file when the last character, a Control-Z, is entered, and Enter is then pressed.

COPY CON: BU.BAT

ECHO ON

:   THIS BATCH FILE WILL HELP YOU REMEMBER HOW TO BACK UP
:   IMPORTANT INFORMATION FROM YOUR HARD DRIVE DAILY.

CD C:\

BACKUP C: B:/S/M/A

>Z

(Be sure to correct ALL typing mistakes before pressing Return at the end of each line. If you mess up a line and hit Return, give a Control-Z, a Return then start all over again.)

Using this method to back up files results in an accumulation of many backup diskettes after only a few weeks. The backup diskettes will have many files on them that are not needed. Perhaps once a month, the hard disk should be purged of all files that are no longer needed, other files copied off the hard disk and filed away for possible future use, and the hard drive trimmed down to the most often used files. Then the entire hard disk should be backed up, as explained previously.

If the hard drive of an operating AT should suddenly become inaccessible, it is a good idea to check the SETUP of the computer, using the SETUP command. Failure of the internal batteries can cause an apparent failure of the hard disk by merely allowing the computer to forget what the hard drive parameters are on power-up. After checking the SETUP and finding it to be incorrect, it is time to check the battery within the AT that remembers the parameters.

If during normal operation or during the installation of a pair of hard drives, one or both of them gives problems, disinstall one of the drives and attempt to get one of them working. This will eliminate the drives as being defective.

If there is an error on power-up called a "1701" error, there may be a mismatch between what the computer thinks is there for a hard drive and what is actually there. This can be an AT SETUP memory failure or an incorrect jumper setting on the controller or the hard drive. Another reason for a "1701" error is the lack of a primary format on the hard drive.

Detailed troubleshooting of the controller might be done with full documentation of the controller, using the built-in diagnostics of the controller, if any. This possibility probably involves changing a jumper on the controller board to invoke a diagnostic program in the controller ROM and watching the hard drive for a code blinked out on the drive access LED.

If the controller and the hard drive seem to be good, swap out the control and data cables, between the controller and the drive, with ones known to be good.

A hard drive can sometimes get "stuck" if it has not been properly parked. This may be because the heads have come to rest on the outer tracks of the drive, a position that allows much better brake action, sometimes even preventing the disks from turning. The cure is to gently remove the hard disk from the computer, remembering that the heads are now on the medium. Disconnect all the cables and hold the drive in one hand. Gently but rapidly, twist the hard disk frame back and forth in the normal rotation plane of the drive. This should, by virtue of the inertia of the disks, cause the disks to move a bit under the heads. Reinstall the drive, turn on the computer, and hope the drive will rotate.

Software problems with hard disks are covered in Chapter 12.

CHAPTER SUMMARY

INSTALLING AND TROUBLESHOOTING HARD DISK DRIVES provides information about handling and installing a hard disk drive. A hard disk drive is extremely fragile and must be handled with great care. It should be parked before turning off the computer. A hard disk drive is sealed and should never be opened if the drive is ever to be used again. Two methods are available to write data on a hard disk: MFM and RLL. MFM writes 17 sectors, while RLL writes data at a faster rate in 26 sectors. Some terms unique to hard disks should be understood, particularly if the manual method of hard disk installation is to be used. Interleaf of the sectors on a hard disk can be changed to improve performance, but only up to a point. DOS version 3.3 recognizes only two hard disk drives, each of which can contain only up to 32 MB of storage. DOS version 4.0 recognizes 4 drives and up to 2 GB. A new hard disk system must be low-level (primary) formatted, a partition established, and then high-level formatted (using the FORMAT program). Manual methods of drive installation can be used utilizing only DOS programs, but commercial software is available to considerably ease the job. An AT computer must be set up to access a hard disk, usually using one of the standard drive types as listed in Appendix E. A hard disk should be periodically backed up to diskettes or a tape drive to guard against the ever-possible hard disk crash.

REVIEW QUESTIONS

1. What is the most involved part of installing a hard disk?
2. What is the mechanism of a hard disk crash?
3. What can be done to minimize the possibility of a crash?
4. How is the capacity of a drive determined?
5. When is it permissible to remove the cover of a hard disk drive?
6. Why might a drive number of "1" be confusing?
7. How many sectors does the MFM recording system usually use?
8. How many sectors does the RLL recording system usually use?
9. What is the most efficient way to install many hard disk drives, such as on an assembly line?
10. When installing two hard disk drives, what should one do about the termination resistors?
11. You wish to install three hard disk drives in a microcomputer. How can this be done?
12. You wish to install a 64 MB drive and a 20 MB drive in a computer. What problems would you have?
13. What does the primary (low-level) format do?
14. What does the partitioning program FDISK do?
15. What does the high-level FORMAT program do to a hard disk?
16. What extra step is necessary for an AT to use a hard disk?
17. What two lines are necessary in the CONFIG.SYS file to utilize the new speed and convenience of the hard drive?
18. What is the gradual dispersal of data in scattered data sectors on a hard disk caused by repeated editing of files?
19. Is data fragmentation undesirable?
20. What is the effect of gradually reducing the interleaf factor of a hard disk?
21. What two programs are used to store and retrieve data from a hard disk to floppies?

chapter eight

Troubleshooting and Replacing the Power Supply

CHAPTER OBJECTIVE

TROUBLESHOOTING AND REPLACING THE POWER SUPPLY prepares the technician to analyze and repair power supply problems. This chapter explains the operation of the unique type of power supply used in microcomputers—the switching power supply (see Figure 8.1). The plugs from the power supply are identified. Typical failure symptoms are given with an explanation of their probable internal causes.

THE TYPICAL MICROCOMPUTER POWER SUPPLY

Today's microcomputers almost always use a switching power supply because of its small size, efficiency, and unique overload characteristics. See Figure 8.2. The switching power supply can produce large output currents, despite its small size. A transformer/rectifier power supply for comparable output currents would be much larger and heavier. While other power supplies blow the input fuse when overloaded, the switching power supply simply ceases to operate, going into an "idling" condition and drawing very little current. This characteristic is a very desirable advantage in providing power for computers. If there is a short or overload, the power supply does not furnish excessive current, possibly causing further damage, and there is no need to replace the fuse when troubleshooting. When the overload is removed, the switching power supply resumes normal operation as though nothing had happened. This kind of power supply is called a self-resetting, foldback power supply.

A WORD ABOUT SAFETY

The power supply within a microcomputer can be dangerous to service. In some instances, it may be more economical to replace the power supply as

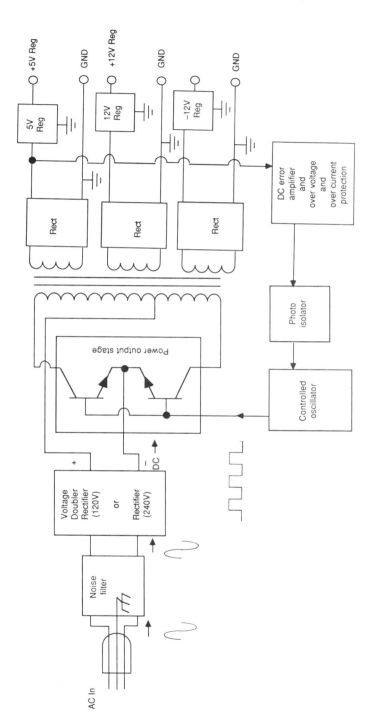

Figure 8.1 Most microcomputers use the switching power supply.

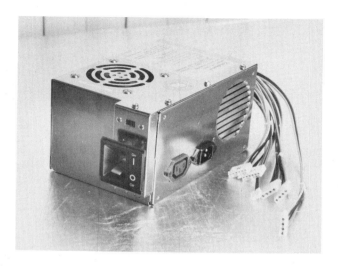

Figure 8.2 A typical microcomputer power supply. (Tom Carney)

a unit. In others, component-level troubleshooting can be done with a very good chance of success, even without a schematic.

If the power supply is to be opened (most are encased in a safety enclosure of some kind), the technician must be careful. These power supplies usually double the 120VAC line voltage, resulting in about 365VDC. This voltage is stored across two series-connected capacitors rated at 200VDC and is quite capable of providing a lethal electrical shock. These two capacitors can be recognized by their large physical size and the 200VDC voltage rating. If the power supply is to be turned on while it is exposed, keep well away from this circuitry. Use caution when using a voltmeter to measure any voltage within these power supplies. Another good precaution is to never work alone when working on dangerous equipment. Be sure to use only small-tipped, sharp test probes to measure voltages, thus making a slip of the probe less likely and preventing damage to the circuitry. Whenever the power supply is turned off and before touching the circuit board, discharge the two large, 200V capacitors by shorting them with a suitable jumper wire.

POWER SUPPLY SPECIFICATIONS

Input Voltage Regulation

The switching power supply regulates all of its output voltages by varying the amount of energy fed through the switching transformer. Because of this regulation, variations in the incoming line voltages are also compensated. The output voltages of a switching power supply used in a microcomputer typically remain constant in spite of input voltage variations from 90 to 135VAC.

Output Voltage Regulation

In addition to a constant amount of energy being coupled through the transformer, several of the output voltages of the power supply are further regulated, resulting in double-regulated output voltages.

The 5V output of the power supply is the principal voltage used in a microcomputer. This is the voltage that powers the chips within the computer and is the supply voltage providing the heaviest current. This voltage *must* be within the range of 4.75 to 5.25V.

The +12V output is regulated and used principally for the operation of the drive motors used in floppy and hard disk drives. In addition, it is used to generate the output voltages of the serial I/O ports of the computer.

The −12V output is also used to generate the output voltages for the serial I/O ports and is available for any special chips that might need this voltage. This −12V is supplied at the expansion slots in the computer.

The −5V output, like the −12V output, is available for special chips at the expansion slots. Very few chips use this voltage.

The first microcomputers used a 63.5 watt power supply. When more drives and cards were added, this power supply could not provide the additional power required. Power supplies of greater capability were designed and sold. Today, a 200 watt power supply is common. It will probably remain adequate, too, since future loads will be more efficient than older loads. This includes disk drives, hard disk drives, and optional cards. The larger power supply may come in a larger enclosure, so be sure it will fit the space available when replacing one.

A comparison of the capabilities of a 63.5 and a 200 watt (actually 204.5 watt) power supply is as follows:

63.5 watt		**200 watt**	
+5V @ 7A	35 watt	+5V @ 20A	100 watt
+12V @ 2A	24 watt	+12V @ 8A	96 watt
−5V @ 0.3A	1.5 watt	−5V @ 0.5A	2.5 watt
−12V @ 0.25A	3 watt	−12V @ 0.5A	6 watt

CONNECTORS AND VOLTAGES

The output voltages from the power supply are generally provided in six cables: Two are intended to be connected to the system board, and the remaining four are all the same, in parallel with each other and intended to connect to floppy and/or hard disk drives.

The System Board Connector

Connections to the system board are made by two connectors that, sadly, can be interchanged with dire results. BE SURE YOU HAVE PROPERLY IDENTIFIED both the connectors themselves and the proper points to connect them on the system board. If there is any doubt, it is always a good idea to check with your distributor before connecting these plugs!

If the two plugs are identified, they may be marked with a "P8" and a "P9" designation. If they are not marked, they can be identified, providing they are "standard," by the color of their wires. It is a good idea to mark these cables and the connectors into which they fit with a permanent marker. When properly marked, future work on the computer is less likely to result in a tragedy caused by accidental switching of these connectors.

The P8 connector should contain 5 wires colored black, brown, yellow, and white. THIS CONNECTOR CONNECTS TO A STANDARD SYSTEM BOARD AT THE REARMOST, RIGHTHAND CORNER, near the rear of the computer.

The P9 connector should have 6 wires colored red, blue, and black. This connector attaches to the system board just forward of where P8 connects.

Note that the +5 and +12V inputs to the system board are doubled-up, using several pins for the connection. This is deliberate: The current is distributed over several pins of the connector, thus preventing overheating and resulting intermittent connection of a single pin having to carry excessive current. The pinouts for P8 and P9 are given in Appendix A.

The Drive Power Connectors

There are probably four more cables coming from the power supply. These cables all have the same kind of connector, each with yellow, black, and red wires. A drive, either floppy diskette or hard drive, will need only two voltages: +5 and +12V.

The wiring of the diskette drive connectors is as follows:

Pin	Use	Wire Color
1	+12V	Yellow wire
2	+12V Ret	Black wire
3	+5V Ret	Black wire
4	+5V	Red wire

The +5 and +12V "Ret" lines are the return lines, or COMMON leads. The "Ret" lines are connected together. This connection point is sometimes inaccurately called "ground," because in the case of these computers, the return is not actually earth ground. It is, however, the point from which the positive voltages must be measured.

TYPICAL POWER SUPPLY PROBLEMS AND SYMPTOMS

The Inadequate Power Supply

Additional loads, such as extra options, can overload power supplies of the older, less powerful variety. When such a power supply is overloaded, the power supply refuses to oscillate, and it goes into an idling state. There are no indications of power to such a computer. Occasionally the load will be such that the computer will begin to boot up, but then fail completely. This might happen when the power supply is on the very edge of operating. A disk drive then comes on and puts the power supply into the idle mode.

A power supply that is acting this way can be confirmed as being inadequate by briefly removing those options not actually necessary. If the computer then operates normally, either the removed options are defective (shorted internally) or the power supply simply cannot handle the additional load.

Internal Power Supply Failures

A power supply can be checked fairly easily for proper output using a voltmeter. A digital or analog meter can be used. The most convenient place to test for proper voltages is at the power connector for one of the drives. In some cases, it may not be necessary to disconnect the drive. See Figure 8.3.

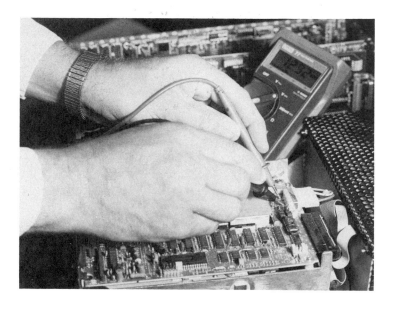

Figure 8.3 The diskette drive power connector often provides a convenient place to check the +5 and +12VDC power supply outputs. (Abbey Enterprises)

Measure the voltages at the drive connector. The +5V supply as measured from the red to the black wires MUST be within the 0.25V (+ 4.75 to 5.25V) at this connector. This voltage is critical, as it is used throughout the computer to power all of the IC chips. A voltage out of tolerance can be the cause of all manner of computer problems and must be corrected. The + 12V supply, between the yellow and black wires, may also be regulated and should be within perhaps 5% to be acceptable.

Another important power supply test is to check the amount of ripple present on the drive voltages. There should be less than 55 millivolts of ripple on these two supplies. Ripple is measured using a digital multimeter by setting the instrument to the AC scales and measuring the DC voltages. An analog meter, on the other hand, must be used on its "output" function, enabling the meter to read AC in the presence of DC.

The −5V and − 12V power supply outputs can be measured at an expansion slot connector using a convenient return connection, which can be the black wire of the diskette drive power connector. Appendix A provides the pinout for the expansion slots for PC/XTs and ATs.

TO REPAIR OR REPLACE, THAT IS THE QUESTION

A new, 200 watt power supply costs about $100. At this price, it is seldom worthwhile to spend much time repairing a power supply. The switching transistors are most often the cause of a switching power supply failure. These transistors have 3 leads and usually are mounted to a heat sink. There may be one or two of them. Check and replace them if one or both are defective.

SYMPTOMS OF POWER SUPPLY FAILURE

Did the Fuse Blow?

The condition of the fuse supplying the 120VAC power to the power supply yields important information on the cause of the problem. If the fuse has blown, the problem will be found in the first half of the power supply. If the fuse did not blow, there is probably an overload on the power supply, either because there is too much connected to it for its capability, or there is a fault and an abnormal overload. This might be a shorted IC, capacitor, or other such failure.

If the Fuse Has Blown

If the power supply has blown its fuse, replacement of the entire supply is the quickest way to get the computer up and running in the shortest possible time. Repair requires that the power supply be removed from the computer and dismantled.

If the Fuse Has Not Blown

When the fuse doesn't blow, this indicates one of two kinds of failures: (a) there is an overload or short on one or more of the power supply output voltages, including the installation of too many options, or (b) there is an open circuit in one or more of the outputs of the power supply.

First, a careful visual check should be made of the cables coming from the power supply. Check to see that each wire goes firmly into the attached connector and that the connectors are firmly seated. The repair of an open circuit is generally obvious: Resolder the loose wire or replace the connector.

Next, check all four voltages produced by the power supply. Presence of all but one of the four voltages indicates that there is either an open circuit in one of the leads coming from the power supply, or there is an internal failure of the power supply. An internal failure of one of the power supplies means removal and repair or replacement of the power supply.

If all of the output voltages of the power supply are missing, this is a strong indication of an overload on the power supply. To eliminate the power supply as the cause, two methods can be used at this point: (a) substitution of another power supply (if another runs well, the original was defective or "weak," not having sufficient current capability) or (b) eliminating the loads on the power supply. This method will disclose a shorted load, printed circuit board, or a drive.

Eliminating Power Supply Loads

Be sure to turn off the computer power before removing or inserting any of the cards within the computer or disconnecting or connecting any connectors.

Eliminate all but the absolutely necessary loads on the power supply to see if the computer will boot up. This means that the floppy diskette drive B can be disconnected by pulling the power supply connector from the rear of the drive. Floppy diskette drive A must remain connected, since this is the drive that the computer boots from. A hard disk drive, if any, can also be disconnected by removing its plug. All of the expansion slots should then be emptied except the video card and the floppy disk controller. With this minimum system setup, the computer should be turned on.

If the computer now boots up and loads the operating system, either one of the cards or the drive just removed is shorted or there is simply too much load for the power supply to handle. Reinstall the cards and drives, one at a time, until one of them results in another overload. (Remember to turn off the power!) Once a card or drive is suspect, substitute a known good one to see if the problem is an overload or a defective unit. Substitution of a good unit and a recurring overload indicates a power supply problem. If another unit works fine with all of the other original cards and drives installed, the suspect unit is shorted. It can then be replaced and the computer restored to normal operation.

REPLACING THE POWER SUPPLY

It is a relatively simple task to replace a power supply. To remove one, however, it may be necessary to temporarily remove other items, such as the floppy diskette drives. MARK DOWN CONNECTIONS to the system board. Note the color coding of the wires before you disconnect them from the system board. This step is particularly important when reinstalling another power supply. Unplug the six internal output connectors from the drives. Remove the screws (two to six of them) and lift out the power supply as a unit. The new power supply slips into place just like the old one.

One item to check is the power input voltage selector. This is usually a special, tiny, slip-in PC board on the back of the power supply, near the input connector. See Figure 8.4.

The fuse size and condition should also be checked. When changing a supply from 240 to 120VAC operation, for instance, the fuse should be doubled in size.

The output voltage connectors should be replaced as they are removed from the old supply. Be particularly careful, however, of the connectors to the system board. Be sure to connect them in exactly the same way as in the old power supply.

Figure 8.4 The input voltage can be selected on some computers by changing the position of a small printed circuit board, using it as a switch to change input connections. (Abbey Enterprises)

CHAPTER SUMMARY

TROUBLESHOOTING AND REPLACING THE POWER SUPPLY indicates that a high percentage of microcomputer failures involve the power supply. The switching power supply is the most common kind of power supply used in microcomputers due to its small size and high efficiency. A 200 watt power supply is a good size to recommend. Two plugs, P8 and P9, supply power to the system board. Four other plugs coming from the supply are for operating floppy or hard disk drives. The power connector on a floppy disk drive is often a convenient place to check the +5 and +12V supplies. The condition of the fuse gives valuable information as to where the power supply problem may lie. An overload on the power supply can be determined by removing printed circuit boards and connectors until the overloading circuit is found. NEVER OPERATE A SWITCHING POWER SUPPLY WITHOUT A LOAD!

REVIEW QUESTIONS

1. What is the type of power supply most often used in microcomputers?
2. What are two advantages of the switching power supply?
3. In the switching power as used in microcomputers, incoming power is first changed to _____, then to _____, then to _____.
4. While power supplies in microcomputers used to be as low as 63 watts, today's computers use power supplies more in the neighborhood of _____ watts.
5. Two connectors supply power to the system board. Are these plugs interchangeable?
6. Which of the four output connectors for drives must be used for a hard drive?
7. If a switching power supply is overloaded, will the fuse blow?
8. If the fuse of a switching power supply blows, this is an indication that there is a short before the _____.
9. What is the method of determining where an overload may be within the computer?

chapter nine

Installing and Repairing Computer Monitors

CHAPTER OBJECTIVE

INSTALLING AND REPAIRING COMPUTER MONITORS explains how the video system of a microcomputer works. Popular types of monitors and adapters are compared. See Figure 9.1 for a block diagram of a TTL monochrome monitor. Installation of any monitor is relatively easy. Methods of troubleshooting monitors and adapters are given, along with a few of the simpler adjustments that can be made within the monitor itself.

WHAT A COMPUTER MONITOR DOES

The computer monitor is a sort of window into the computer. The computer's CPU leaves information in digital form in an appropriate area of memory. This information is scanned and processed by the *video adapter*, then sent in an appropriate format to the monitor. The processing necessary to convert the memory information into a stream of information suitable for a monitor is accomplished by a large-scale integrated (LSI) circuit called a *video controller*, located on the video adapter card. The video adapter must also interpret color and intensity information in some cases. The cursor is produced and controlled by the video controller.

While monochrome text displays require only 4K of RAM memory, an enhanced graphics adapter (EGA) display can use up to 128K of memory, depending on specific program requirements and capabilities. There are three memory areas for video information. Monochrome text automatically begins using its 4K of RAM at address B000. A color graphics adapter (CGA) also always begins at memory location B800 and it uses 16K of RAM. The video graphics adapter (VGA) and the EGA can be operated several ways: 32K of memory beginning at the monochrome address of B000 or the color address B800. If started at A000, these adapters can use up to 64K of RAM within the A segment.

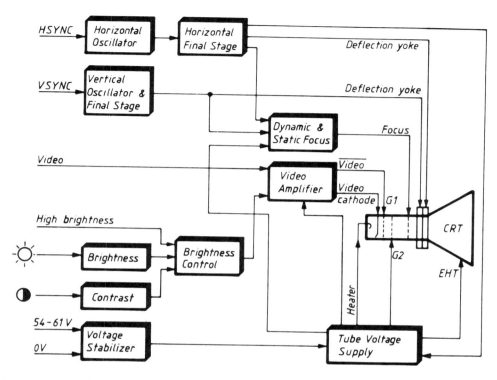

Figure 9.1 Block diagram of a TTL monochrome monitor. (Courtesy of Ericsson Information Systems)

Up to 128K can be used if the entire A and B segments are used. The multicolor graphics adapter (MGCA) uses only the 64K of the A000 segment.

The video controller and its circuitry are quite complex. The circuitry is a plug-in card that seats in one of the system board expansion slots. When the CPU writes information for display on the monitor, the information is placed into video memory chips located on the video board. From there, the video controller has access to the information and integrates that information with the cursor, horizontal and vertical synchronizing pulses, color, and other information including blinking, underlining, and intensifying characters. All of the resulting signals come out the back of the adapter in a 9-pin plug for a direct-drive monitor. See Figure 9.2. The composite video signals of a CGA, on the other hand, come out of a single RCA-type connector. See Figure 9.3.

While the video adapter is the real "brain" of the video system, the monitor has a different job: providing the visual part of the display. Any kind of computer monitor must take the information produced by the video controller and place that information in a visual form. While some liquid crystal displays are used

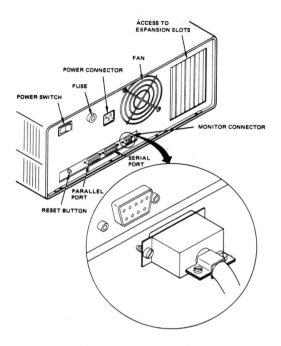

Figure 9.2 This 9-pin connector is commonly used to connect a monochrome or color monitor to a microcomputer. (Courtesy of Corona Data Systems, Inc.)

Figure 9.3 This RCA jack is used to get composite video signals and synchronizing pulses to the monitor with a single coaxial cable. (Tom Carney)

on laptop and portable computers, the cathode ray tube (CRT) is the standard monitor for microcomputer use.

The CRT cathode produces the electrons that are eventually splashed onto the front screen, where they produce light. The electrons exit the cathode area through a hole in the cylindrical CRT grid (Figure 9.4). Video monitors usually operate the cathodes near ground potential since the input to these CRTs involves putting the video signal into the grid or cathode circuit to turn the CRT beam on and off. The accelerating anodes operate at very high positive voltages with respect to ground.

Normal CRT voltages require that the tube element voltages increase in positive steps from the cathode to the screen with the exception of the grid, which is held at a negative voltage with respect to the cathode. This negative voltage is adjustable to control the intensity of the spot on the screen through a brightness control.

The difference in voltage between the focusing and accelerating elements determines the focus of the spot. Troubleshooting focusing problems begins with measuring these two voltages. The CRT circuits may have regulators on several voltage sources to hold critical ones constant. Failures of these regulator circuits can cause brightness fluctuations and unstable focusing of the spot. The higher the final accelerating voltage, the brighter the spot. If the spot on a CRT is dim and unfocused, the high-voltage supply should immediately be suspected to be too low. This may also be confirmed by the CRT showing images too large. Below-normal final accelerating voltage makes the image larger because the electron beam is moving more slowly and is more easily deflected.

BE CAREFUL WHEN MEASURING THE VOLTAGES ASSOCIATED WITH THESE TUBES. Read the following information carefully before proceeding with

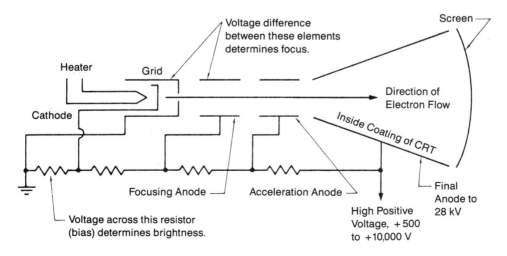

Figure 9.4 Internal structure of the CRT.

any voltage measurement; high voltages may be present where they are not expected. Cathode ray tubes require much higher voltages than those used with semiconductors. Familiarity with the following safety rules will help avoid a shock hazard.

1. When using a voltmeter on high voltages, be sure to attach the ground lead to the chassis or common point before checking voltages. Failure to do this first may produce a hot negative lead that can be dangerous if touched.
2. When measuring voltages up to perhaps 200V, remove any metal jewelry and keep your left hand (assuming you are right-handed) in your back pocket. This helps avoid the possibility of accidental current flow through the chest.
3. In addition to the rules above, when measuring voltages higher than about 200V, other precautions are necessary. Turn off the equipment, discharge the filter capacitors, attach the meter, and then turn on the power and take the reading. Do not touch the meter or the leads until the power is again turned off and the capacitors are discharged.
4. Electrical insulating rubber matting on the floor in front of the bench to stand on is also advisable.

The information for the video adapter can be in one of two forms: characters or graphics. When characters are left for display, the adapter gets the ASCII value of that character and looks up the bit pattern necessary to make up that character from within a ROM on the video adapter. Using several (typically eight or nine) scanning lines across the face of the CRT, the bit patterns are generated on the screen by turning the CRT beam on and off at precisely the right times to produce the characters that the operator sees. Graphics patterns are interpreted on a bit-for-bit basis, with each tiny picture element (pixel) of the CRT individually written to, including color if applicable. The size of the dots determines the resolution of the monitor. The more dots of resolution, the finer grained the picture is and the more pleasant it is to use.

An adapter other than a simple monochrome adapter must be switched from the text mode to the graphics mode. This is done by the software in use.

A COMPARISON OF VIDEO ADAPTERS AND MONITORS

The Monochrome Display Adapter (MDA)

The purely monochrome adapter uses only 4K of RAM memory per page of text display. The ASCII coded characters are contained in this area and are read by the adapter. The adapter converts the ASCII codes into bit patterns that are then sent in serial format to the monitor for display. Only text, including 128 special "extended" characters, can be displayed by a purely monochrome adapter. This adapter displays 80 columns on 25 lines at high resolution. The individual scan lines and dots that make up the characters are so small they are hard to see. There are 720 pixels horizontally and 350 vertically.

The monochrome monitor can also intensify individual characters or groups. This is particularly helpful since the monochrome monitor cannot, of course, display color. An extra signal line to the monitor is provided to support this feature.

The lack of graphics capability was a serious disadvantage. It was not long before the Hercules card became available. This adapter can display both text and graphics of 720 × 348 with high resolution on a monochrome monitor. A Hercules card can use up to 64K of RAM memory, beginning at the same place as the monochrome area, B000.

If color is not particularly desired for a specific application, a monochrome monitor with a Hercules graphics card is the best choice for the money.

The Television Monitor

The first microcomputers were put together with the idea that they would be little more than toys. High-resolution, high-quality graphics were thought to be unnecessary. Some of the first microcomputers could use a color television as a monitor. All that was needed, if not already provided with the computer, was a small black box called an "RF modulator." While this approach may have been very inexpensive, it was very, very poor in visual quality. No more than 40 columns of characters could be put side by side on the screen even on a "good" TV, before the quality suffered and the letters became difficult to read. For even occasional use, the TV monitor is obsolete and should not even be considered.

The Color Graphics Adapter (CGA)

The need for color and graphics capability led to the development of the CGA. This adapter was intended to be used with a simple red, green, and blue gun monitor. These three colors were mixed to produce other colors; at least in theory, up to 16 colors were possible. The final result was short of the mark, however. The color graphics display was pretty bad. It flickered because it scanned the text for 1/30 second, then blanked the screen with black for another 1/30 second before repeating. The resolution was poor, resulting in a display that was excessively grainy in appearance. And there were not enough color combinations.

The CGA used 16K of memory beginning at B800. It could be switched from an 80-column display to a 40-column display to allow the use of a TV as a monitor. This capability had little practical use for text, however. The graphics were the only good reason to use a CGA display because the text display, even using the 80-column mode, was less than pleasant to use.

The Enhanced Graphics Adapter (EGA)

The EGA card rapidly became the standard for serious color users. This adapter was designed to use with an enhanced color display (ECD). While normally used with 80 columns and 25 lines of text, it can display up to 132 columns and 43 lines. All of this capability is shown on a display that is stable (does not flicker) and has a high resolution of either 640 × 200 dots or, in the interlaced mode, 640 × 350 lines. Interlacing is the process of displaying two separate frames of the display alternately, showing the even lines in one vertical sweep, then the odd lines on the next. The overall effect is to show a flicker-free display with great detail.

Depending on the initial jumper settings and the program in use, the EGA card can use 32K, 64K, 128K, or 256K of RAM.

The ECD monitor can be either a high-resolution color monitor for EGA or it can display monochrome data. The monitor is capable of 64 different color combinations. However, because of the way color is encoded within the video controller, only 16 colors are readily available at any one time. These 16 colors are changeable as a group, called palettes.

When an EGA video adapter is operating a CGA or multisync monitor as though it were a CGA monitor, the adapter can be described as being in "mode 1" operation. This results in a display resolution of 640 columns × 200 lines. When connected to an ECD or a multisync monitor, the adapter can be operated in "mode 2." In this mode, the display runs at 640 column × 350 line resolution and interleafs the frames of the display. The EGA video adapter senses the difference between CGA and EGA video and automatically generates the proper signals for the monitor to follow. A multisync monitor follows the synchronizing signal changes and shows the display accordingly.

An EGA card and a multisync ECD monitor are probably the best buy for a serious computer user.

The Multicolor Graphics Array (MGCA)

There are a few other video displays available that have not yet come into widespread use. One of these is available on some of the newer models of microcomputers. The MGCA display is capable of 256 colors with 320 horizontal dots and 200 vertical, or it can be operated in the high-resolution mode and provide 640 dots horizontal and 480 vertical. It uses 64K of video RAM.

The Video Graphics Adapter (VGA)

This is another adapter that may come into more widespread use in the future. This video adapter handles video intended for display on MDA, CGA,

A Technical Comparison of Monitors*

Type	Bandwidth (MHz)	Horizontal Sweep	Vertical Sweep	Character Box
MDA	16.257	18.432	50	9 × 14
HGC	16.257	18.432	50	9 × 14
CGA	14.318	15.75	60	8 × 8
EGA Color				
Mode 1	14.318	15.75	60	8 × 8
Mode 2	16.257	21.85	60	8 × 14
EGA Mono	16.257	18.432	50	9 × 14
MCGA	25.175	31.5	60 to 70	8 × 16
VGA	25.175 to 28.322	31.5	60 to 70	8 × 8, 8 × 14, 9 × 14, 9 × 16

*From "DOS Power Tools," *PC Magazine*, Paul Somerson, Executive Editor.

and EGA monitors. It is capable of 256 colors and may become the most popular monitor in the future.

GETTING THE SIGNALS TO THE MONITOR

Appendix A gives the pinouts for the standard connectors used to connect a monitor to an adapter that is mounted inside the computer.

Composite Video Monitors

The composite video signal contains all information necessary for a monitor: the video, intensity, synchronizing, and color information. The video signal is an analog signal of about 1 volt peak-to-peak and should be sent through a 75 ohm video cable. Figure 9.5 shows what this signal might look like on an oscilloscope. The signal jack used for composite video is usually an RCA jack, shown in Figure 9.3. The horizontal sweep frequency of a composite monitor is 15.75 MHz and the vertical is 50 to 60 Hz.

The block diagram (Figure 9.6) of a composite monitor shows where the video and synchronizing signals are separated from the main composite signal flow. Some of the original monitors used with the CGA had a composite video drive. The block diagram of such a monitor is similar to Figure 9.6 with the addition of color circuits within the video section.

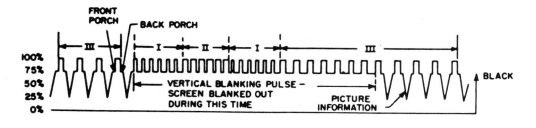

Figure 9.5 The composite video signal contains all the signals needed by the monitor.

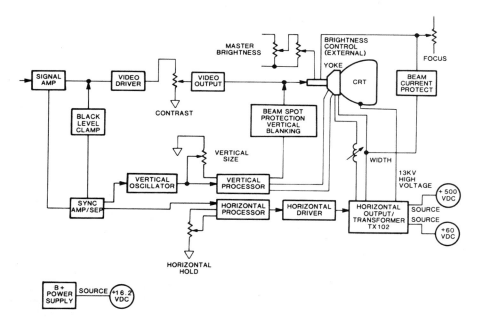

Figure 9.6 Block diagram of a composite monochrome monitor. (Courtesy of Zenith)

Direct-Drive Monitors

A monitor using composite feed cannot quite produce the sharpness of characters that a direct-drive monitor is able to display. Sending the video and synchronizing signals over separate lines is a better way to drive the monitor.

Direct drive of a monitor simply means that the synchronizing signals for the horizontal and vertical sweeps, the video, intensity signal (if any), and color information for color monitors are all sent on separate lines. These lines are generally TTL-compatible voltages and are either on or off—truly digital in nature. Figure 9.1 shows a block diagram of a monochrome monitor using direct drive. Figure 9.7 shows a similar diagram for a color monitor, used with a CGA.

The connector used for passing signals between the video adapter and the monitor for all kinds of monochrome and color monitors has standardized on the 9-pin "D" connector. The use of the pins varies with the kind of monitor to be connected, however. These pinouts are given in Appendix A.

DUAL-MONITOR OPERATION

Two monitors can be used at the same time. Typically, a monochrome monitor can be used to display text at the same time that a CGA monitor is used to show graphics. The software used must be able to drive both monitors, however. A good example of such software might be a computer-aided drafting program.

The two monitors must use different areas of memory. The original microcomputer system was able to operate a monochrome and a color monitor at the same time, since the monochrome used 4K of RAM memory beginning at B000, while the color graphics portion used 16K of memory beginning at a later address of B800.

The EGA and VGA adapters are able to use memory beginning at several selectable addresses. The software used with the two monitors must match the selected addresses. When considering operating two monitors with a given program, test for compatibility of the video addressing and the program before the program is purchased, if at all possible.

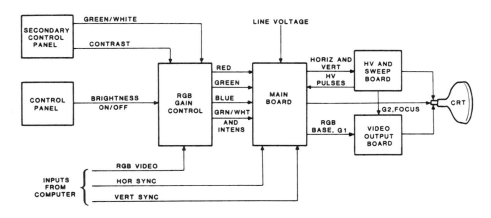

Figure 9.7 Block diagram of RGB color monitor. (Courtesy of Zenith)

For testing purposes, the display of video information can be switched between the monochrome and the color areas of memory at the DOS level with the following commands:

MODE CO (to switch to address B800)

MODE MO (to switch to address B000)

TROUBLESHOOTING VIDEO ADAPTERS AND MONITORS

Check the Obvious

Difficulties with monitors can often be cured by checking and correcting simple problems. The cables feeding signals to the monitor should be checked first, along with the monitor operating controls. Be sure the plugs are firmly seated in their connectors. Check the brightness and contrast controls. These controls are sometimes conveniently placed for idle twiddling, resulting in a control setting "accidentally" misadjusted. In other cases, the controls are hidden behind a panel, and a deliberate adjustment of the control is forgotten or someone is not aware that the control has been moved.

If the monitor is operating but the colors displayed seem to be defective or if the video signal has a seemingly minor problem, a video diagnostic program may identify the problem more definitely. Colors should show as they are labeled. If the colors do not match, there is a problem with either the video adapter or the monitor. Missing portions of a character, for instance, might be an indication of a failing video ROM, which would show when running the video diagnostic program.

Try Substitution Next

If a monitor is "dead," the next step is to try operating a different monitor with the microcomputer. Be sure to turn off power to both units before disconnecting or reconnecting the new monitor.

If the problem is no longer evident with a new monitor, the old one must have a problem within it. If changing the monitor does not affect the situation, the video adapter within the microcomputer must be at fault. The best way to definitely determine whether the video adapter is bad is to open the computer and substitute a known good video adapter in its place.

The Defective Video Adapter

If the video adapter is causing the problem, it is probably not worth the effort to repair the card. It is usually most economical to purchase a new adapter and install it, discarding the old card. A possible exception might be to change the chips on the card that are installed in sockets, in the hope that one of them is causing the problem. In this case, it is necessary to have a stock of replacement chips on hand, an improbable situation in most cases.

The Defective Monitor

When the monitor is at fault, some of the same reasoning may apply. If the monitor is not expensive, simple replacement is a valid alternative.

Internal repairs of CRT monitors involves some danger: possible implosion of the tube and flying glass, and electrical shock. Be extremely careful not to strike or even bump the fragile neck on the rear of the CRT. The glass in this area is relatively thin and easily broken. Be especially careful when adjusting the deflection yoke and centering magnets on the neck of the CRT.

When removing the cover from a monitor, be careful of internal wiring. Do not touch any circuitry without first disconnecting the power cable. Be careful not to touch the ultrahigh-voltage circuits providing voltage to the high-voltage cap on the side of the CRT bell. Visually check the internal workings of the monitor, looking for burned parts and poor solder joints on the printed circuit boards.

Adjustments inside a monitor can consist of the following:

Power supply adjustments

Sub-brightness (secondary brightness)

Vertical hold

Vertical linearity

Horizontal hold

Horizontal linearity

Convergence adjustments, static and dynamic

Electrical and mechanical focus

Mechanical centering

Mechanical tilt

Power supply adjustments can be checked with a voltmeter, but only if the proper test points and the voltages to be expected are known. Without this information, the adjustments should not be changed. Failure of the power supply to provide the listed voltages, particularly if it cannot provide the voltages within the normal range of the adjustments provided, indicates a problem that must be repaired.

Besides the normal low-voltage power supply outputs, the monitor also requires an ultrahigh-voltage supply for the CRT final anode. This voltage is typically 13 kV in a monochrome monitor, and can be as high as 28,000V in a large-screen color monitor. This voltage is derived as a by-product of the horizontal sweeping waveform produced in the monitor. A DC voltage is used to build up a current in a special transformer called a flyback transformer. When this current is interrupted by the horizontal sweeping waveform, a very high voltage pulse is produced, much like the spark of an ignition coil. This pulse is rectified by a special high-voltage diode and sent to the CRT where it is filtered by the CRT itself. See Figure 9.8.

Measurement of this ultrahigh voltage should not be attempted with a "normal" meter, as it is far too high to be safely read. A special probe must be used to safely reduce this voltage to one that a voltmeter can handle. See Figure 9.9.

The internal sub-brightness control is an auxiliary control of the brightness of the monitor. The CRT can produce a wide range of brightness, only part of which should be available to the operator. As the CRT ages, however, the front panel brightness control needs to be operated at maximum brightness to get a usable display. Further aging may make it necessary to open the monitor and increase this internal brightness control. The control is a potentiometer that controls the voltage difference between the grid and the cathode elements of the CRT.

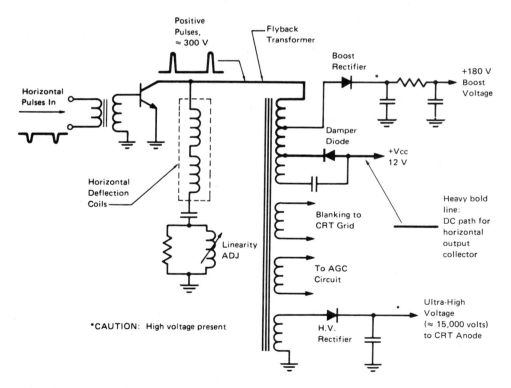

Figure 9.8 The horizontal oscillator circuit also provides very high voltage for the CRT.

Figure 9.9 An ultrahigh-voltage probe is necessary to measure the voltage on the CRT accelerating anode. (Reproduced with permission from the John Fluke Mfg. Co. Inc.)

A monitor that will not hold the picture vertically (the display flips up or down) may need only a small adjustment of the vertical hold control. This control should be adjusted to the middle of the range, approached from either direction, where the display holds still. This adjustment is particularly important when a display is used to synchronize with 2 different sweep frequencies.

A misadjustment of the vertical linearity control is evident if the characters at the top of the screen are taller or shorter than those at the bottom of the screen. Adjusting the vertical linearity control may, however, affect the vertical hold, necessitating back-and-forth adjustment of both controls until the display is correct.

Similar adjustments may be provided for the horizontal circuit, the horizontal hold, and horizontal linearity. Tearing of the picture horizontally is a symptom of lack of horizontal synchronization, sometimes requiring only a small horizontal hold adjustment. Horizontal linearity can be adjusted so that characters are the same width on the left and right of the screen. Again, there may be interaction between the hold and linearity controls.

A color CRT has several more adjustments than a simple monochrome CRT. These adjustments ensure that the color guns within the CRT all hit the front screen at the same exact position. These controls are called convergence controls and they consist of both mechanical and electronic adjustments. Adjustment of the convergence controls of the monitor requires the instruction book for the monitor. The static adjustments, small mechanical adjustments on the deflection yoke, are done first. The dynamic adjustments are electronic adjustments and are made with the help of a special convergence signal generator, not often found in the field. Without a way to provide the convergence signals and without an instruction book, it is best to return the monitor to the dealership or manufacturer for adjustment of the internal color controls.

The focus control of a monitor is a simple adjustment, needing to be manipulated until the sweep lines on the CRT are most visible. This requires looking very carefully at the characters on the screen, adjusting for the sharpest edges possible.

The display of a monitor can be tilted by loosening the yoke on the CRT and rotating the yoke assembly carefully, resnugging the clamp GENTLY when the display is straight. See Figures 9.10 and 9.11.

The monitor display can be centered by changing the adjustment of the centering magnets individually or as a unit, around the neck of the CRT. See Figure 9.12.

Repairing a monitor beyond this point should be attempted only if full documentation is available. The block diagram of the monitor under repair should be thoroughly understood and signals from a microcomputer (preferably a diagnostic program) should also be available.

Figure 9.10 Turning the deflection yoke after loosening the clamp allows the picture to be vertically adjusted on the screen. (Tom Carney)

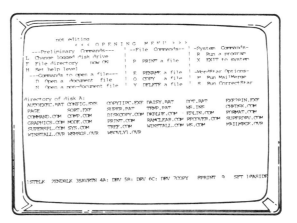

PICTURE TILTED

PICTURE TOO FAR LEFT

PICTURE TOO HIGH

Figure 9.11 Yoke tilt and centering problems.

Figure 9.12 The centering magnets are two rings, each with an adjusting tab. Their relationship to each other and as a unit determine the centering of the raster. (Abbey Enterprises)

CHAPTER SUMMARY

INSTALLING AND REPAIRING COMPUTER MONITORS explains the differences among various types of monitors. The EGA monitor and adapter is becoming the most popular high-resolution color monitor for microcomputers. The higher the resolution, the more pleasant the display is to view. Other less expensive monitors are available without color or with less resolution. The CGA display is disappointing because of poor resolution and excessive flickering. Substitution of units is the fastest, easiest way to determine where a video problem lies. Direct-drive monitors are better than composite monitors. A few of the adjustments within a monitor can be easily made, but internal color adjustments must be done with a special signal generator.

REVIEW QUESTIONS

1. Data to be displayed is placed into memory by the _____.
2. The reading of memory and generation of the monitor display accordingly is done by the _____.
3. True or False? The monochrome monitor can display two different levels of intensity.
4. True or False? The monochrome monitor can display graphics.
5. What is the worst display to use in terms of resolution?
6. How does the EGA monitor get such good resolution in "mode 2"?
7. How many signal lines are necessary to feed a composite display?
8. What is the most common video display connector?
9. How might a monitor with a tilted display be repaired?
10. What control would compensate for a display that showed too tall letters at the top of the screen and with compressed letters at the bottom?
11. What adjustments would help in centering the display on a monitor?

chapter ten

Installing and Repairing Computer Printers and Plotters

CHAPTER OBJECTIVE

INSTALLING AND REPAIRING COMPUTER PRINTERS AND PLOTTERS prepares the technician to troubleshoot and make limited repairs to these machines. The kinds of printers are discussed, emphasizing the most common types used with microcomputers. The control of printers is explained, along with the software that uses them. The use of drivers is also explained. See Figure 10.1 for a diagram of a "smart" dot-matrix printer.

A WORD ABOUT SAFETY

There are two principal dangers in working with printers. The mechanical parts of a large printer can be very strong, and thus they present the possibility of pinching or crushing unwary fingers. Long hair can get caught in the paper roller or other mechanisms, pulling one's face into the mechanisms or removing the hair. Be careful. Do not bypass the interlocks when provided unless it is absolutely necessary to do so.

Another danger in some printers, especially laser printers, is the high-voltage power supplies necessary for their operation. The standard precautions of turning off power and short-circuiting high-voltage capacitors should be followed. Testing high-voltage power supplies should be done with one hand in a back pocket to prevent current from accidentally flowing through the chest and heart. All metal jewelry, particularly metal watchbands and rings, should be removed during printer servicing.

MT-160 BLOCK DIAGRAM

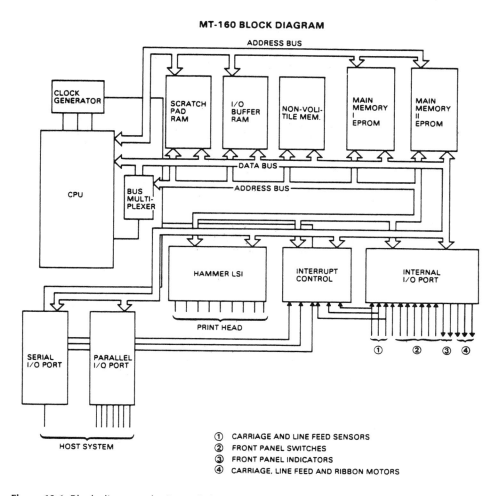

Figure 10.1 Block diagram of a "smart" dot-matrix printer. (Courtesy of Mannesmann Tally)

TYPES OF PRINTERS

The Dot-Matrix Printer

The dot-matrix printer in Figure 10.2 is representative of many brands now on the market. Its operation consists of "firing" the ends of print wires against a ribbon that carries ink onto the paper behind it. By the proper selection of possible dot positions in a 5 × 7 matrix, uppercase letters may be formed. A 7 × 9 or 9 × 9 matrix can be used to form all upper- and lowercase letters.

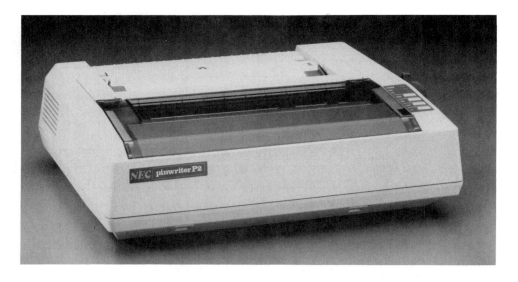

Figure 10.2 A typical dot-matrix printer used with a microcomputer. (Courtesy of NEC Information Systems)

DOT MATRIX

Now is the time for all
Now is the time for all
Now is the time for all
Now is the time for all

FULL FORMED

Now is the time for all
Now is the time for all
Now is the time for all
Now is the time for all

Figure 10.3 Dot-matrix printing is not as easy to read as that of a fully formed character printer.

The operation speed of the dot-matrix printer is limited by the time needed for the wires to fire, make the impression, and recover, ready for the next row of dots.

The printing of a dot-matrix printer (shown in Figure 10.2) is actually made up of tiny dots strung together to give the impression of characters (Figure 10.3). Characters are "scanned" from left to right and, in the case of a bidirectional printer, also from right to left. The speed of any printer, dot-matrix or fully formed character, is enhanced if the printer is able to print a line from either direction, left to right or "backwards" from right to left. Reversed-direction printing saves the time usually needed for the carriage to return to the left between lines.

To make dot-matrix printing more attractive and easier to read, special techniques may be used to fill in between the dots making up the characters. This entails at least two passes along a line of print and a very slight position shift of either the paper or the printhead (see Figure 10.4).

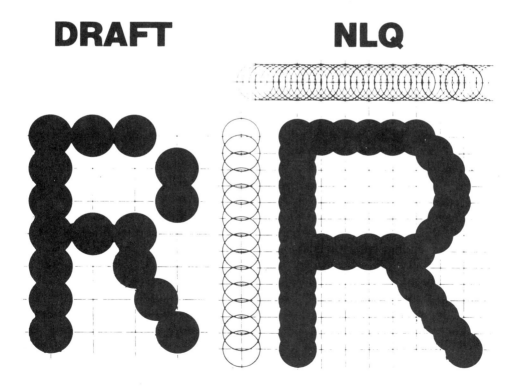

Figure 10.4 Multiple passes of a dot-matrix pattern in slightly different locations produce a much more attractive copy. The resulting copy is called NLQ, for near letter quality, also called correspondence quality. (Courtesy of Mannesmann Tally)

The Fully Formed Character Printer

Fully formed character printers are usually of the daisy-wheel or thimble types (Figure 10.5). The daisy-wheel printhead is very popular and is the principal fully formed character printhead discussed here.

The operation speed of fully formed character printheads is limited by the speed in which the next character can be brought into position under the striking solenoid. To minimize the time needed for this task, the microprocessor chip in the printer notes the present location of the printhead and the location of the next character, then determines the shortest direction to rotate the print wheel to bring the next character into proper position.

The principal advantage of the fully formed character printer is that the printed characters are fully formed and pleasing to read. Because of the attractive print quality, these printers produce what is commonly called letter-quality printing. Special character wheels can be used to change the type font, producing different printing effects (see Figure 10.6). The major disadvantage of the fully formed character printer is that it is slower than a dot-matrix printer. A fully formed character printer may type as fast as 100 words per minute, not much faster than a fast typist.

Table 10.1 summarizes advantages and drawbacks of the two most frequently used printers.

Figure 10.5 Two fully formed character printing methods, the daisy-wheel and the golfball-style printheads. (Abbey Enterprises)

Table 10.1 Relative Merits of the Dot-Matrix and Fully Formed Character Printers

Dot-Matrix Printer	Fully formed character Printer
Fast*'	Slow
Hard to read*	Attractive printing
Flexible type fonts	Restricted type fonts
Graphics capability	No graphics

*Except in the special NLQ mode, which is slower in operation but easier to read.

```
EXTENDED PRINT
ABCDEFGHIJKLMNOPQRSTUVWXYZ  abcdefghijklmnopqrstuvwxyz  1234567890
!"#$%&'():*-=;+,<.>/?

PICA (DRAFT)
ABCDEFGHIJKLMNOPQRSTUVWXYZ  abcdefghijklmnopqrstuvwxyz  1234567890
!"#$%&'():*-=;+,<.>/?

ELITE (DRAFT)
ABCDEFGHIJKLMNOPQRSTUVWXYZ abcdefghijklmnopqrstuvwxyz 1234567890
!"#$%&'():*-=;+,<.>/?

SEMICONDENSED
ABCDEFGHIJKLMNOPQRSTUVWXYZ abcdefghijklmnopqrstuvwxyz 1234567890
!"#$%&'():*-=;+,<.>/?

ULTRACONDENSED
ABCDEFGHIJKLMNOPQRSTUVWXYZ abcdefghijklmnopqrstuvwxyz 1234567890
!"#$%&'():*-=;+,(.)/?

HEADLINE
ABCDEFGHIJKLMNOPQRSTUVWXYZ  abcdefghijklmnopqrstuvwxyz  1234567890
!"#$%&'():*-=;+,<.>/?

PICA PROPORTIONAL (DRAFT)
ABCDEFGHIJKLMNOPQRSTUVWXYZ abcdefghijklmnopqrstuvwxyz 1234567890
!"#$%&'():*-=;+,<.>/?

ELITE PROPORTIONAL (DRAFT)
ABCDEFGHIJKLMNOPQRSTUVWXYZ abcdefghijklmnopqrstuvwxyz 1234567890
!"#$%&'():*-=;+,<.>/?

PICA (NLQ)
ABCDEFGHIJKLMNOPQRSTUVWXYZ abcdefghijklmnopqrstuvwxyz 1234567890
!"#$%&'():*-=;+,<.>/?

ELITE (NLQ)
ABCDEFGHIJKLMNOPQRSTUVWXYZ abcdefghijklmnopqrstuvwxyz 1234567890
!"#$%&'():*-=;+,<.>/?

PICA PROPORTIONAL (NLQ)
ABCDEFGHIJKLMNOPQRSTUVWXYZ abcdefghijklmnopqrstuvwxyz 1234567890
!"#$%&'():*-=;+,<.>/?

ELITE PROPORTIONAL (NLQ)
ABCDEFGHIJKLMNOPQRSTUVWXYZ abcdefghijklmnopqrstuvwxyz 1234567890
!"#$%&'():*-=;+,<.>/?
```

Figure 10.6 A fully formed character printer type font can often be changed by changing the print wheel.

The Laser Printer

The laser printer is the next technological step in the progression from the typewriter to the graphics-capable dot-matrix printer. The laser printer offers more attractive text than the dot-matrix printer, while offering the ability to print very high-resolution graphics. See Figure 10.7.

The laser printer is similar in many ways to the familiar copying machine. Rather than taking an image from an original printed page, however, a laser imprints an image from RAM memory onto a light-sensitive drum. After this, the process is nearly the same as that of the copier. The rotating drum electrostatically attracts toner (ink) on the appropriate areas, then transfers the toner onto a sheet of paper by a combination of heat and pressure.

The software end of a laser printer writes a pattern of dots representing the entire printed page into RAM memory, where it can be scanned and written by the extremely finely focused light of a laser directed at the light-sensitive drum. With appropriate software fonts, the type style of the laser printer can be easily changed by simply writing a different font dot pattern into an appropriate area of RAM, where it can then be used to place text, dot by dot, onto the

Figure 10.7 The laser printer is capable of excellent printing quality and also offers very high-resolution graphics. (Photo courtesy of Hewlett-Packard Company)

proper areas of a page, ready to be scanned. Thus, the laser printer lends itself very well, via software, to changing type fonts. The default font, unless changed, is usually the "Courier" font.

The laser printer needs the same supplies and maintenance as a copier— toner, lubrication, periodic overhauls, etc.—similar to the copier. The similarity to copier machines also extends to the size of paper that can be used. Single sheets are used, rather than the often more convenient continuous, pin-feed paper of other printers. The laser printer excels in printing on good quality, preprinted letterhead paper. The paper must be dry, however, as damp paper tends to jam inside the printer.

In text-only applications, the less expensive dot-matrix printer with as many as 24 printing pins, for a price of perhaps $550, will suffice. Those needing higher speeds and high-resolution graphics, typically 300 dots per inch, might wish to consider the laser printer. A laser printer currently costs between $1500 and $10,000. Generally speaking, the costlier the printer, the more features it will have available and the faster and more heavy duty it will be. These printers can produce 6 to 12 pages of text and graphics per minute, compared with the 30 to 45 seconds required for each page from a dot-matrix printer.

The laser printer is a particularly good choice for desktop publishing, which uses intermixed graphics and text. It is also much quieter than the dot-matrix and daisy-wheel printers.

The laser printer depends heavily on large amounts of RAM memory for the storage of different type fonts and perhaps several pages of text waiting to be printed. The use of graphics requires much more memory than simple text. Where 512K of memory might be sufficient for text-only printing, graphics can use as much as 2 or 3 MB of memory. It is better to have too much memory rather than too little, to avoid such problems as "locking up" part way through a job or a sudden, unscheduled change of type font.

It is best to try a laser printer on location before purchasing it, if possible. Try the kind of paper and the software with which the printer will be used. One of the best tests of a laser printer for compatibility is to print out WordPerfect's PRINTER.TST file, using an appropriate printer driver. Some laser printers are able to emulate, or imitate, the printer operating codes of such industry standards as-the Hewlett Packard LaserJet, Epson, or IBM dot-matrix, Qume, or Diablo printers.

Troubleshooting a laser printer requires some mechanical skill. First, check to be sure that there is sufficient toner. If the printer prints in blobs, try changing the toner cartridge. When replacing the cartridge, clean the corona wires (recognizable by the extreme insulation and hair-thin single wire tightly strung betwen them) with a cotton swab. Replace the fuser roller cleaning pad while you are inside the machine. Some laser printers have an internal diagnostic program that can help troubleshoot the machine. If the paper jams inside the printer frequently, try using different or drier paper.

Other Printer Types

Other kinds of printers are available for use with computers, but for various reasons they are not as popular as the two types mentioned above. They include

Line printers

Inkjet printers

Thermal printers

Electrostatic printers

Line printers are used with large computers where a great volume of material must be printed in a short time. Line printers such as the one shown in Figure 10.8 are capable of very high speed operation: This one operates at 600 *lines* (about nine pages of solid text) per minute. The text is printed in horizontal rows, not unlike the scanning of a video monitor, from the top of the

Figure 10.8 A commercial line printer such as this one is used with mainframe computers to print large quantities of data. (Courtesy of Mannesmann Tally)

page down. This printer uses 66 print wires similar to those of a dot-matrix printer. Each print wire covers the space occupied by two matrix spaces. Thus, as a particular print wire passes down through a line, it prints two adjacent characters. All 66 print wires operate simultaneously, which enables very high printing speeds.

The inkjet printer is very quiet in operation in contrast to both the dot-matrix and fully formed character printers. It forces a minute amount of ink directly onto the paper from tiny nozzles. This kind of printer is relatively new and is not yet in widespread use.

Thermal printers heat special paper, making a dark mark on the paper. Although quiet, the thermal printer cannot be used with standard paper, its principal disadvantage. The electrostatic printhead places a mark on special metalized paper. Like the thermal printer, this printer is relatively quiet but also requires special paper, again a major disadvantage.

COMPUTER DATA OUTPUT CONCEPTS

Typing a letter on a computer gives the operator flexibility in working with printed material that cannot be obtained with a simple typewriter. But unless the document can be taken out of the computer and placed on paper, the problem is only half solved. This is the purpose of the computer printer. Information is sent from the computer to the printer and then placed on paper in a mechanical form. Information placed on paper by a computer is sometimes called "hardcopy."

To work with printers, a technician should know some new terms and memorize a few simple facts:

1. The usual print size is known as *pica*. This is slightly larger than the also popular size of print called *elite*.
2. The length of a piece of paper, so far as the printer is concerned, is 66 lines. These 66 lines include the usual margins at the top and the bottom of the paper.
3. When a sheet of paper is held as it normally is written upon, it is in the "portrait" orientation, while it is in the "landscape" orientation if rotated 90 degrees.
4. There are 80 columns of characters across a standard 8½ × 11 inch sheet of paper when held in portrait orientation.
5. When using computer-wide paper, 132 columns of characters are available, while the height of the sheet remains at 11 inches.

DOS-Level Outputs to a Printer

When a computer is first turned on and booted up with the operating system, it is immediately able to operate a printer—with some limitations. First, the printer must be connected to the first parallel output port, LPT1, which is ASSUMED to have a printer connected. Two other printer ports are recognized by the operating system: LPT2 and LPT3. But LPT1 is the only one that is assumed to have the printer connection.

A serial printer can also be connected instead of, or in addition to, a parallel printer. Any data bound for printer port LPT1 can be redirected to the serial port by using the MODE command (an external command file found on the DOS diskettes). Before using a serial port, it is necessary to set it up with several parameters with a command such as

MODE COM1:12,N,8,1

This command is typical for most printers and simply means that the first serial port (COM1) is to be operated at a rate of 1200 baud, there will be no parity checking of the data, there will be 8 bits (a full byte) within each character, and there will be the usual single stop bit. This prepares the port to pass data to the serial printer. The following command is now required:

MODE LPT1:=COM1:

This command takes the digital information that was originally bound for the parallel port by default and redirects it to the serial data port COM1.

The serial printer will now respond to the data from the computer. If the serial printer is the only one used, the two previously listed commands (modified to fit the precise situation) should be put into the AUTOEXEC.BAT file for automatic execution each time the computer is booted up.

Redirected data going out the serial port can be directed back to the original LPT1 port by the command

MODE LPT1:

By alternating between these two commands, two printers can be operated independently via the computer keyboard while operating at the DOS level.

"Dumb" Printers

A "dumb" printer is one that, simply put, does not have a microprocessor within it. Such a printer is capable of operating only at the basic level of accepting ASCII characters and printing them. A few other functions such as form feed, carriage return, and line feed will be supported, but that is about it. No other capabilities such as compressed type, graphics mode, alternate (foreign) character sets, or different fonts are available via software. A dumb printer works well at the DOS level when printing simple ASCII characters from a text file.

"Smart" Printers

Putting a microprocessor in the printer opens all sorts of possibilities, particularly when used with a dot-matrix or a laser printhead. While the addition of a microprocessor to a daisy-wheel printer can enable some additional functions such as microspacing of characters and bidirectional printing, the daisy-wheel printer still cannot print graphics because of the fixed characters on the daisy wheel. The dot-matrix printer can, by firing each pin independently, make almost any dot pattern on paper, including normal and special font letters.

Control Codes and Escape Sequences

The ability to print any dot pattern in addition to normal text characters opens all sorts of possibilities. Controlling the printer, however, means that the stream of data going to the printer has to have a special code that tells the printer NOT to print the next few characters, but to interpret them internally and change the operation of the printer.

One of the first companies to solve this problem has set the "standard" for control codes for printers. The Epson printer is now the standard that most other printer manufacturers try to match. Doing so ensures that programs will also easily operate their printers, thus greatly enhancing sales.

The characters listed on the ASCII chart (see Appendix C) below the numbers (binary 00110000) are called *control codes*. These include line-feed, carriage return, and form-feed characters. While these control codes are certainly used, there are too few of them (31) available to tell a printer to do all of the special things of which it may be capable, such as changing to graphics mode and back to normal type again, changing to an italics font and back again, etc.

The solution to the problem of too few characters available is to send a special character called an *escape character*. When the printer gets this character, it interprets the ASCII characters following it as control codes rather than as characters to put on the paper. For instance, the sequence

ESC [4 w

causes a DEC model LA120 printer to print 16 characters per inch rather than the usual 10. This is, effectively, a compressed print. Sending the same printer an escape sequence of

ESC [w

resets the printer back to 10 characters per inch, the normal pica size for letters.

Appendix H lists the control sequences for the Epson printer.

Sending Printer Escape Codes at the DOS Level

When operating at the DOS level, control and escape codes can be sent directly to a printer if the printer is toggled on. The printer can be toggled on by pressing the control key (Ctrl) and hitting the printscreen key (PrtSc). Nothing will happen immediately, but if a letter key is pressed, the printer should respond by printing it. This is a good test to make. Enter the escape sequences and control codes by first looking up their decimal equivalents. Hold the alternate key (Alt) down, then key in the decimal numbers on the righthand number pad. When the keys are entered, release the Alt key. The code will proceed to the printer. A strange character will probably appear on the screen since the monitor also interprets the keyboard entry.

If you have a problem entering the codes, try substituting the number 155 decimal for the escape code rather than the 27 as listed on the ASCII chart. The addition of 128 to the 27 code may be necessary because of the way the computer interprets the low (less than 31) characters of the ASCII chart before putting it out to the printer.

There are many programs available in the public domain for operating a printer at the DOS level. These programs make it easy to manipulate an Epson-compatible printer. The best way to operate a printer is by using an applications printer that has a *driver* for the printer actually in use, Epson-compatible or not.

Applications Programs Run Printers Best

An applications program is written to serve a particular purpose, such as a word processing program like WordPerfect. These programs are able to operate any printer for which they have the driver interface software. A driver is a program that interfaces between the main program (like WordPerfect) and the machinery of the printer. The driver uses the full capability of the given printer.

While large, expensive word processors can use almost any printer through any of the installed ports on the computer, smaller applications programs (such as many of the public domain programs) assume the use of the LPT1 port and an Epson-compatible printer—period. They do not have drivers or the ability to fully utilize different printers, although most of a particular printer's capability will probably be usable. Using such a small program with a printer on the serial COM1 port rather than the assumed parallel LPT1 port requires *prior* setup and redirection of data to the serial port before loading the program.

Large applications programs require *configuring* of the software to use the facilities available. A word processor, for instance, might be configured to use a dot-matrix printer on LPT1 and a serial letter-quality printer on COM1. The setup or configure options during the installation of the software have prompts that lead the technician through the process of "telling" the software what is out there on the ports.

In addition to configuring the program for the hardware, the program may have the drivers necessary to use the given printer to its full capability. The drivers are usually slightly different for each make or model of printer. In a directory listing, drivers often have a *.DRV file extension. Only the drivers for the printers installed need to be available during the configuration of the software. Other drivers that are not needed should be kept on the original diskettes and stored away when using the program. There is no reason, for . instance, to put all of the drivers for a program on a hard disk. Most of them will never be used, so why take up space on the hard disk? The same goes doubly for a computer without a hard disk: Load only the needed drivers onto a working diskette, storing the rest with the original diskettes.

Only one driver program needs to be available for each different printer connected to the computer. Any one of several connected printers can be selected from within a program. The selection of the proper printer to use is made from within the program.

A program such as a word processor does some intricate manipulations of the control and escape codes of a printer. Text that has to be underlined, for instance, has to first be printed. Then, the printhead is told, via escape codes, to return in the opposite direction and begin striking the underline character at the proper time and the printhead moves across the paper from right to left. At the end of the line, the paper is advanced one line, and printing resumes. The program is actually merging the control codes and the text into a single stream of data going to the printer. The printer parses or filters out, the controlling escape sequences from the data bound for printing.

Using this method of merging the printer codes and the text itself, it can be seen that the applications program must be used in this case to properly print the document. Otherwise, the control and escape codes would not be sent. This is why a word processor document file does not print properly at the DOS level. Besides not having the proper codes to control the printer, other characters within the document will print strangely.

An alternate way of printing a document with all sorts of fancy things like underlining, double-striking, and bolding of the text, is to have the applications program *print to disk file*. This merges both the printer instructions and the text together into a file that can be printed at the DOS level *without* reloading the applications program.

THE MECHANICS OF PRINTERS

The mechanical side of printers consists of four major functions:

The printhead mechanism

The paper-feed mechanism

The carriage movement mechanism

The ribbon-feed mechanism

While the carriage mechanism moves across the width of the paper, the print-head puts characters onto the paper. At the end of each line, when the carriage prepares to begin another line, the line-feed mechanism moves the paper up one or more lines. During the actual printing, the ribbon-feed mechanism moves the ribbon to ensure fresh ink for the next character.

Printheads

Careless operation can damage printheads. Operating a printer without paper or ribbon can damage the print wires of a dot-matrix printhead. The wires can mushroom at the tip, causing them to jam and to make poor characters— particularly where the printhead fires against a metal platen or bar. The daisy wheel, too, should have the cushioning of the paper and a ribbon. Any kind of printer should be kept clean of ribbon and paper debris, dust, and dirt. A small amount of denatured alcohol applied with a cotton swab makes a good cleaning tool.

The Daisy Wheel. Probaby the most common problem the daisy wheel causes is the missing character. This occurs when the wheel has a broken "petal" and there is no character to be struck against the paper. The only cure is, of course, replacement of the daisy wheel itself. A related problem is one or more characters out of horizontal position, caused by a bent petal. The printing of scrambled letters can have at least two causes: The wheel has lost track of where it is due to a paper jam or the serial data (baud) rate of a serial printer is incorrect. If the printer has worked well and the serial data rate has not been changed, the head has likely lost track of where it is and the printer must be reinitialized by turning it off and back on again. If, however, the printer has never worked with that particular computer or software, the software may be inappropriate. In a serial printer, check the printer parity selection switches and the number of data bits being sent by the computer.

Another common problem with a daisy-wheel printer is the printing of the same character at each strike of the strike solenoid, regardless of the character sent. This is caused by the failure of the daisy wheel to turn. This in turn is often caused by a mechanical jamming of the wheel that prevents its turning or the failure of the driving mechanism for the daisy-wheel stepper motor.

If the printhead seems to be working but little or no impression is being made on the paper, the head-to-paper distance may be too great. Check the printer instruction book for details of setting this adjustment. A failure such as binding of the strike solenoid can also cause these symptoms.

The Dot-Matrix Printhead. The dot-matrix printhead may run quite hot in normal operation due to the high speed and continuous use of the driving solenoids. Common problems include missing or broken print wires, evidenced by a missing horizontal row of dots. The defect is easiest to identify if a repeating series of diagonals are printed: / / / / / / / / / / /. Another cause for missing dots in the matrix might be a binding solenoid or defective driving circuitry for that wire.

Paper Feeds

One of the common problems that arises with printers is improper paper feed. This could be the result of gearing caused by the operator. Since the paper feed is often driven by a stepper motor that is often geared down a great deal, the stepper motor is not only able to turn the platen with great torque but also takes a great deal more torque than normally applied. Operators of printers should be aware of this potential damage to the printer and be trained to avoid it. Sometimes this means turning off the printer before turning the platen; at other times it is necessary only to disengage the stepper mechanically by pressing inward or pulling outward on the platen knob.

The printhead must have something to strike against, behind the paper. This is often a rubber roller for a friction-feed system similar to that of a typewriter. Such paper-feed systems are used when the paper has no holes along the edge. See Figure 10.9.

Figure 10.9 Friction paper feed is used with paper that has no holes along its edges, such as ordinary typing paper. (Abbey Enterprises)

Dot-matrix printers usually have a paper-feed system that feeds the paper precisely according to the advancement of the holes along each side of the paper. See Figure 10.10.

Some printers offer the option of using either method of paper feed: friction for letter-quality printing on single sheets of paper and tractor feed for long strings of data printing using paper with holes along the edge. Some operators have problems with these printers because either one or the other of these methods can be used, but not both at the same time. If friction and tractor feeds are used together, the paper will eventually wrinkle and pull from the tractors, jamming the printer. See Figure 10.11.

Typical problems with the paper-feed mechanism include the usual out-of-paper error message and jamming of the paper in the printer. Jamming can cause the printhead of a daisy-wheel printer to go out of synchronization and requires reinitializing the printer by turning it off and back on after the jam is cleared. Damage can occur to the paper feed, carriage, and printhead mechanisms if the printer is not cared for. Turn off the power, clear the jam, and turn the printer on again. Remember not to turn the printer on without paper feeding into it as the printer may begin typing against the bare platen and cause printhead damage.

Another cause of paper-feed problems is too much drag on the paper for the printer to pull against. Such a problem might be caused by the printer sitting on the paper, for instance.

Carriage Mechanisms

The carriage mechanism of a printer is built to very close tolerances. The carriage must go across the width of the paper without play or backlash in order for the printed characters to be in their proper places. The suspension bars in particular are carefully machined.

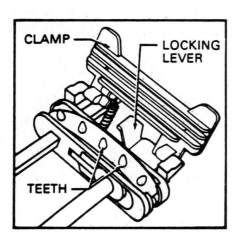

CLAMP — LOCKING LEVER

TEETH —

Figure 10.10 Tractor feeds make automatic feeding of long strings of paper precise and trouble-free. (Courtesy of Mannesmann Tally)

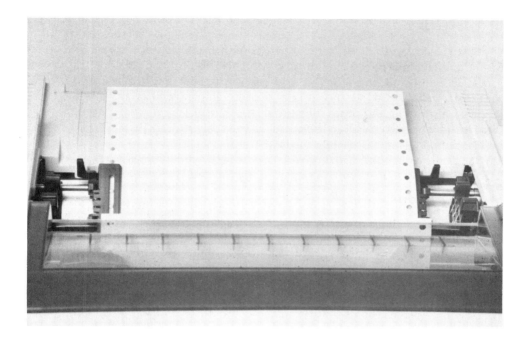

Figure 10.11 Do not use both the friction and tractor paper feeds at the same time. (Tom Carney)

The carriage is moved across the paper by one of several methods. A lead screw, toothed belt, and cable are common methods. In many cases, the motor that moves the carriage is a stepper motor. When the printer is first turned on, the carriage is brought to the left end of the carriage and its presence is detected by a switch or a photocoupled device. This is the starting position from which all further movement is calculated.

The horizontal spacing of the printer is sometimes programmable, commonly occurring in steps of 10, 12, or 15 characters per inch. Other printers, called microspacing printers, offer customizing of the horizontal carriage movement in increments as small as 1/120th of an inch for special uses. Sophisticated printers are also available that determine the horizontal spacing according to the width of the individual letters. For instance, an *i* would occupy less horizontal space than a *w*. This is called *proportional spacing* of letters.

Common problems with carriage movement mechanisms include buildup of sticky residue on the carriage suspension bars from careless lubrication of the suspension shaft and the dust from the paper feeding through the printer. A broken cable or toothed belt or one that has come off one of the pulleys is another problem that can occur with some regularity. A more subtle problem is the carriage that does not consistently move the distance it should because of a slipping setscrew in a drive pulley.

Ribbon Feeds

Two basic kinds of ribbons are in common use for dot-matrix and fully formed character printers: the fabric ribbon and the carbon ribbon. The fabric ribbon in Figure 10.12 is rugged and can be used many times through the printhead mechanism. As the ribbon is used, the printed characters become progressively lighter and more difficult to read. This is the most common ribbon used with dot-matrix printers because of their heavy and high-speed use for draft copies and large amounts of data.

The carbon ribbon in Figure 10.13 is sometimes used in typewriters that double as printers. These machines are fully formed character machines, used mostly for typing formal correspondence. The carbon ribbon can be used only once because the carbon is completely removed from its plastic backing and placed upon the paper at each strike of the printhead. The advantage of this ribbon is that the printed character can be easily removed from the paper using a special sticky tape. This type of ribbon is sometimes called a correctable ribbon.

There are two common methods of installing ribbons. Sometimes they are packaged in cartridges and replaced as a unit. This makes them quick, clean, and easy to replace. The other alternative is the older method of providing the ribbons on individual spools. These require more work since they must be fed through the printing mechanism by hand and threaded onto a takeup spool at the opposite end. See Figure 10.14.

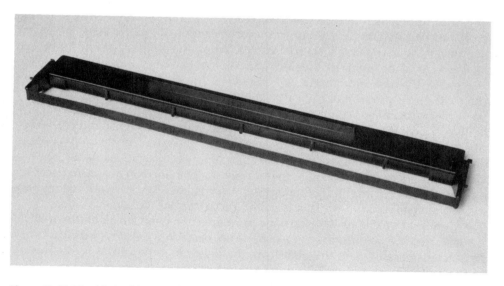

Figure 10.12 The fabric ribbon is rugged and often used in dot-matrix printers. It is also often messy to change. (Tom Carney)

Figure 10.13 The carbon ribbon is often used in fully formed character printers that double as typewriters. These ribbons are sometimes "erasable" with special lift-off tape. (Abbey Enterprises)

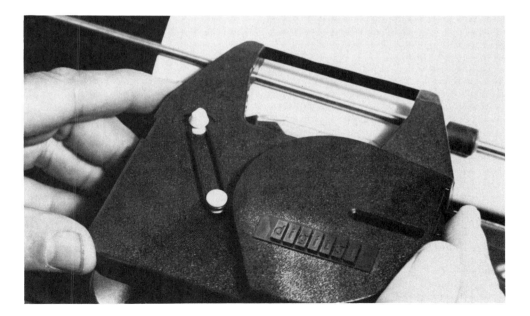

Figure 10.14 The ribbon cartridge is more convenient but often more expensive than the spool-to-spool ribbon mechanism. (Abbey Enterprises)

Common problems relating to the ribbon mechanism include jamming and running out of ribbon. Jamming eventually causes all of the ink on the ribbon to be depleted in one spot. In severe cases, there may be a hole in the ribbon because of the constant pounding of the printhead. This is usually a mechanical problem in the feed mechanism, but occasionally a ribbon that is binding can cause such a problem.

Interlock Switches

Interlock switches are often provided so that operators cannot get their fingers, ties, or hair caught in the mechanisms. Some of the carriage-return and paper-feed mechanisms are quite powerful and could cause injury. When the interlock switches are open, indicating the presence of a human in the works, the printer cannot operate. A common problem causing service calls is the misadjustment or failure of this interlock switch (see Figure 10.15).

Figure 10.15 The interlock switch is a common cause of service call due to its failure or misadjustment. (Abbey Enterprises)

INSTALLING A PRINTER

Installing a printer amounts to doing two things: connecting the printer to the computer with a suitable cable and setting any DIP switches within the printer to the correct settings.

The selection of a printer cable depends on the kind of feed the printer requires: parallel or serial feed. If parallel feed is used, the cable connects from the usual LPT1 port (a 25-pin female connector on the back of the computer) to an appropriate connector on the printer. The typical cable is described in Appendix A.

A serial cable, on the other hand, can be one of two types, a simple extension or a *null-modem* cable. See Appendix I for an explanation of RS-232C. Appendix A shows the connections necessary for extension and null-modem cables.

The printer may have DIP switch settings, too. These switches may have the following functions, together with the recommended settings for the average computer user:

1. Auto LF: Off (let the computer program advance the paper; don't let printer do it automatically when a carriage return is received).
2. Ser/Par: As necessary to select the method of feeding the printer from the computer. When optional, use the one that is most convenient or for which a cable is available.
3. Baud Select: As necessary to support the baud rate from the computer (1200 is typical). Baud rate does not affect the speed of actual printing.

These switches are read only during power up. If changed, the printer must be turned off and then turned on again to reread the switches.

Serial data transmission requires that one end transmit, the other receive. According to the standard for feeding serial data from a microcomputer, the data comes out of the computer as a data terminal equipment (DTE) on pin #2 of a male DB-25 connector. It is intended to enter the #2 female pin of a data communications equipment (DCE) connector of the same type. A straight-through connection of like-numbered pins results in the data being sent normally. Although the original RS-232C standard was intended to be used with a computer terminal and a modem, it is now being used for a microcomputer to any serial device.

Printers can be made with serial input ports, similar to a modem. The choice as to how the printer should be configured, DTE or DCE, is up to the manufacturer. It is up to the technician to determine which way the printer is actually wired. Although the standard provides for a female connector on a DCE and a male on a DTE, manufacturers have apparently disregarded the intent of the standard in this regard. The microcomputer, fortunately, appears to have stood by this standard properly, thus enabling a technician to reasonably depend on the computer serial port to be a male connector.

There is another source of confusion in the marking on the connector of a serial device. The connector *may* be marked to indicate how it is wired or it may be marked as to *what it should be connected to*, which would be just the opposite of how it is wired!

The bottom line is to determine how the connector on the printer is wired internally. The most reliable source of information is a good instruction manual or a schematic. The manual usually only implies the type of connection, rather than coming right out and specifying it. For instance, if the cable shown for the serial printer indicates a straight-through connection from a microcomputer or a data terminal, then the printer must be a DCE device. The use of a null-modem (crossover) cable indicates that the printer is a DTE device. Once a device is definitely determined to be either a DTE or a DCE, that designation should be marked next to the connector using a permanent marking pen. This will greatly help in future changes in the system.

If a schematic of the printer is available, the kind of device can be easily determined by noting what is connected to pin #2 of the interface connector. If pin #2 is an input to the printer, the printer is a DCE device. On the other hand, if signals come out of pin #2, it must be a DTE device. A simple memory aid of use here is to keep track of the Ts in the sentence, "A DTE TRANSMITS ON TWO."

The wiring of the cable for a serial device is a simple extension cable (straight-through connections) or a crossover or null-modem cable. Wiring of a null-modem cable is shown in Appendix A.

INSTALLING A PLOTTER

A plotter processes data much like a printer. Data in the proper format (determined by the software used) is converted into drawings using a pen. The major difference between a printer and a plotter is that the plotter primarily draws geometric figures, where the printer responds to simple ASCII characters. A plotter can, in some cases, use its pen to draw ASCII characters, acting like a printer, but this ability is seldom used. The plotter is intended for drawing pictures with a pen.

A plotter can be fed data in either the parallel or serial format, depending on the port configuration of the plotter and the ports available on the computer. Some plotters can accept either data format.

A plotter may have DIP switches to set, similar to those of a printer. Only the instruction book gives complete information on how the switches should be set. Parallel feed of a plotter should be simple, merely requiring the setting of a single switch to select this method. Serial feed, on the other hand, requires setting the baud rate, number of data bits, etc. as for a serial printer.

Because of its complexity, a plotter must contain a microcontroller. This means that there will probably be an internal self-test or diagnostic routine that can be initiated to test the plotter. This internal self-test is usually initiated by holding down one or more buttons normally used for completely different purposes, while power is applied. For instance, all of the four pen movement buttons on an Amdek plotter are held down while power is applied to begin this test.

PRINTER SPOOLERS

Printing a file takes time. Plotting a file takes even longer. During the actual printing or plotting of a file, the computer spends perhaps 98% of its time waiting for the printer or plotter to catch up. It would be nice if the computer operator could use this 98% for something useful, such as continuing the program that is in operation.

As an example, a word processing program is in use. A long document, perhaps a dozen pages, needs to be printed. This may take 25 minutes to print on a slow, letter-quality printer. This may mean that the word processing program cannot be operated during this time, forcing a 25-minute break. Although this is great for the operator, it is very inefficient in terms of computer time.

The printer spooler cures these problems. A print spooler is a software routine that will do the following:

1. Merge the document with the proper printer codes.
2. Place the data into RAM rather than outputting it, a byte at a time, directly to the printer.
3. Divide the computer CPU time between continuing the word processor program and putting information out to the printer.

When the printer needs more data, it is provided from RAM very quickly, without the operator even being aware of it. The computer seems to be doing two things at once, continuing the word processing program, yet "at the same time" running the printer.

The larger the block of RAM set aside for a print spooler, the larger the document that can be held within it. Programs such as WordPerfect automatically set up the print spooler and manage it, regardless of the number or the size of the documents to be printed.

Installing an External Printer Buffer

If there is a shortage of internal RAM available for a print spooler due to running large programs, an external spooler can be used to hold the data bound for the printer. This external memory can take data as quickly as the computer can put it out. The printer on the output side of the spooler takes the data at its own rate. With such a spooler, the computer is again ready for use much sooner than it would be without it. External spoolers are particularly useful when using a plotter, because of the slow plotting speed.

Another benefit of using an external spooler is that, if the total memory of the spooler has not been used, a simple touch of a front panel button begins dumping all of the data out again, thus easily making several copies of a document or drawing without reloading the spooler from the computer. In fact, the computer can be shut down after the data is loaded into an external spooler, and as many copies as needed can be made by hitting the Copy button on the spooler.

If very large documents or drawings are put through an external spooler, the memory within the spooler will fill up. When this happens, the computer must wait while the printer empties and processes the data at the other end, byte by byte. When this happens, the computer operates as it would without a spooler—very slowly. When the computer loads the final data of the file into the spooler, however, the computer is then released for any other use. The spooler then simply continues to output data to the printer, often for a long time.

TROUBLESHOOTING PRINTER PROBLEMS

While ordinary paper will run through a printer without too many problems, running gummed labels through a printer can easily mess it up. Some printers jam the labels, particularly if the operator turns the platen or paper feed backward by hand. The labels then come off the backing sheet and begin sticking in the printer, usually in the paper path, behind the printhead. This jams the printhead, and the printer is out of service until someone cleans it out. If this is a recurring problem, try changing the brand or the size of the labels used. Also caution operators *not* to back up the label strip in the printer.

Printers that contain a microprocessor will undoubtedly have some kind of internal or self-test. This test can be run whenever there is a suspected problem with the printer. Invoking such a test usually requires that one or more pushbuttons be held down while power is applied. This is an unusual thing to do, holding down a button while applying power, but it is an ideal way to do something unusual such as starting a special test routine.

The specific combination to use to start the self-test must be found in the operator's manual for the particular printer. External cabling does not need to be connected. Just hold the correct button and turn on the machine. If paper is provided, the printer (or plotter) will go through a specially programmed sequence designed to test as much of the equipment as possible.

Most problems with printers and plotters are caused by improper installation or operation by the computer operator. Perhaps the largest problem is the proper configuration of the software running on the microcomputer.

Configuring the software to be used on the computer means that the proper printer driver (interfacing software between the program and the computer) must be used. The proper *default parameters* must also be used. These parameters are in effect for printing, yet their presence may not be evident. For instance, a printer might always line up the right ends of lines of text, although the text appearing on the screen does not line up. This is the result of setting up a default of *right justify* for the printer. Unless this is recognized and corrected, the printer will always "screw up," regardless of how the text appears on the computer monitor.

Here are some of the more important *printer defaults* that the technician must be able to recognize and manipulate, if necessary, to correct apparent printer malfunction:

Justification

Margins (top, bottom, right, and left)

Letter quality/draft quality (dot-matrix printers only)

Form length (66 lines for pica, on an 8½ × 11 inch sheet)

PRINTER PREVENTIVE MAINTENANCE

Printer maintenance is mainly a matter of keeping the printer clean, inside and out. The keyboard of a printer, if it has one, can be cleaned with a soft brush, taking care to brush lint and dust away from the keys as much as possible rather than pushing it down between and under the keys.

The interior of the printer can usually be reached only partially without dismantling the cabinet. A thorough job of cleaning can be accomplished by removing the cabinet and vacuuming out the interior with a small vacuum cleaner. Be careful not to damage any small mechanisms such as levers and cables. Take it slow and easy, and do not move around too quickly inside the printer. The printhead can be cleaned using a small cotton swab and denatured alcohol. The mechanisms of the printer such as the carriage rails should *only* be lubricated in accordance with the manufacturer's instructions. Use of improper lubricants can result in these rails and mechanisms becoming contaminated with sticky residue, countering any good intentions of the service technician by creating more problems than would have resulted if there were no lubrication applied in the first place. Remember that the printhead of some printers may be hot if the printer has recently been in full high-speed service. It may be wise to wait for a while for the head to cool off.

CHAPTER SUMMARY

INSTALLING AND REPAIRING COMPUTER PRINTERS AND PLOTTERS describes the various printers available. The dot-matrix printer is popular due to its low cost and ability to print graphics. The letter-quality printer produces print that is easier to read than the dot-matrix printer. The laser printer is gaining in popularity. Pica and elite are the two sizes of print most commonly used with letter-quality printers. There are 66 lines of text possible on an 8½ × 11 inch sheet of paper, the most common size of paper used.

The parallel and serial ports support printers. Default printer output goes to the first parallel port, the LPT1 port. Printer output may be redirected to a serial port using the MODE command. If a serial printer is a DTE device, a null-modem cable is required to operate it from the computer's DTE serial port. A DCE-configured serial printer uses a straight-through extension cable from the serial port of the computer.

"Smart" printers look for escape codes in the data stream to control them. The number pad keys of a microcomputer can be used to send special characters to a printer. Complex operations on a printer are best handled by an applications program such as a word processor. Printer spoolers save the operator time, making the computer apparently do two tasks at once: printing and interacting with the operator. The printer's self-test can determine whether a problem lies within the printer or is caused by external cables, software, or the computer hardware.

REVIEW QUESTIONS

1. What are two advantages of the dot-matrix printer?
2. What is the main advantage of letter-quality printing?
3. What is NLQ and how is it produced?
4. What are the two most common sizes of print produced by a letter-quality printer?
5. What is the most versatile printer available?
6. How many lines are available on a standard 8½ × 11 inch sheet of paper?
7. What is the default printer output port?
8. When working at the DOS level, how can a serial printer be used if the printer output defaults to the parallel port?
9. How can data be made available back at the parallel port if the commands of question 8 are issued?
10. How can a smart printer be told to change defaults, such as the size of its print, or to go into or out of the graphics mode?
11. How can special codes be sent to a printer at the DOS level?
12. Applications programs must have the ability to operate many different printers, each of which may have different control codes and escape sequences. How is this accomplished for a given computer installation?
13. Is it necessary or desirable to put all of the drivers provided with a given applications program on the hard disk?
14. What is the difference between a file saved by a word processor and the same file "printed to disk"?
15. What are the two kinds of data feed to a printer or plotter?
16. When deciding what kind of cable to use with a serial printer, what is the determining factor?

17. What is the usual kind of output, DTE or DCE, that the microcomputer is configured for on its serial ports?
18. If a serial connector is labeled DTE, does it mean that the connector is a DTE configuration?
19. What software or hardware improvements can be made to make a computer more efficient when printing or plotting documents?
20. What is the quickest way to determine whether the printer is causing a problem?
21. New software has just been purchased for word processing. Will the program work properly with your printer when first attempted?

chapter eleven

Installing and Using a Modem

CHAPTER OBJECTIVE

INSTALLING AND USING A MODEM will help the technician get one of these amazing units on-line and operating in a minimum time with a minimum of mistakes. There are many special terms used for data communications. Each is explained and, where appropriate, examples are given. Recommended protocols to use during microcomputer data communciations are explained. The internal chain of events are followed as the modem dials, locks onto a remote modem signal, and begins passing data. Common switch and default settings are explained. Use of the host mode of operation is covered. The packing of files into a shorter version that is more efficient to send over telephone lines is explained. The configuration of a modem in preparation for data communications is covered in detail. A brief discussion of computer viruses warns of possible problems that may be enabled by the use of a modem. Figure 11.1 shows a block diagram of a modem.

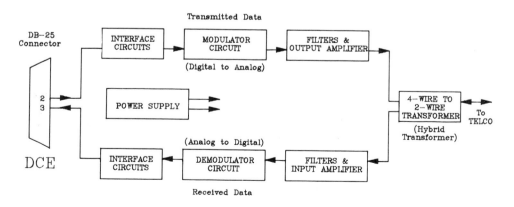

Figure 11.1 Block diagram of a modem.

AN OVERVIEW OF MODEM COMMUNICATIONS

A modem is a piece of equipment installed to interface between a digital device and the telephone company. It enables the digital device to "talk" to another digital device anywhere in the world. Here we assume that the digital device is a microcomputer, although the modem is also commonly used with data terminals in communicating with mainframe computers. See Figure 11.2.

While it is a simple matter to hook up eight data lines and transmit ASCII and binary information over short distances (typically less than 50 feet) with a parallel port, it is impractical to use such methods for longer distances. It would be necessary to have more than a dozen wires between devices to transmit information in a parallel format. Using a single telephone circuit and transmitting each bit of a data file, one at a time, is far more practical for long distances. The wiring standard used for connecting a modem to a terminal or microcomputer is the RS-232C standard. The wiring of an RS-232C connector and an explanation of the RS-232C standard is given in Appendix A.

The telephone company can handle analog signals very well. It will not, however, handle the very high frequency components of a digital signal. Digital signals must be converted into analog tones that the telephone company can handle. This is the primary job of the modem: converting digital signals into analog and analog signals to digital.

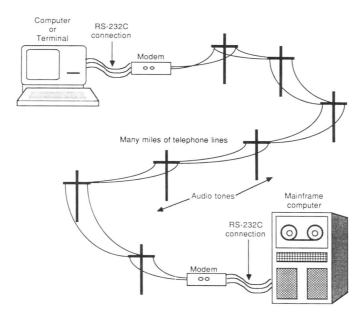

Figure 11.2 How modems can link computers over great distances.

THE HAYES MODEM STANDARD

In a new field, the first company to produce a quality, reliable, complete product is the one that other manufacturers try to copy. Years ago, the Hayes Company produced such a product, a modem. Since that time, others have boasted that their modems are "Hayes-compatible." In other words, they copied the Hayes modem, changing the circuitry slightly, but retaining the same set of commands to control it. In this way, software written for the Hayes modem would also work on the copied modems.

In order for a modem to respond to commands and be reprogrammable, it must contain a microprocessor. The microprocessor interfaces the commands sent to the modem to the hardware of the modem. Since the modem is so programmable and flexible in its operation, it is referred to as a "smart" modem. This was, in fact, part of the brand name of Hayes modems, "Smartmodems."

The instructions that the modem is capable of carrying out are listed in Appendix G.

How a "Smart" Modem Works

The modem has two principal states of operation, the command state and the on-line state. When the modem is first turned on, it is ready to accept commands. This is the command state. The commands come from the computer or terminal to which the modem is connected, via the RS-232C cable. See Figure 11.3.

When the modem is communicating with another modem, however, it cannot accept commands, since all the information sent to the modem during

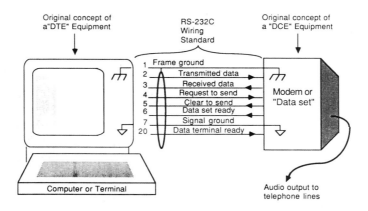

Figure 11.3 Commands pass between the terminal or microcomputer and the modem via the RS-232C cable.

this time is assumed to be meant for transmission to the distant modem. There is one exception, the "break" command, which will bring the modem out of the on-line state back into the command state. See Figure 11.4.

MODEM HARDWARE INSTALLATION

There are two types of modems, internal and external. Both are shown in Figure 11.5.

Each kind of modem has advantages:

Internal Modem ("Bus" Modem)	**External Modem** ("Port" Modem)
Saves desk space outside the computer	Does not require an expansion slot
Does not require an actual serial port	Shows modem status on LEDs

Internal and external modems are easy to install. A telephone set can also be connected in the setup. In this way, the telephone handset can be used in the normal way when the modem does not need the telephone line.

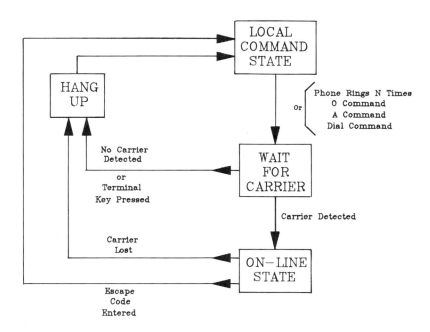

Figure 11.4 Flowchart of the states of operation of a Hayes-compatible modem.

Internal Setup Switches

The initial settings and default states of a modem for normal communications can, in some cases, be determined by the appropriate setting of a bank of DIP switches within the modem. Removing the front plate or taking the cover

Figure 11.5 Internal and external modems. (Courtesy of Hayes Microcomputer Products, Inc.)

off the modem may be necessary to gain access to these switches. It is often possible to override these hardware settings by sending software commands to the modem during initialization. The Hayes 2400-baud modem, on the other hand, has only a few internal DIP switches, and the majority of the necessary default settings are accomplished in software during initialization. If a software command is given that varies with the settings of the switches, the modem will operate according to the new software command. If the power to the modem is turned off and on, the modem reverts to the settings dictated by the switches.

The switches of a 1200-baud Hayes modem, as an example, are as follows:

1. Switch #1 determines whether the modem will monitor the ready-or-not status of the microcomputer via pin #20 of the interconnecting cable. Placing this switch in the DOWN position "lies" to the modem, telling it that the computer is always ready to communicate. This signal allows the modem to execute commands at all times. If the switch is UP, however, the computer can cause the modem to hang up the telephone line through software. This is valuable when operating in the host mode, accessing the computer from a remote location.

2. Switch #2 determines how the modem communicates information back to the computer. There are two ways to do this: using ASCII strings (real words) with or numbers. The software used in the computer determines which method should be used. Words are normally used, so this switch should be in the UP position.

3. Switch #3 should be left in the DOWN position, which enables the modem to send responses to the computer. Placing the switch in the UP position disables this capability, an option seldom used.

4. Switch #4 determines whether or not the modem will repeat (echo) each keystroke back to the computer screen. This capability is usually used, so the switch should be in the UP position. Using the modem in this way "checks out" the data path between the computer and the modem with each keystroke. An optional and less desirable method is to have the keystrokes of the computer appear directly on the screen without the echo capability. This, of course, does not confirm that the commands go via the modem to the screen. Incorrect placement of this switch results in no characters appearing on the screen (echo needs to be turned on) or double characters (echo needs to be turned off; the software of the computer is already sending characters to the screen directly).

5. Switch #5 is particularly important in that it determines whether the modem will answer a telephone ring. The modem should answer the phone only when the computer is in the host mode, ready to access from a remote location without local operator intervention. Normally, the modem will not answer the telephone, and this switch should be in the DOWN position.

6. Switch #6 should normally be in the DOWN position. This tells the computer that the modem is always receiving a signal from a remote modem and that the computer should process the information from the modem accordingly.

7. Switch #7 should be in the UP position, indicating that the modem uses a standard telephone line connection. To use the modem on a multiple-line installation, the instruction book is needed.

8. Switch #8 should be in the DOWN position. This enables the modem to recognize commands. The reason for this switch is rather obscure.

CONFIGURING COMMUNICATIONS SOFTWARE FOR DATA TRANSFERS

Communication software must be configured for use with a specific modem. Among the items that must be initialized within the software are the following:

Port to be used (COM1 or COM2)

Baud rate to be used (typically 1200 or 2400 baud)

Whether or not parity is to be checked (normally no)

Number of data bits (usually 8)

Number of stop bits (normally 1)

These items enable the microcomputer to "talk" to the modem at the proper rate and via the proper port.

The modem sends ASCII information back to the communications program in the microcomputer. The communications program must be configured accordingly.

The following messages must be entered into the communication program under a heading something like MODEM REPORTS:

CONNECT ∧M   (message when modem connects with another at 300 baud)

CONNECT 1200   (message when modem connects with another at 1200 baud)

CONNECT 2400   (message when modem connects with another at 2400 baud)

The Hayes-compatible modems are actually as many as three different modems in a single package. The simplest modem is the 300-baud modem. This modem operates on an old communications mode called frequency shift keying (FSK). The 1200-baud modem operates on the communication mode called phase shift keying (PSK). The 2400-baud modem is the most complex of all and it operates with the quadrature/amplitude modulation (QAM) mode. As the complexity of the modem increases, so does the chance of data transmission errors. Excessive data errors at a higher baud rate can sometimes be cured by changing to a lower baud rate.

Initializing these CONNECT messages properly within the communications software is important because the modem can operate at only one of several possible baud rates when locking onto another modem. The selection of the baud rate between the modems usually begins at 2400 (if capable of that data rate) and drops to 1200 baud if they cannot lock at the higher rate. The modems may drop to the lowest rate of 300 baud as a last resort. The baud rate from the communications program running on the computer to the modem MUST match to send and receive data with the modem. The modem report messages lets the computer software change its baud rate to match that of the now locked-on modem.

Baud rates slower than 300 are no longer used, being vestiges of the old mechanical teletype network. Baud rates faster than 4800 may require special high-quality lines for data transfer that do not use a telephone dial tone, but are always connected to the modems at both ends. These lines are called leased lines. These lines are expensive to lease, and use of these data rates will probably also require that the modems in use must be identical at each end due to the lack of stringent data standards for these data rates.

Note that the CONNECT message for 300 baud includes a carriage return symbol (∧M), which may also have to be specified during the setup of the communications program.

In order to actually use these modem messages, the program setup must also specify that AUTO BAUD DETECT will be used.

ORIGINATING A MODEM COMMUNICATIONS CONNECTION

There are two ways to make a connection to another digital device via the telephone company. One way is to originate the call by dialing the telephone number of the other equipment. The other way is to make the computer an answering equipment, awaiting an incoming call.

To explain what happens when establishing communications with other digital equipment, we assume that a microcomputer and a Hayes modem are used to originate a call to another computer at a remote location via modems and the telephone company.

There are several steps involved in making contact with a remote computer:

1. Initialize the modem.
2. Dial the telephone number.
3. Wait for answer carrier.
4. Send originate carrier.
5. Report modems locked-on.

The modem is initially in the command state. It will accept ASCII commands sent to it from the microcomputer. An initializing string of ASCII characters is sent to the computerized modem to instruct it on how to react. See Figure 11.6. A typical initializing string might be

AT E1 L1 V1 X4 S0=0 M1   M

Explanations of these codes can be found in Appendix G. Spaces between commands are optional as they are ignored by the modem.

The modem is instructed to dial the telephone number of the remote equipment. See Figure 11.7. A typical command to dial might be

AT DT 235 2300

Dialing commands can also include pauses and area codes.

Watch for an answering carrier tone from the remote equipment. See Figure 11.8.

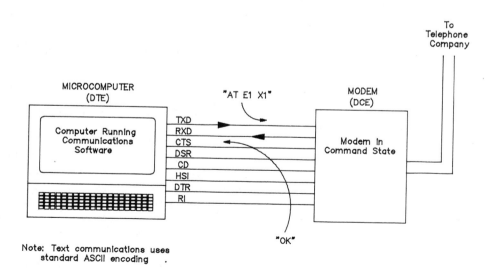

Figure 11.6 Block diagram of microcomputer sending initializing string to modem.

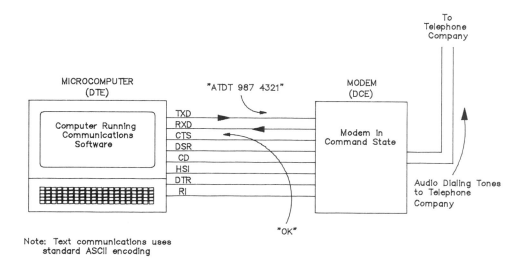

Figure 11.7 Block diagram of dialing a number with a modem.

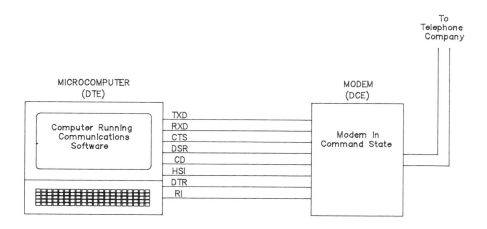

Figure 11.8 Block diagram of waiting for an answer tone from the remote computer.

If an answer carrier from the remote location is received, send out an originate carrier in return. See Figure 11.9. (If no carrier is heard within a specified time, the modem hangs up the telephone, goes back into the command state, and sends a report to the local computer that the answer carrier was not detected.)

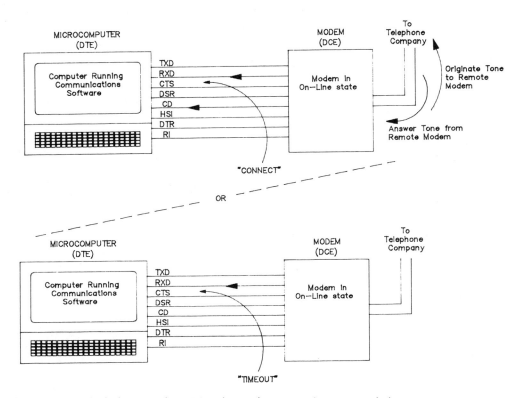

Figure 11.9 Block diagram of receiving the modem answering tone or timing out.

The modem reports to the local computer when the connection has been made. The modems are "locked" on one another and data communications begin. The modem is now in the on-line state and will no longer accept commands from the microcomputer. All of the digital information sent to the modem is passed through into the phone line. Once contact is established between two modems, data sent into either modem appear at the output of the other. Data files and programs can be sent over the telephone lines. See Figure 11.10. With appropriate software at both ends, a remote computer can even be controlled, to some extent, from next door or from thousands of miles away. This is called operating a computer in the HOST mode, to be covered later.

Three things can cause a modem to disconnect, terminating the "lock" on the other modem:

1. Turning off the power or disconnecting the telephone line to the modem
2. Loss of carrier from the remote modem (it disconnected the telephone line)
3. Detection of a unique character string, including pauses, that should not occur in a normal string of data bound for the remote computer.

ANSWERING A MODEM COMMUNICATIONS CONNECTION

The following information applies only when the data communication is to be run in reverse—when a computer is to be set up to answer the telephone and respond to commands coming in via the telephone line. The computer is operating entirely without a local operator. If this is not the intent, proceed to the next heading and skip this information.

It may be sufficient to use a modem only to communicate with other modems, with the operator sitting at the keyboard, controlling the computer and the communications. Many modems are operated only in this manner. It is also possible, with appropriate software, to make a microcomputer available for file transfers from any remote location. Operating a microcomputer in this manner is called operation in the *host mode*. This is a valuable capability for the businessperson who wishes to have access to microcomputer files from the office or from any location in the world. All that is required on the road is a computer and modem. Tiny laptop computers equipped with a modem, for instance, can be used at a motel to access the person's home computer, and files can be passed in either direction. Written reports prepared while on the road can be sent directly to the home computer and stored there for use at the end of the trip. To make the modem an answering modem rather than an originating modem, the initializing string must contain a command to answer the telephone.

There are five steps to answering an incoming telephone call with a modem:

1. Initialize the modem.
2. Answer on specified ring.
3. Provide the answer carrier.
4. Listen for an originate carrier.
5. Report modems locked-on.

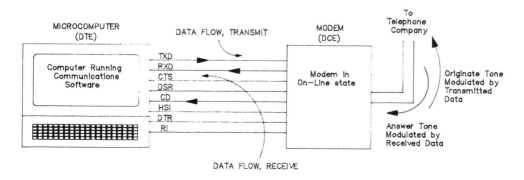

Figure 11.10 Block diagram of the modem handling data flow.

The modem will initially be in the command state, able to accept ASCII commands sent to it from the local computer. An initializing string of commands is sent to the modem to instruct it on how to act. See Figure 11.6.

The modem must be told that it is supposed to answer the telephone when it rings. A Hayes-compatible modem will do this if the following initializing string is sent to the modem:

AT E1 L1 V1 X4 M1 S0 = 1 &C1 &D2   M

Note that the initializing string is similar to that used for an originating modem, except that the S0=0 command is now S0=1. The number following the equal sign is the number of the ring on which to answer the telephone. When the telephone rings the specified number of times, the modem goes into the on-line state, picking up the telephone. The commands beginning with the ampersand (&) are necessary when operating in the host mode. The code &C1 makes the modem report the receipt or absence of an answering carrier from the remote modem. The code &D2 enables the computer to control the modem. When the computer drops the data transmit/receive (DTR) pin, the modem hangs up the telephone line, ceases to automatically answer the telephone next time it rings, and returns to the command state. The modem then immediately sends an answer carrier down the telephone line. The modem on the other end should reply with the originating carrier.

It is interesting to note what happens when the telephone rings because of a person wishing to speak to someone at the called number. The answering modem has no way of knowing that a person, not a modem, is making the call. The answer carrier is still sent down the line, right into the ear of the person calling. A knowledgable person will realize that a modem is connected and hang up. The modem, not receiving an originate carrier for a predetermined time, eventually hangs up. Callers will probably think something is wrong with the telephone line and may call several times before becoming discouraged.

Once the modems have locked onto one another, files can be passed between the modems, and to some extent, a microcomputer can be operated from a remote location. The remote user can change default drives, view directories, and execute some of the DOS programs. Limitations of DOS, however, prevent the execution of most programs from a remote location. These same limitations prevent using the computer effectively in the host mode with other than those serial ports specifically recognized by DOS, COM1 and COM2 with MS-DOS version 3.3.

PASSING DATA DOWN THE LINE

Communications software is required to run a modem. While it may be possible to dial a modem without special software, the complex file transfer protocols require communications software. Several such programs are available in the public domain. Software may also be provided with the modem when it is purchased. Such software may or may not be able to operate the computer in the host mode, however.

COMMUNICATIONS PROTOCOLS

The telephone company is rapidly moving from mechanical relays to microwave and fiber optic data transmission. Some portions of the telephone system are still electrically "noisy" because of the old relay contacts and aging connections in the central offices. The decaying magnetic field of a relay can induce spikes of noise in adjacent wiring, contributing to the accumulation of electrical impulses. While these noise impulses are easily ignored during a normal voice telephone communications, they may become critical when transmitting digital data. A noise pulse can be interpreted as a digital bit, introducing a foreign character into the data file. If the data file is simple ASCII letters, a person reading the characters can probably figure out that a particular character is wrong and no meaning is lost. If the file is a computer program, however, a misplaced bit will probably render the program completely useless.

It is possible for noise to appear in only one direction of a modem hookup, causing data scrambling at only one of the locations involved rather than at both locations.

If an error in transmission can be detected, the portion of the file containing the error can be sent again. This is the common way microcomputer data transmission errors are avoided. Data files are commonly broken up into blocks of 128 or 1024 characters for transmission over modems. If a transmission error occurs in a block of data, the defective block is simply retransmitted.

There are three principal ways in which errors en route from one location to another are detected. Both of the following methods depend on performing a mathematical operation on each block of data to be sent and then sending the result of this operation along with each block of data. At the opposite end, the same mathematical operation is performed on the block of data as it arrives. The math operations are then compared. If the results are the same, the file is assumed to have arrived without error. If the results are different, the receiving computer requests retransmission of that block of data. This entire operation is like sending a deposit of money to the bank along with a deposit slip that shows the total amount of cash. If the bank teller counts the cash and finds that the amount of money matches that on the deposit slip, the deposit is accepted. If there is a disagreement, then a correction must be made. The deposit is not accepted without a correct total.

Half-Duplex Communication Protocols

Parity Checking of ASCII Files. If a data file consists entirely of ASCII characters, each byte of data can be encoded using the unused high bit (D7) of the byte.

Remember that ASCII characters use only the least significant 7 bits of an 8-bit byte. The unused bit can be forced high or low to maintain a consistent even or odd count of the entire byte. For instance, if an ASCII byte of 7 bits for the letter "A" are to be sent, those 7 bits would be

100 0001

If *even parity* were agreed upon at both ends of the communication, the byte sent down the line would be have the highest bit forced to a "0":

0100 0001

This results in an overall even number of bits (2) being set. If the letter "C" were being sent, it would be

100 0011

to begin with. This would be an odd number of bits (3). Having agreed upon an even parity, the high bit would be combined with this ASCII character and sent as follows:

11000011

This arrives at the receiving end as an even number of bits.

Parity checking is no longer used for microcomputer data communications since other protocols are much more reliable and efficient.

XMODEM. The first significant transmission protocol was the XMODEM protocol. Using 128-byte data blocks, this method of data transmission originally used CHECKSUM error detection. Although this allowed some errors to be undetected, it worked. XMODEM later became available using the CRC error detection method. Both CHECKSUM and CRC detection methods (XMODEM and XMODEM CRC) are available for use. Initially, the receiving end attempts a match using CRC, reverting to CHECKSUM if unsuccessful in obtaining a match. XMODEM is compatible with most communications software. This protocol will automatically terminate due to line after ten attempts to transmit a block of data.

MODEM7. MODEM7 is a variant of XMODEM, but it supports multiple-file transfer using DOS wild cards and both CRC and CHECKSUM error detection methods, similar to XMODEM. It is used mostly on CP/M operating systems.

TELINK. TELINK is a variation of both XMODEM and MODEM7, but includes the file attributes of file size and date. It is used widely with FIDO bulletin boards.

YMODEM. YMODEM was the next improvement of data communication protocols. This method uses blocks of 1024 characters, reducing the time required for block verification. If there is too much line noise, YMODEM automatically steps down to a block size of 128 bytes. This occurs after a block fails to arrive error-free after three tries.

YMODEM BATCH. YMODEM BATCH is a further improvement in file transfers, allowing the use of wild cards to sequentially send a group of files without typing data file names and sizes manually at both ends of the communication. YMODEM BATCH is probably the best protocol for most microcomputer data transmission jobs. Just put all your files to be sent into a specific directory or on a specific diskette and send the entire contents of that directory using DOS wild cards (*.*). Once the transfer is begun, all the contents of that directory or diskette are sent, one after the other. Each file also includes the file attributes, size, and the date of last revision.

Full-Duplex Communication Protocols

Full-duplex protocols send information and verification data simultaneously along the line. In so doing, the time required for the transmission of given data is reduced.

ZMODEM. ZMODEM is a sophisticated method of data transfer developed principally for data transmission via time-sharing systems, satellites, and packet-switching networks. If using ZMODEM at either end of a data transfer where it is not supported at the other end, ZMODEM reverts to YMODEM protocol. ZMODEM uses the full-duplex capability of a network or telephone line and sends data in 256 byte blocks, automatically stepping this number down on "bad" lines. Rarely supported by communications programs, it is also complex to learn and use.

KERMIT. KERMIT is also a packet-oriented protocol. It is a full-duplex protocol, sending and receiving verification information simultaneously. It can handle multiple, sequential file transfers including file attributes (file size, date, etc.) like YMODEM BATCH. KERMIT has either 7 or 8 bit data bit transmission and can be used on many older systems. KERMIT also has data compression capability, passes file attributes, uses full duplex, and includes "server mode" and "sliding windows." The KERMIT block size is about 90 characters.

Special Communications Protocols

Other protocols are popular for specific applications, such as the following:

SEALINK. This is a variation of XMODEM, developed to overcome transmission delays of satellite-relayed or packet-switched networks. It can send up to 6 of the 128 byte blocks before verification.

COMPUSERVE B. This is used only on the COMPUSERVE network. It is sometimes called the CIS B protocol.

WXMODEM. Used on the PEOPLE LINK, TYMNET, TELENET, and DATAPAC networks because it can hand network flow control and has a sliding window feature to reduce transmission delays. Sends four 128 byte blocks before verifying error-free reception.

Protocols Without Error Detection

There are three protocols that are used only for modems that have special hardware to detect and to correct transmission errors.

YMODEM-G. A full-duplex protocol, this protocol sends data continuously without verification. It will send a data file until the full-duplex mode requests a stop.

YMODEM-G BATCH. This is the same as YMODEM-G, with multiple file capability.

IMODEM. This is very similar to YMODEM-G.

All this time, you are telling the remote computer how to send a file or group of files. Once these details are out of the way, the local computer user will be prompted to specify which file on the remote computer is selected for transmission. The file name, (or wild cards if a group of files) is then selected. The remote computer then goes into a timing loop, awaiting the local computer to begin the transfer.

The local computer must also be instructed to receive the file. This is done with some software by hitting the Page Down key, indicating a download (from host to local computer) direction of data flow. Following the prompts at this point in the file transfer process should result in the computers actually passing the file through the telephone line.

FILE ARCHIVING

Data files need time to send through a telephone line, regardless of the data rate. Logically, a data rate of 2400 baud requires half the time to send when sending a given file compared to a data rate of 1200 baud. Data files are not as compact as they could be, however. A program using one of several schemes, called crunching, packing, or squeezing, can reduce data files so that they take less time to transmit through the telephone network, saving transmission cost.

Several programs are available to do this. Among the best is a small program called PKARC. This program takes files and packs them into a single file, rather like packing clothes into a suitcase. The single large file containing the smaller ones inside is called an ARCHIVE file. (Note: This use of the word ARCHIVE is not to be confused with the archive bit, one of the attributes of a data file, which is used to indicate whether or not that program has been backed up using the DOS BACKUP program.)

COMMUNICATIONS PROBLEMS

Most problems with modem and computer installation are caused by the software not being configured properly. A technician must learn all of the intricate steps necessary to get the modem installed properly.

Modem Hardware Problems

The configuration of a modem is of critical importance. The internal switches must, of course, be set properly. Check these switch settings and change them, if necessary, as a first step.

In the case of an external modem, be sure that the cable used is a simple extension cable, NOT a null-modem cable. The connector on the computer should be a DTR connection, which transmits data on pin #2. The modem connector should be the complement, the DCE connection, which receives data on pin #2. With this setup, the computer and the modem are connected with a simple one-to-one cable. A given pin on one end is connected to the same number pin on the other end.

An internal modem, of course, does not use a cable. It must, however, be configured for an available communications port address by means of a jumper on the internal modem card. This address should be set for the communications port to be used, usually either COM1 or COM2. This address is actually used, even though there is no port hardware or a connector brought out to the back of the computer.

If no dial tone is obtained when the modem is instructed to dial out, the telephone line should be checked. Use a standard telephone set (not a special, multiline instrument) and connect it to the telephone circuit to determine whether the line is active. A dial tone should be available if the line is suitable for modem use.

Some modern central telephone switching equipment [private business exchanges (PBX)] will not provide a normal telephone line and a dial tone to a modem, instead seeking a special kind of telephone instrument. These central telephone switching units are sometimes used in office buildings. If this is the case, a dedicated telephone line may have to be installed for modem use.

Modem Software Problems

The next step is to properly configure the parameters of the communications software used in the computer. This software must "look for" the modem at the correct communications port. In addition, the baud rate, number of data bits, and number of stop bits must be properly set for communicating with the modem. First determine which port the modem is using. Configure the communications software with either COM1 or COM2, as appropriate. Using the wrong communications port will result in no response from the modem when commands are given.

Configuring the software includes the communications baud rate, whether or not parity checking is to be used, the number of data bits, and the number of stop bits. Configure the software for these as follows:

1200,N,8,1   or   2400,n,8,1

These exact parameters should satisfy perhaps 95% of computer communications requirements. The choice of either 1200 or 2400 baud as shown is determined by the highest speed capability of the modem used.

Selection of the improper baud rate or number of data bits results in communicating, but the characters sent and received will be garbled.

The number of stop bits should always be 1. Other options for stop bits became obsolete long ago, vestiges of the teletype days.

Parity checking can be done only when transferring pure ASCII files. An ASCII file can be sent with 8 data bits just as any other file. There is no particular advantage in using other than 8 data bits for any data transfer, mainly due to the inconvenience and complexity of changing data transmission protocols.

The Initializing String

When the modem is first used, the communications program sends a string of characters to the modem to instruct it in how to act for that session. The string is sent while the communications program is loaded into the computer. The contents of this string are critical to the proper operation of the modem.

Note that the modem must be turned on *before* loading the communications program in order for the modem to accept the commands sent to it during program loading. In the same manner, any changes made to the initializing string within the communications program will not be sent to the modem until the computer program is exited and reloaded.

In a Hayes-compatible modem, the initializing string contains a single AT or attention command, followed by individual commands and terminating with a carriage return.

If communications are basically good but contain occasional errors, the software should simply report a few bad blocks during the data transfer between the modems. Excessive errors can often be cured by reducing the speed of transmission, the baud rate. Dropping from 2400 to 1200 baud or from 1200 to 300 baud may decrease errors, but will result in increased transmission time for a given file size.

Other Important Configuration Items

The communications software used in the microcomputer must know several other important items to effectively communicate with the modem.

The dialing command is the ASCII string that commands the modem to dial a specified telephone number. For a Hayes-compatible modem, this string is ATDT for tone access lines or ATDP for the older pulse-type lines. The dialing command suffix for a 2400-baud Hayes-compatible, used to tell the modem the end of a string, or the "do it now" character, is a carriage return, a control-"M" or ^M. This may be entered in some software by two keystrokes, an uppercase number 6, followed by an uppercase "M." The Hayes 1200, on the other hand, uses the exclamation point (!) as the end-of-string character.

When sending data files through a modem, any combination of characters is possible in the data stream. Once in the locked-on mode, the modem can no longer be given commands; it is in the on-line state. Getting the modem to leave this mode and drop back to the command mode requires a unique character string. The communications software needs to know what this string is. For a Hayes modem, this string requires a pause in addition to the code to return to the command state. This is encoded as three pauses, a break character, and three pauses. Returning to the command state does not hang up the telephone. Hanging up is a separate command. This entire string as encoded for entry into the communications software for a Hayes 2400-baud modem is:

~ + + + ~ATH~ + + + ~^M

where the tilde (~) represents a pause of 2 seconds and the + + + is the break character. The actual command to hang up is the "AT" (Attention) "H" (Hang it up.)

The Hayes 1200, on the other hand, uses a code of

, + + +,ATH

where the comma (,) represents a pause of about 2 seconds (also programmable).

Occasional errors during a file transfer between computers is taken care of by the software at both ends. Bad blocks of data, corrupted by line noise, are simply sent again up to a maximum of typically ten times, until it arrives correctly. Excessive errors may cause the file transfer operation to abort. If too many errors occur, it may help to reduce the baud rate, passing data at 1200 or even 300 baud if noise is really bad.

If All Else Fails

Substitution of the modem, the cables (if any), and the software is always a viable troubleshooting option. After changing one of these possible sources of a problem, try communicating. Intelligent substitution will disclose the problem. Keep in mind also that the modem MUST have its own communication port. If there is a COM1 port installed and you attempt to use an internal modem at the same address, you cannot expect the modem or the port to work properly, even though all the hardware and software are good.

COMPUTER VIRUSES

Once in a great while, a data file is transferred over the telephone line and arrives defective, in spite of every precaution. Although this is inconvenient, it is not the end of the world. There is, however, a more insidious danger when getting software from outside sources. It is possible to load up and run software that, completely unknown to the operator, changes vital files on your computer, programming them to cause deliberate damage. Such damage might be to unexpectedly format your hard disk, thus losing ALL of the data on it! This computer "viruses," as they are called, infect your computer and can be inadvertently passed on. Since they can be programmed to do their damage after, say, the 14th time you turn on your computer (a simple software counter can do this), the original virus program can be passed on to dozens of other computers before being detected!

The primary source of microcomputer viruses is the electronic bulletin board, but ANY computer equipped with a modem is susceptible to this vandalism. This even includes our Wall Street, Internal Revenue Service, and national defense computers!

Any bulletin board software should be suspect. Such software can have a virus that is very effectively passed all around the nation—even the world—via modems and the telephone network! Users of bulletin boards must keep this in mind. Irreplaceable data on the computer MUST be backed up before running untried software.

Software is available to help the computer user guard against some viruses. One of the prime targets for a virus is the system files and COMMAND.COM since these files are used predictably and their location is known (in the root directory) of most computer users. These files are an excellent place to place a virus. In order to "plant" the virus into a program, it must modify or write to that program. Watching for unauthorized writing to such files is a good way to detect viral infection of your computer.

CHAPTER SUMMARY

INSTALLING AND USING A MODEM takes some time and "fritter" to tune up. Hardware and software must be configured. Two modem transfer rates are common today for microcomputer data: 1200 and 2400 baud. The standard configuration for a 2400 baud modem is 2400 baud, no parity, 8 data bits, and a single stop bit. The best protocols to use are XMODEM for single files and YMODEM BATCH for multiple files.

REVIEW QUESTIONS

1. Where is a modem installed when connecting one computer to another over the telephone network?
2. What does the modem do?
3. What company has become the standard for modem operation?
4. What are the two states of operation of a modem?
5. What is meant by hardware configuration of a modem?
6. Besides a modem, what else is needed to get on-line with a modem?
7. Which modem, the originating or the answer modem, provides the first tone on the telephone line?
8. What three things can being a modem off-line?
9. Each end of a data communications network must agree on the details of data transfer. What are these data transfer formats called?
10. What is the best protocol to use for a single file?
11. What is the best protocol to use for multiple-file transfer?
12. Is it a good idea to use ASCII format protocol, with parity checking, for the passing of ASCII data files?
13. How is the reception of a bad block of information handled with microcomputers?
14. What protocol would you use when dialing the COMPUSERVE net?
15. Why would anyone use a protocol that does not allow for resending of a bad block of data?
16. What is the purpose of file archiving as it pertains to data communications?
17. What is the most common cause of communications problems?
18. Generally speaking, when changing defaults, the hardware or software may not use the new settings. Why?

part four

Troubleshooting Computer Software Problems

chapter twelve

Troubleshooting Computer Software Problems

CHAPTER OBJECTIVE

TROUBLESHOOTING COMPUTER SOFTWARE PROBLEMS gives the technician background information necessary to determine where a software problem may lie, how to verify a suspected problem, and what to do about it.

SOME NECESSARY DEFINITIONS

There are basically two kinds of computer files: those for the machine to execute and those for humans to interpret, using ASCII characters and numbers.

A byte, the basic unit of information for a microcomputer, can represent 256 different combinations. Of these, only about half are used by the computer monitor as letters or numbers. The remainder are control codes for peripheral equipment and for special displays, such as foreign characters and primitive graphics characters.

Program Files

Programs use the entire range of byte values from 0 to 255. Programs are shown on a directory listing as having a *.SYS, *.COM, or *.EXE file extension. If such a file is displayed on the monitor using the TYPE command, the file will display many odd characters. This can be done by issuing the following command with an appropriate file name and extension:

TYPE FILENAME.EXT

Binary files are the instructions for a microprocessor, none of which make any sense to a human. Incidently, the TYPE command stops showing the file when it encounters the first binary byte 00011010. The TYPE command is intended to be used only with ASCII files. This binary combination is a Control-Z, an end-of-file marker byte. Binary files are defined by their length, not by a unique character. The entire binary file can be displayed by using the following command:

COPY FILENAME.EXT CON:/B

The /B option used with the COPY command forces the file to terminate at its actual length.

There may be ASCII strings within a program. These are various messages the program places on the screen for the operator and are not instructions for the microprocessor itself. They are often error messages.

Data Files

There are three general types of data files:

ASCII files

8th bit word processor files

Graphics files

ASCII Files. The simplest of files, the ASCII file, consists entirely of ASCII characters and control codes. These files are necessary for some applications and represent a generic data file. An ASCII file is simple and can be interpreted by many different kinds of applications software. Software compilers, for instance, require a pure ASCII input file as the original program. The ASCII file is terminated by a special control character, the Control-Z, or ∧ Z as it is sometimes shown.

8th Bit Files. A word processing program needs special codes that mean something only to itself. Codes are required to be placed in a text file which is basically an ASCII file, for such things as soft carriage returns, soft hyphens, margin codings, indents, and so forth. The word processor may also imbed printer control codes into the document. Displaying such a document on the monitor with the TYPE command shows the text, but many strange characters are also included for these special functions. To generate these special codes, the upper half of the byte, decimal values above 127, are used.

Graphics (Picture) Files. Graphics files are encoded pictures. The generation and display of graphics depends entirely on the program used. Graphics in themselves cannot be displayed without at least a program to load the graphic picture into video memory and to tell the video adapter to switch to the graphics mode. Displaying a graphics picture with the TYPE command results in what appears to be a binary file, just a bunch of strange characters.

DEFINING THE PROBLEM—HARDWARE OR SOFTWARE

The first step in troubleshooting a computer problem is to localize the problem to a program, a data file, or the hardware of the computer itself. To this end, the first question is, "Will it boot up to DOS?"

If the computer reaches the DOS prompt, the computer hardware is probably working properly and the software or its data are probably in error. On the other hand, failure to reach the DOS prompt probably means that something in the hardware is defective.

HARDWARE FAILURES

When attempting to boot up a computer, a defect may occur immediately. The hard drive comes up to speed, but there is no response from the disk drives. The lack of access to drive A, evidenced by the drive's activity LED not coming on, indicates that the operating system is not loading from diskette. It is also possible that the drive may come on and remain on. This can be caused by a failure of the power supply or of any of the major chips on the system board.

Chapter 8 covers the troubleshooting of the power supply. If the power supply is normal, the computer can be stripped to its barest essentials to eliminate problems that could be caused by extra, unnecessary boards. Remember to reset the system board switches as necessary when changes are made to the amount of memory, the kind of display, the number of drives installed, and the presence of a math coprocessor. See the end of Chapter 4 for the system board switches and how to set them.

Exchanging the system ROM with another ROM from an identical computer may cure the problem, indicating a ROM failure. Be sure to replace the ROM with one that has an *identical* CHECKSUM number on the ROM, thus ensuring that the internal programming is identical.

The major chips of the system board could also be changed, one at a time, if replacement chips are available. If not, the entire system board should be replaced to verify that it is causing the problem.

Power Supply Failures

If the computer makes no sound at all when turned on, thoroughly check the power outlet and the power cord to the computer. Be sure both ends are firmly seated.

If the computer fan comes on, this shows that power is reaching it and that the power cord is all right. Lack of any other response, such as the hard disk drive not coming up to speed with its characteristic whirring sound and the lack of any of the floppy diskette drives temporarily accessing during boot up, strongly indicates that the power supply has failed. See Chapter 8 for information on troubleshooting the power supply.

Hard Drive Failures

Chapter 7 relates some of the problems that may occur with a hard drive. The hard drive can be determined to be a problem if the computer previously booted up using the hard drive, but does not now. Insert a bootable floppy diskette in drive A and see if the system will now boot. If it does, the smartest thing to do is to IMMEDIATELY BACK UP ALL DATA ON THE HARD DRIVE. You may be lucky and get all of the irreplaceable files off the drive before it deteriorates any further, assuming there is damage to the hard drive. This problem may, however, just be an error within one of the system files on the hard drive.

Another symptom of hard drive problems is occasional error messages on the monitor relating to the hard drive.

A hard drive crash is the result of the read/write heads of the hard drive striking the rotating platters of the drive with sufficient force to damage the heads or the recording surface, or both. In this case, any data on the platter surfaces are lost, and the heads themselves can be ruined. Symptoms of a hard drive crash are repeated head-seek noises, buzzing sounds that are repeated several times while the drive unsuccessfully attempts to read the platter surface. This is one of the most ominous sounds a hard drive can make, other than silence (simply ceasing to operate, without rotation) or a sudden screeching sound.

One exception is the noise that some drives eventually make due to the grounding clip touching the end of the rotating shaft. If this connection begins making noise, the drive can be carefully removed (remember to park it first!) and the spring clip taken out. Touch up the contact surface with a pencil eraser and put a very tiny drop of oil on the end of the shaft just before reinstalling the spring clip. This repair should last many months.

The lack of motor noise, indicating that the platters are not turning at their design speed of 3600 rpm, may only be due to not parking the heads after use. See the end of Chapter 7 for a possible cure for this problem.

Replacement of the hard drive is the only practical cure if it has crashed. Although some companies repair hard disks, the cost of a new one is often about the same. The files of a crashed hard drive are probably gone forever. Some hard disk repair facilities may offer data recovery from a crashed disk. One could expect to pay a premium price for such a service, particularly if the data is needed as soon as possible.

Hard Disk Operating System Won't Boot

The failure of a hard drive to ever boot up the computer without the insertion of a bootable floppy disk is a problem caused by improper initializing of the hard drive during the low- and high-level formatting.

The failure of the hard drive to boot up the computer after it has worked previously is a problem often caused by the deletion or the moving of the hidden system files, BIOS and DOS, from their proper places as the first two files on the hard drive. Even though they may be present, these files will not boot the computer unless they occupy the first two entries in the root directory of the drive.

The system files can be disturbed by restoring old files on the hard drive after a different operating system has been installed on the drive. Tampering with the files with any software can produce the same results.

If the system files are present (CHKDSK can see the hidden system files, as can some other software) and the computer still does not boot on the hard drive, it is necessary to use the SYS command to attempt to replace the files. Boot up on a good floppy disk with the proper operating system and version, then use the SYS command to transfer the operating system to the hard drive. Copy COMMAND.COM to the hard drive, too. If this approach does not result in proper hard drive booting, it is necessary to back up all of the files on the hard drive and do a new FORMAT with the /S option. A last option may be to use one of the Norton's Utilities to clean out the system files area, readying it for writing new system files.

Prevention of Data Loss

A hard drive should always be parked before shutting down the computer. This places the read/write heads over a nondata portion of the drive, where the disk rotates the slowest.

Back up your new programs and data frequently. The use of the BACKUP command is covered at the end of Chapter 7. Be sure to have plenty of pre-formatted diskettes available before attempting a large backup of the entire hard drive.

Restoring Data to a New Hard Drive

If the hard drive fails, a new drive must be installed. Once the new drive is in the computer and has been low- and high-level formatted, be sure that the computer will now boot from the hard drive. If it does not, check to be sure that the operating system is installed. See Chapter 7 for details.

Once the computer boots up on the hard drive, use the RESTORE command to place all of the files originally saved with the BACKUP command. BACKUP stores data in a somewhat compressed form and can also split files between diskettes. Files in the BACKUP format cannot be used without first RESTOREing them.

The default directory on the hard disk must be the same as that used when the files were originally backed up, before using the RESTORE command, usually the root directory. A typical command to restore all files is

RESTORE B: C:/S

Hard Disk Data Recovery

Accidental Erasure of a File. Files accidentally erased can often be easily reclaimed, particularly if no new files have been written to the disk since the erasure. Once a file is erased, its data sectors are marked as being available. If no new data are written, the old data are still there. If written over, however, the old data are gone forever. Norton's Utilities include a program to unerase files. Other programs such as PC TOOLS also make erased data recovery possible.

Accidental High-Level Format of Hard Drive. In spite of precautions, it is possible, particularly for new computer users, to format the hard drive. Formatting a hard drive does not remove the data as it does with a floppy disk—the data are still there. Chapter 7 suggests ways to recover from this problem by using a program such as MACE.

Damaged File Allocation Table. If the file allocation table located on track 0 of the disk is damaged, an error message may report it. In this case, the data is reclaimed using the second copy of the file allocation table, also on track 0 of the drive. In the process of recovering the files, however, original file names are lost. The program to recover data (forget trying to reclaim program files this way) is the RECOVER command. DO NOT USE THE RECOVER COMMAND UNLESS ABSOLUTELY NECESSARY! All of the recovered files will have names like

FILE0001.REC

FILE0002.REC

FILE0003.REC

These do not indicate the kind of file: The files may be executable, graphics, or ASCII files. The only way to find out what they are is to use other software to view and edit them, then to rename them accordingly.

Lost Clusters. It is a good idea to periodically run the CHKDSK program to check on the status of the hard drive. Running this program now and then makes you aware of lost chains of sectors. It may also warn of more serious problems. Just run the following command

CHKDSK C:

Nothing can be done to fix problems without the /F option, but just getting a report is nice at this point. If all is well, no lost chains will be reported.

If lost chains are reported, rerun the program like this:

CHKDSK C:/F

This enables you to fix the problems automatically. Old chains of sectors that had been lost to the system will now have names such as

FILE0001.CHK

FILE0002.CHK

FILE0003.CHK

You may examine each of these new files to see if there is any ASCII information there that you may need. Otherwise, you can probably just delete them with a blanket command like

DEL *.CHK

FLOPPY DRIVE FAILURES

Symptoms

When the floppy diskette drive access LED comes on, the floppy diskette is supposed to rotate within its jacket. Sometimes the floppy will not rotate, causing an apparent malfunction of the drive. Changing the diskette should cure this problem.

If the A drive access LED never comes on, this could indicate a failure of the power supply (see Chapter 8), the floppy drive adapter, or the drive itself. Typical symptoms of diskette drive failures include the following:

One drive won't read diskettes written on by another.

The A drive runs all the time, and the computer won't boot.

One or both drives give error messages.

On IBMs only, the computer won't boot and "falls through" to the BASIC prompt "Ok."

For any of these symptoms, see Chapter 6.

If, however, a single diskette is producing problems, the suggestions made above for the hard disk are applicable to floppies, too. Using CHKDSK and RECOVER are possible cures for similar floppy problems.

A special case bears mentioning. If a drive won't read a sector of a diskette, it is possible that a fingerprint in the access slot of the diskette has caused the problem. Some of these fingerprints can be removed, often enough to reclaim the data underneath, by careful cleaning with a very soft tissue with an extremely small amount of moisture on it. Once the data is recovered from such a diskette, discard the diskette.

Prevention of Floppy Diskette Data Loss

The same precautions apply for data stored on floppy diskettes as on hard disks: Back up the information frequently on other diskettes. Store the backup diskettes separately from the working diskettes, so that a calamity to one set of diskettes cannot befall both sets.

MEMORY FAILURES

The occasional report of a parity error on the monitor or the unexplained freezing up of the computer keyboard may be an indication of a memory defect. The failure of a single bit of memory in the right place can cause a computer crash.

Memory failure can be verified by running memory diagnostic programs. The defective bank of memory chips should be replaced together as a unit. Once the defective bank is verified, each original chip within that bank can be replaced, one at a time, until the offending chip is identified.

Chapter 5 gives useful information on memory expansion that is applicable to the replacement of a bank of memory.

SOFTWARE FAILURES

Symptoms

Software failure is relatively easy to verify. If a given program runs well on another computer that has *identical* hardware attached, then the software is good. Failure of this software to run on the first computer indicates a problem with the first computer's hardware.

Lacking two identical computer systems to identify bad software still leaves another option. Successfully running similar software that uses the same hardware clears the computer as the cause of the problem. For instance, if a particular word processing program runs fine on the computer, but another different word processing program does not, the second program must be the problem.

Old Software

Old software is software that at one time ran just fine on a given computer, but now does not. One of the common causes for this kind of a problem, other than damage to the floppy diskette or the hard drive, is the inadvertent erasure of a support file for the program at hand. Often, the program will report that the needed file is now missing.

About the only cure for a program malfunction is to restore the program from backup diskettes or to recopy the original program from the original program diskette. It is not practical to try to modify a program to repair it.

When possible, the program should be restored from backup diskettes, using the RESTORE program. Be sure to have the proper default directory before restoring programs. It is preferable to use a copy of the working program rather than using the original program diskettes because the original program will not be configured for the computer hardware used. The software from an original diskette must be configured before it can be used.

New Software

New software must often be configured before it will perform properly with given hardware. Programs such as a word processor, for instance, need to know whether the software must work with a monochrome or a color monitor and whether the dot-matrix printer is an Epson or an IBM.

The method of software installation varies with the program. Although some programs attempt to have easy installation procedures, they can sometimes modify your CONFIG.SYS or AUTOEXEC.BAT files in a way that you do not want. They can also make directories and place files into them where you do not wish to have directories.

Manual Software Installation

Although many software packages come with installation programs, often a file with the name INSTALL.BAT, it is sometimes better to manually install the programs. The "automatic" installation files that can cause problems are often batch files. You can see what the files are doing by typing them to the screen rather than invoking them. At least look them over to determine how they may be setting up your directories and changing your CONFIG.SYS or AUTOEXEC.BAT files.

Batch Files

It is important for the technician to understand batch files. These files, particularly the AUTOEXEC.BAT file, often affect the computer's hardware responses. To add to the subtlety of the problem, these responses are usually transparent to the operator.

An example of the importance of understanding batch files is as follows. A parallel port has been redirected to a serial port in a batch file. Such a command can be given in the AUTOEXEC.BAT file. The parallel port has thus become "inoperative." The technician must be aware of such a possibility. It becomes evident that this file or any other batch file that has been executed should be reviewed for possible causes of apparent hardware problems.

CHAPTER SUMMARY

TROUBLESHOOTING COMPUTER SOFTWARE PROBLEMS is perhaps the most important chapter of this book. The technician can determine whether a problem is within the hardware or the software of a given computer system with a few tests: Does the computer boot up to the DOS prompt? If so, the hardware is probably OK. Did the software run before, but now fails? The program is damaged. What happens if a file is now inaccessible? Use unerase software to regain the files. What if the file allocation table is reported damaged and no files are available? Use RECOVER (only when needed, please!) to regain the files. Typical failures of the hard drive and the floppy drives are also covered.

REVIEW QUESTIONS

1. What are the two basic kinds of computer files?
2. What determines the end of a file as far as the TYPE command is concerned?
3. What are the three general type of data files?
4. What is the significance of a computer problem that results in the inability of the computer to boot up to the DOS system prompt?
5. If a microcomputer is absolutely silent when turning on the computer and none of the drive or control panel LEDs ever comes on, what is the probable cause of the problem?
6. The computer will boot on a floppy drive, but not, as it did before, on the hard drive. The hard drive does not sound as if it is turning. What is the possible cause?
7. The computer used to boot on the hard drive. Now it will not. It does, however, boot on a floppy diskette. Once booted, files on the hard disk appear to be normal. What is the probable problem?
8. What is the primary defense against hard disk data loss?
9. What is meant by the error message "bad or missing command interpreter?"
10. An important file is accidentally erased. Can it be recovered?

11. What program can help if the file allocation table is reported damaged and files are no longer available?
12. What program will test floppies and hard disks for "lost" chains of clusters?
13. What can be done to prevent data loss on floppies?
14. What is a parity error mean?
15. You suspect a program on a diskette is defective. How can you verify this?
16. Can new software be expected to run the first time on a given computer system?
17. Old configured software on a diskette used to work on a given system. Now it does not. What is the likely problem?
18. What is the possible disadvantage of using the setup or install options provided with new software?

appendix a

Microcomputer
Interconnection Standards

This appendix lists some of the most common connections made to microcomputers. It is not, however, infallible. Manufacturers are not bound to these standards, and considerable deviation may be noted in actual use. These listings are to be used only as a guide. Color codes, in particular, can vary greatly among manufacturers.

SERIAL PORT CABLES

Note: See Appendix I for explanations of the RS-232C standard.

Only about half of the 25 commonly used DB-25 serial connector wires are likely to actually be used. The remaining pins and wires may not be connected or they may be missing altogether.

Remember that the microcomputer is usually a DTE device. An extension cable (wired through from like-numbered pins on each end) is used to connect to a DCE device. When connecting the computer to another DTE device, however, a null-modem cable must be used. See Appendix I for further explanation.

Minimum Microcomputer Serial Port Wiring

Pin	Use
1	Frame (earth) ground
2	Transmit data
3	Receive data
4	Ready to send
5	Clear to send
6	Data set ready
7	Signal ground
8	Data carrier detected
12	High-speed indicator
20	Data terminal ready
22	Ring indicator

To save rear panel space, some computers use a 9-pin connector and have a short cable to a full-sized 25-pin connector for one of the serial ports. The wiring of that short cable is as follows.

Microcomputer 9-Pin to 25-Pin Serial Port Pigtail

DB-9S	DB-25P
1	8
2	3
3	2
4	20
5	7
6	6
7	4
8	5
9	22

PARALLEL PORT CABLES

A cable to operate a parallel printer from a microcomputer will probably be wired as shown in the following table.

Microcomputer Parallel Port Wiring

Female DB-25P	Centronics[a,b] 36-Pin Plug	Use
1	1	(−)[c] Data strobe[d]
2	2	D0
3	3	D1
4	4	D2
5	5	D3
6	6	D4
7	7	D5
8	8	D6
9	9	D7
10	10	(−) Acknowledge strobe from printer[e]
11	11	(+) Busy signal from printer[f]
12	12	(+) Out-of-paper error from printer[g]
13	13	(+) "Printer on" signal from printer[h]
14	14	(−) Auto feed[i]

Continued

Female DB-25P	Centronics[a,b] 36-Pin Plug	Use
15	32	(−) General error from printer[j]
16	31	(−) Initialize to printer[k]
17	36	(+) Select input to printer[l]
18	33	Signal ground
19	19	Signal ground
20	21	Signal ground
21	23	Signal ground
22	25	Signal ground
23	27	Signal ground
24	29	Signal ground
25	30	Signal ground

[a] The connector is an Amphenol #57L-40360-2700.

[b] Centronics connector lines not used: 15, 16, 17, 18, 20, 22, 24, 26, 28, 34, 35.

[c] (−) and (+) indicate whether the signals are active low or high, respectively.

[d] Data strobe: A short negative pulse sent by the computer to signify that the logic levels on the data lines are stable and ready to be read by the printer.

[e] Acknowledge strobe: A short negative strobe to the computer that indicates that the printer is ready for the next byte of data.

[f] Busy: A logic high on this line indicates that the printer cannot accept more data. It is sometimes called a not-ready line, and it is used in conjunction with the acknowledge line.

[g] Paper end: A signal from the printer to the computer when the printer is out of paper.

[h] Select: May be used as a signal from the printer to inform the computer that the printer is turned on.

[i] Auto Feed XT. When this line is held low by the computer, the printer automatically advances the paper one line when a carriage return is received. When high, the printer requires a separate line-feed command to advance one line.

[j] Fault (Error): May be used as a signal to the computer for any kind of printer problem, including when the operator takes the printer off-line.

[k] Initialize: Initialize the printer. Clear buffers, reinitialize printhead to starting (Home) position.

[l] Select In: Normally low; When high, this line causes the printer to respond to XON (DC1 in the ASCII chart) and XOFF (DC3 in the ASCII chart) codes by ignoring all characters received between an XOFF and an XON.

A close inspection of the Centronics plug shows that the high-speed circuits of the data strobe, the data bits, and the acknowledge and busy signals are all on one side of the plug with the corresponding grounds for those signals directly across from the plug nearest them. This provides isolating grounds between all of the data and strobe lines for shielding when using a ribbon cable or twisted-pair wire cables.

VIDEO MONITOR CABLES

The standard pinouts for EGA, CGA, and monochrome are as follows.

The EGA Video Signal Connector

Pin	Use
1	Ground
2	R'
3	R
4	G
5	B
6	G'
7	B'
8	Horizontal synchronization pulse
9	Vertical synchronization pulse

Note: Each color intensity is governed by two bits, thus providing four different intensities.

The CGA Direct Drive Signal Connector

Pin	Use
1	Ground
2	Ground
3	R
4	G
5	B
6	Intensity
7	Not connected
8	Horizontal synchronization pulse
9	Vertical synchronization pulse

The Monochrome Direct Drive Signal Connector

Pin	Use
1	Ground
2	Shield ground
3	Not connected
4	Not connected
5	Not connected
6	Intensity
7	Video
8	Horizontal synchronization pulse
9	Vertical synchronization pulse

The light pen cable should be wired as follows.

Standard Light Pen Wiring

Pin	Use
1	+ Light pen signal to computer
2	Not connected
3	+ Light pen switch
4	Ground
5	+5VDC supply (from computer)
6	+12VDC supply (from computer)

The RF modulator, if provided, may be wired as follows.

Standard RF Modulator Wiring

Pin	Use
1	+12VDC supply (from computer)
2	Not connected
3	Composite video signal output
4	Ground

THE KEYBOARD CABLE

The keyboard cable of most microcomputers uses a European DIN connector, wired as follows.

Standard Keyboard Cable Pinout

Pin	Use
1	TTL signal, keyboard clock (from computer)
2	TTL signal, keyboard output
3	Keyboard reset (from computer)
4	Ground
5	+5V supply (from computer)
Shell	Shield

The pinout of the keyboard connector, looking at the computer end of the keyboard cable, clockwise from 12 o'clock, is 1,4,2,5,3.

POWER SUPPLY CONNECTORS

The power supply has two connectors to attach to the system board, commonly called "P8" and "P9." There are usually four additional connectors, all the same, to provide power to the floppy and hard disk drives.

The system board connectors are wired as follows.

Power Supply P8 Connector

Pin	Use
1	TTL "Power Supply OK" signal, white wire
2	Not connected
3	+12VDC, yellow wire
4	−12VDC, brown wire
5	Ground, black wire
6	Ground, black wire

Power Supply P9 Connector

Pin	Use
1	Ground, black wire
2	Ground, black wire
3	−5VDC, blue wire
4	+5VDC, red wire
5	+5VDC, red wire
6	+5VDC, red wire

Floppy and Hard Disk Drive Power Connectors

Pin	Use
1	+12V, yellow wire
2	12V return, black wire
3	5V return, black wire
4	+5V, red wire

OTHER CONNECTORS

The Speaker Connector

Pin	Use
1	Speaker "Hot"
2	Not connected
3	Ground
4	+5VDC (not used)

The AT Battery Holder Connector

Pin	Use
1	Ground
2	Not connected
3	Not connected
4	+6VDC (four 1.5V cells)

The system board edge-connector for an AT is as follows. The long connector is numbered A1 thru A31 on the right side and B1 thru B31 on the left side, counting from the rear toward the front. The short connector is numbered on the right side, as C1 thru C18 and on the left side as D1 thru D18, from the rear to the front.

The AT System Board Long Connector

Pin	Name	I/O	Pin	Name	I/O
A1	− I/O CH CK	I	B1	Ground	Ground
A2	SD7	I/O	B2	Reset drive	O
A3	SD6	I/O	B3	+5VDC	Power
A4	SD5	I/O	B4	IRQ9	I
A5	SD4	I/O	B5	−5VDC	Power
A6	SD3	I/O	B6	DRQ2	I
A7	SD2	I/O	B7	−12VDC	Power
A8	SD1	I/O	B8	OWS	I
A9	SD0	I/O	B9	+12VDC	Power
A10	− I/O CH RDY	I	B10	Ground	Ground
A11	AEN	O	B11	− SMEMW	O
A12	SA19	I/O	B12	− SMEMR	O
A13	SA18	I/O	B13	− IOW	I/O
A14	SA17	I/O	B14	− IOR	I/O
A15	SA16	I/O	B15	− DACK3	O
A16	SA15	I/O	B16	DRQ3	O
A17	SA14	I/O	B17	− DACK1	O
A18	SA13	I/O	B18	DRQ1	I
A19	SA12	I/O	B19	− REFRESH	I/O
A20	SA11	I/O	B20	CLK	O
A21	SA10	I/O	B21	IRQ7	I
A22	SA9	I/O	B22	IRQ6	I
A23	SA8	I/O	B23	IRQ5	I
A24	SA7	I/O	B24	IRQ4	I
A25	SA6	I/O	B25	IRQ3	I
A26	SA5	I/O	B26	− DACK2	O
A27	SA4	I/O	B27	T/C	O
A28	SA3	I/O	B28	BALE	O
A29	SA2	I/O	B29	+5VDC	Power
A30	SA1	I/O	B30	OSC	O
A31	SA0	I/O	B31	Ground	Ground

The AT System Board Short Connector

Pin	Name	I/O	Pin	Name	I/O
C1	SBHE	I/O	D1	− MEM CS 16	I
C2	LA23	I/O	D2	− I/O CS 16	I
C3	LA22	I/O	D3	IRQ10	I
C4	LA21	I/O	D4	IRQ11	I
C5	LA20	I/O	D5	IRQ12	I
C6	LA19	I/O	D6	IRQ15	I
C7	LA18	I/O	D7	IRQ14	I
C8	LA17	I/O	D8	− DACK0	O
C9	− MEMR	I/O	D9	DRQ0	I
C10	− MEMW	I/O	D10	− DACK5	O
C11	SD08	I/O	D11	DRQ5	I
C12	SD09	I/O	D12	− DACK6	O
C13	SD10	I/O	D13	DRQ6	I
C14	SD11	I/O	D14	− DACK7	O
C15	SD12	I/O	D15	DRQ7	I
C16	SD13	I/O	D16	+ 5VDC	Power
C17	SD14	I/O	D17	− MASTER	I
C18	SD15	I/O	D18	Ground	Ground

The system board connector for a PC or XT is as follows. The PC/XT connector is numbered A1 thru A31 on the right side of the long connector and B1 thru B31 on the left side, counting from the rear toward the front.

The PC/XT System Board Connector

Pin	Name	I/O	Pin	Name	I/O
A1	− I/O CH CK	I	B1	Ground	Ground
A2	D7	I/O	B2	Reset drive	O
A3	D6	I/O	B3	+ 5VDC	Power
A4	D5	I/O	B4	IRQ9	I
A5	D4	I/O	B5	− 5VDC	Power
A6	D3	I/O	B6	DRQ2	I
A7	D2	I/O	B7	− 12VDC	Power
A8	D1	I/O	B8	OWS	I
A9	D0	I/O	B9	+ 12VDC	Power
A10	I/O CH RDY	I	B10	Ground	Ground
A11	AEN	O	B11	− MEMW	O
A12	A19	I/O	B12	− MEMR	O
A13	A18	I/O	B13	− IOW	I/O
A14	A17	I/O	B14	− IOR	I/O
A15	A16	I/O	B15	− DACK3	O
A16	A15	I/O	B16	DRQ3	O
A17	A14	I/O	B17	− DACK1	O

Continued

Pin	Name	I/O	Pin	Name	I/O
A18	A13	I/O	B18	DRQ1	I
A19	A12	I/O	B19	DACK	I/O
A20	A11	I/O	B20	CLK	O
A21	A10	I/O	B21	IRQ7	I
A22	A9	I/O	B22	IRQ6	I
A23	A8	I/O	B23	IRQ5	I
A24	A7	I/O	B24	IRQ4	I
A25	A6	I/O	B25	IRQ3	I
A26	A5	I/O	B26	−DACK2	O
A27	A4	I/O	B27	T/C	O
A28	A3	I/O	B28	ALE	O
A29	A2	I/O	B29	+5VDC	Power
A30	A1	I/O	B30	OSC	O
A31	A0	I/O	B31	Ground	Ground

appendix b

DOS Commands for the Technician

To be proficient in assembling and repairing computers, a technician must also be able to operate them. To attain competency, the following commands are the minimum that a technician must be able to use. Detailed instructions on their use and the options available within these commands can be obtained from any good DOS reference manual.

INTERNAL COMMANDS

DIR: Used to find out what files are on a diskette or hard drive.

REN: Rename files.

CLS: Clear the screen; used mostly in batch files.

COPY: Make copies of files. This can also be used to change the name on the second copy of the file during the copy procedure. It can be dangerous, copying old data over new when files have same name.

VER: Tells what version of DOS you are using.

TYPE: Put contents of a file on the screen; terminates at the first   Z in the file. This is useful for checking the contents of data files.

BATCH FILES: A powerful feature, consisting of lines, each a DOS command, in a text file whose name ends with ".BAT." Typing the file name causes DOS to execute each line consecutively.

DEL: Erase (delete) files.

PATH: A "standing instruction" to the computer: If this program is not available in this directory, look for it in...

CTTY: A primitive way of controlling the computer via one of the serial ports; limited in its capabilities.

MD, RD, CD: Commands to make, remove, and change the default specified directories.

Root Directory Symbol (\ ): When leading, used to indicate "starting from the root directory...." and as a separator when listing successive directories.

Using Wild Cards (?), (*): When designating groups of files, ? is a single-character wild card, and * is a multiple-character wild card.

Dot (.) and double dot (..): A single dot means the same as *.* when referring to the current directory. Double dots refer to the directory above the default. As a result, don't try to delete these symbols or you will delete all of the files in either directory!

EXTERNAL COMMANDS

RECOVER: A dangerous program to be used only when problems are reported due to damaged file allocation tables.

FDISK: A dangerous program to be used to divide a hard disk; to be used only when all hard disk files are properly backed up.

FORMAT: A dangerous program that will remove all old data from a floppy disk or remove the directory of a hard disk.

DISKCOPY: A potentially dangerous program that will copy entire diskettes from one to another. Be sure you do not copy from a bad diskette to a good one, however, or you will have two copies of the bad diskette.

MODE: A particularly useful program used to set up the technical parameters for serial ports and to redirect the data heading for one port to a new one.

BACKUP: An important program to provide emergency copies of everything on a hard disk and to later add the files that have been updated since the last backup. One of the few programs that can split very large files between two or more diskettes.

RESTORE: The complement of backup, this program puts the files from backup diskettes back on to a hard drive. May copy an old file over a new one.

CHKDSK: An important program that will run some basic checks on a diskette or hard drive, reporting lost data areas due to improper computer operation such as a shutdown of the computer without properly exiting some programs.

SYS: An important program that will place the two hidden files of the operating system onto a diskette or hard disk. Copying of the file COMMAND.COM will usually be necessary to make a proper bootable disk.

SPECIAL FILES

COMMAND.COM: Part of the operating system, this file is required to interpret and execute all of the internal commands listed above.

AUTOEXEC.BAT: A batch file with this special name will execute all of the DOS commands within it automatically on power-up of the computer. One of the important commands to include in this file is the location of your utility programs, a line beginning with the PATH command.

CONFIG.SYS: A file containing information on how the computer should be customized for the operator's software and hardware. If using a hard disk, this file should include command lines such as BUFFERS=25 and FILES=20.

DEDICATED DEVICES

CON: The console, the keyboard, and monitor as one unit.
LPT1: or PRN: refers to the first parallel port, by default the printer port of a PC. LPT2: and LPT3: are the designation for the second and third possible parallel ports.
COM1: or AUX: refers to the first serial port. COM2: is the second possible serial I/O port.
A:, B:, C:, etc. refer to the storage media drives. Most commonly, A: and B: refer to the first two diskette drives and C: is the first hard drive.

appendix c

An Explanation
of the ASCII Chart

The computer manages information by a series of bits, which may be set or reset (high or low). While this allows the computer to manipulate numbers easily once they are converted into this binary (two-state) format, it does not apply to letters.

Letters are not like numbers. They are never added or subtracted. Their presence is acknowledged and they are manipulated within the computer as coded groups of bits. There are several different standards of text encoding, but the code used within microcomputers is called the American Standard Code for Information Interchange (ASCII).

The ASCII code requires 7 bits to express any given character. In addition to characters, controlling codes are also available. While only 7 bits are required to code an ASCII character, an extra 8th bit is usually present, but set to a value of "0." This highest order 8th bit is used within word processors to represent special characters required by the program.

To find the bit pattern for a given character, assume a "0" for the highest bit, find the character in the following table, and then use the bits represented along the top of the corresponding column for the next 3 bits, moving from left to right. The remaining low-order bits are found to the left of the character, along the left column of the table.

Explanations of the special characters listed in the Control columns follows the table. These codes are used to provide control of data communications over modems and telephone lines, and in some cases to control printers.

Note that holding down the Control key of a computer keyboard results in forcing bit D6 low. Thus, one can hold the Control key down and hit the "L" key to produce an LF code, a printer line-feed command. This technique works in most Control cases, but not all, due to hardware limitations and programming of the keyboards of microcomputers.

Note also that holding the Shift key down and hitting a letter forces bit D5 low, producing upper case letters rather than lower case.

Most of the characters within the ASCII table can also be generated by holding the Alternate key down, generating the decimal code for a character with the right-hand number pad of a microcomputer, then releasing the Alternate key. When decimal numbers greater than 127 are entered in this manner, you will be seeing the extended ASCII codes available within the computer. These will allow you to generate special symbols such as degrees, foreign characters, etc.

D6 D5 D4	0 0 0	0 0 1	0 1 0	0 1 1	1 0 0	1 0 1	1 1 0	1 1 1
BITS D3 D2 D1 D0	CONTROL		NUMBERS SYMBOLS		UPPER CASE		LOWER CASE	
0 0 0 0	0 NUL 0 0	20 DLE 10 16	40 SP 20 32	60 0 30 48	100 @ 40 64	120 P 50 80	140 ` 60 96	160 p 70 112
0 0 0 1	1 GTL SOH 1 1	21 LLO DC1 11 17	41 ! 21 33	61 1 31 49	101 A 41 65	121 Q 51 81	141 a 61 97	161 q 71 113
0 0 1 0	2 STX 2 2	22 DC2 12 18	42 " 22 34	62 2 32 50	102 B 42 66	122 R 52 82	142 b 62 98	162 r 72 114
0 0 1 1	3 ETX 3 3	23 DC3 13 19	43 # 23 35	63 3 33 51	103 C 43 67	123 S 53 83	143 c 63 99	163 s 73 115
0 1 0 0	4 SDC EOT 4 4	24 DCL DC4 14 20	44 $ 24 36	64 4 34 52	104 D 44 68	124 T 54 84	144 d 64 100	164 t 74 116
0 1 0 1	5 PPC ENQ 5 5	25 PPU NAK 15 21	45 % 25 37	65 5 35 53	105 E 45 69	125 U 55 85	145 e 65 101	165 u 75 117
0 1 1 0	6 ACK 6 6	26 SYN 16 22	46 & 26 38	66 6 36 54	106 F 46 70	126 V 56 86	146 f 66 102	166 v 76 118
0 1 1 1	7 BEL 7 7	27 ETB 17 23	47 ' 27 39	67 7 37 55	107 G 47 71	127 W 57 87	147 g 67 103	167 w 77 119
1 0 0 0	10 GET BS 8 8	30 SPE CAN 18 24	50 (28 40	70 8 38 56	110 H 48 72	130 X 58 88	150 h 68 104	170 x 78 120
1 0 0 1	11 TCT HT 9 9	31 SPD EM 19 25	51) 29 41	71 9 39 57	111 I 49 73	131 Y 59 89	151 i 69 105	171 y 79 121
1 0 1 0	12 LF A 10	32 SUB 1A 26	52 * 2A 42	72 : 3A 58	112 J 4A 74	132 Z 5A 90	152 j 6A 106	172 z 7A 122
1 0 1 1	13 VT B 11	33 ESC 1B 27	53 + 2B 43	73 ; 3B 59	113 K 4B 75	133 [5B 91	153 k 6B 107	173 { 7B 123
1 1 0 0	14 FF C 12	34 FS 1C 28	54 , 2C 44	74 < 3C 60	114 L 4C 76	134 \ 5C 92	154 l 6C 108	174	7C 124
1 1 0 1	15 CR D 13	35 GS 1D 29	55 - 2D 45	75 = 3D 61	115 M 4D 77	135] 5D 93	155 m 6D 109	175 } 7D 125
1 1 1 0	16 SO E 14	36 RS 1E 30	56 . 2E 46	76 > 3E 62	116 N 4E 78	136 ^ 5E 94	156 n 6E 110	176 ~ 7E 126
1 1 1 1	17 SI F 15	37 US 1F 31	57 / 2F 47	77 UNL ? 3F 63	117 O 4F 79	137 UNT _ 5F 111	157 o 6F 111	177 RUBOUT (DEL) 7F 127
	Addressed Commands	Universal Commands	Listen Addresses		Talk Addresses		Secondary Addresses Or Commands	

octal	25	PPU	GPIB code
	NAK		ASCII character
hex	15	21	decimal

Some of the abbreviations in the ASCII table are not obvious, so here they are in more digestible form. Note that these are really single-byte messages that can be used in communications between a computer and a modem, a printer, or other peripheral.

NUL = All zeros. Used for idle marking time without occupying buffer space.

SOH = Start of a heading

STX = Start of the text

ETX = End of the text ("End of data, did you receive it?")

EOT = End of a transmission. May be used as a turn-around for half-duplex.

ENQ = Enquiry. Solicits automatic identification from a remote terminal.

ACK = Acknowledgment ("Data has been received OK")

BEL = Bell or attention signal (nowadays a speaker "beep")

BS = Backspace or < --- key (may or may not erase on the way)

HT = Horizontal Tab or -- > | key (normal keyboard Tabulator key)

LF = Line feed on a printer (paper up a line)

VT = Vertical Tab (jump lines on a page)

FF = Form Feed (go to beginning of next page)

CR = Carriage return (Return to left margin of paper)

SO = Shift out (Go to alternate character font set)

SI = Shift in (Shift back to normal character font set)

DLE = Data Link Escape. May be used prior to EOT for an automatic disconnect.

DC1 = Device Control 1 (Also called "XON," used in software handshaking)

DC2 = Device Control 2

DC3 = Device Control 3 (also called "XOFF," used in software handshaking)

DC4 = Device control 4

NAK = Negative acknowledgment

SYN = Synchronous/idle

ETB = End of transmitted block

CAN = Cancel (error in data). May be used to cancel an escape sequence.

EM = End of medium

SUB = A character used in place of a character received in error.

ESC = Escape. An introducer for an escape or control sequence.

FS = Information File Separator

GS = Information Group Separator

RS = Information Record Separator

US = Information Unit Separator

DEL = Delete (backspace and erase too)

appendix d

Microcomputer Error Codes

The following list of error codes may be applicable to your computer. It is a "standard" list of error codes originally developed by IBM and now used by some other computer manufacturers. It is a table of codes used by the diagnostic routines within the system ROM. These routines are executed during power-up of the machine. Not all computers will have the thoroughness of testing that may be implied by this list, nor is any guarantee made of the accuracy or applicability of these codes to any specific computer.

Error Code	Description
01x	Undetermined problem errors
02x	Power supply errors
101	Main system board failed, interrupt failure
103	Timer interrupt failure
104	Protected mode failure
105	Last 8042 command not accepted
106	Converting logic text failed
107	Hot NMI test failed
108	Timer bus test failed
109	Direct memory access test error
121	Unexpected hardware interrupts occurred
131	Cassette wrap test failed
161	System options error (run SETUP) (battery failure)
162	System options not set correctly (run SETUP)
163	Time and date not set (run SETUP)
164	Memory size error (run SETUP)
199	User-indicated configuration not correct
201	Memory test failed
202	Memory address failed
203	Memory address failed
301	Keyboard did not respond to software reset correctly or a stuck key failure was detected. If a stuck key was detected, the scan code for

Error
Code   **Description**

          the key is displayed in hex. (Error 49 301 indicates key 73,
          PgUp failed.)
302   User-indicated error from the keyboard test
303   Keyboard or system unit error
304   Keyboard or system unit error; CMOS does not match system

401   Monochrome memory test, horizontal synchronization frequency
          test, or video test failed
408   User-indicated display attribtues failure
416   User-indicated character set failure
424   User-indicated 80 × 25 mode failure
432   Parallel port test failed (monochrome adapter)

501   Color memory test failed, horizontal synchronization frequency test,
          or video test failed
508   User-indicated display attribute failure
516   User-indicated character set failure
524   User-indicated 80 × 25 mode failure
532   User-indicated 40 × 25 mode failure
540   User-indicated 320 × 200 graphics mode failure
548   User-indicated 640 × 200 graphics mode failure

601   Diskette power on diagnostics test failed
602   Diskette test failed, boot record is not valid
606   Diskette verify function failed
607   Write-protected diskette
608   Bad command, diskette status returned
610   Diskette initialization failed
611   Timeout, diskette status returned
612   Bad NEC, diskette status returned
613   Bad direct memory access (DMA), diskette status returned
621   Bad seek, diskette status returned
622   Bad cyclic redundancy check (CRC), diskette status returned
623   Record not found, diskette status returned
624   Bad address mark, diskette status returned
625   Bad NEC seek, diskette status returned
626   Diskette data compare error

7xx   8087 math coprocessor

9xx   Parallel printer adapter errors
901   Parallel printer adapter test failed

Error Code	Description
10xx	Reserved for parallel printer adapter
11xx	Asynchronous communications adapter errors
1101	Asynchronous communications adapter test failed
12xx	Alternate asynchronous communications adapter errors
1201	Alternate asynchronous communications adapter test failed
13xx	Game control adapter errors
1301	Game control adapter test failed
1302	Joystick test failed
14xx	Printer errors
1401	Printer test failed
1404	Matrix printer failed
15xx	Synchronous data link control (SDLC) communications adapter errors
15xx	SDLC communications adapter errors
1510	8255 port B failure
1511	8255 port A failure
1512	8255 port C failure
1513	8253 timer 1 did not reach terminal count
1514	8253 timer 1 stuck on
1515	8253 timer 0 did not reach terminal count
1516	8253 timer 0 stuck on
1517	8253 timer 2 did not reach terminal count
1518	8253 timer 2 stuck on
1519	8273 port B error
1520	8273 port A error
1521	8273 command/read timeout
1522	Interrupt level 4 failure
1523	Ring indicate stuck on
1524	Receive clock stuck on
1525	Transmit clock stuck on
1526	Test indicate stuck on
1527	Ring indicate not on
1528	Receive clock not on
1529	Transmit clock not on
1530	Test indicate not on
1531	Data set ready not on
1532	Carrier detect not on
1533	Clear to send not on
1534	Data set ready stuck on

Error
Code   **Description**

1536	Clear to send stuck on
1537	Level 3 interrupt failure
1538	Receive interrupt results error
1539	Wrap data miscompare
1540	DMA channel 1 error
1541	DMA channel 1 error
1542	Error in 8273 error checking or status reporting
1547	Stray interrupt level 4
1548	Stray interrupt level 3
1549	Interrupt presentation sequence timeout
16xx	Display emulation errors (327x, 5520, 525x)
17xx	Fixed disk errors
1701	Fixed disk post error
1702	Fixed disk adapter error
1703	Fixed disk drive error
1704	Fixed disk adapter or drive error
1780	Fixed disk 0 failure
1781	Fixed disk 1 failure
1782	Fixed disk controller failure
1790	Fixed disk 0 error
1791	Fixed disk 1 error
18xx	I/O expansion unit errors
1801	I/O expansion unit post error
1810	Enable/disable failure
1811	Extender card wrap test failed (disabled)
1812	High-order address lines failure (disabled)
1813	Wait state failure (disabled)
1814	Enable/disable could not be set on
1815	Wait state failure (enabled)
1816	Extender card wrap test failed (enabled)
1817	High-order address lines failure (enabled)
1818	Disable not functioning
1819	Wait request switch not set correctly
1820	Receiver card wrap test failure
1821	Receiver high-order address lines failure
19xx	3270 PC attachment card errors
20xx	Bisync communications adapter errors
2010	8255 port A failure
2011	8255 port B failure

Error Code	Description
2012	8255 port C failure
2013	8253 timer 1 did not reach terminal count
2014	8253 timer 1 stuck on
2016	8253 timer 2 did not reach terminal count or timer 2 stuck on
2017	8251 data set ready failed to come on
2018	8251 clear to send not sensed
2019	8251 data set ready stuck on
2020	8251 clear to send stuck on
2021	8251 hardware reset failed
2022	8251 software reset failed
2023	8251 software "error reset" failed
2024	8251 transmit ready did not come on
2025	8251 receive ready did not come on
2026	8251 could not force "overrun" error status
2027	Interrupt failure-no timer interrupt
2028	Interrupt failure-transmit, replace card or planar
2029	Interrupt failure-transmit, replace card
2030	Interrupt failure-receive, replace card or planar
2031	Interrupt failure-receive, replace card
2033	Ring indicate stuck on
2034	Receive clock stuck on
2035	Transmit clock stuck on
2036	Test indicate stuck on
2037	Ring indicate stuck on
2038	Receive clock not on
2039	Transmit clock not on
2040	Test indicate not on
2041	Data set ready not on
2042	Carrier detect not on
2043	Clear to send not on
2044	Data set ready stuck on
2045	Carrier detect stuck on
2046	Clear to send stuck on
2047	Unexpected transmit interrupt
2048	Unexpected receive interrupt
2049	Transmit data did not equal receive data
2050	8251 detected overrun error
2051	Lost data set ready during data wrap
2052	Receive timeout during data wrap
21xx	Alternate bisync communications adapter errors
2110	8255 port A failure

Error Code   **Description**

2111	8255 port B failure
2112	8255 port C failure
2113	8253 timer 1 did not reach terminal count
2114	8253 timer 1 stuck on
2116	8253 timer 2 did not reach terminal count or
2117	8251 data set ready failed to come on
2117	8251 clear to send not sensed
2118	8251 data set ready stuck on
2119	8251 clear to send stuck on
2120	8251 hardware reset failed
2121	8251 software reset failed
2122	8251 software "error reset" failed
2123	8251 transmit ready did not come on
2124	8251 receive ready did not come on
2125	8251 could not force "overrun" error status
2126	Interrupt failure-no timer interrupt
2128	Interrupt failure-transmit, replace card or planar
2129	Interrupt failure-transmit, replace card
2130	Interrupt failure-receive, replace card or planar
2131	Interrupt failure-receive, replace card
2133	Ring indicate stuck on
2134	Receive clock stuck on
2135	Transmit clock stuck on
2136	Test indicate stuck on
2137	Ring indicate stuck on
2138	Receive clock not on
2139	Transmit clock not on
2140	Test indicate not on
2142	Data set ready not on
2142	Carrier detect not on
2143	Clear to send not on
2144	Data set ready stuck on
2145	Carrier detect stuck on
2146	Clear to send stuck on
2147	Unexpected transmit interrupt
2148	Unexpected receive interrupt
2149	Transmit data did not equal receive data
2150	8251 detected overrun error
2151	Lost data set ready during data wrap
2152	Receive timeout during data wrap
22xx	Cluster adapter errors

Error Code	**Description**
24xx	Enhanced graphics adapter errors
29xx	Color matrix printer errors
33xx	Printer errors

appendix e

Standard Hard Drive Types

The following is a coded summary of drives that share the same characteristics.

Standard Hard Disk Codes for XT Computers

Standard Type Code	Number of Cylinders	Heads	Precomp	Landing Zone	Unformatted Capacity	Formatted Capacity
1	306	4	128	305	12.2	10.6
2	615	4	300	615	24.6	21.4
3	615	6	300	615	36.9	32.1
4	940	8	512	940	75.2	65.4
5	940	6	512	940	56.4	49.0
6	615	4	None	615	24.6	21.4
7	462	8	256	511	36.9	32.1
8	733	5	None	733	36.6	31.9
9	900	15	None	901	135.0	117.5
10	820	3	None	820	24.6	21.4
11	855	5	None	855	42.7	37.2
12	855	7	None	855	59.8	52.0
13	306	8	128	319	24.4	21.3
14	733	7	None	733	51.3	44.6
15			Do not use — reserved			
16	612	4	None	663	24.4	21.3
17	977	5	300	977	48.5	42.5
18	977	7	None	977	68.3	59.5
19	1024	7	512	1023	71.6	62.3
20	733	5	300	732	36.6	31.9
21	733	7	300	732	51.3	44.6
22	733	5	300	733	36.6	31.9
23	306	4	None	336	12.2	10.6

Standard Hard Disk Codes for AT Computers

Standard Type Code	Number of Cylinders	Heads	Sectors	Precomp	Landing Zone	Formatted Capacity
1	615	4	17	300	670	21.3
2	820	6	17	None	819	42.7
3	733	5	17	None	732	31.8
4	977	5	17	None	976	42.4
5	925	9	17	None	924	72.3
6	989	5	17	None	988	42.9
7	969	10	17	None	968	84.2
8	969	14	17	None	968	117.9
9	830	10	17	512	829	72.0
10	754	11	17	None	753	72.0
11	1024	3	17	None	1023	26.7
12	1024	5	17	None	1023	44.5
13	1024	6	17	None	1023	53.4
14	1024	7	17	None	1023	62.3
15			Do Not Use			
16	1024	8	17	None	1023	71.2
17	1024	9	17	None	1023	80.1
18	1024	10	17	None	1023	89.0
19	1024	12	17	None	1023	106.8
20	1024	14	17	None	1023	124.6
21	918	15	17	None	917	119.7
22	1224	7	17	None	1023	74.5
23	1224	11	17	None	1023	117.0
24	1224	14	17	None	1023	149.0
25	1224	15	17	None	1023	159.6
26	615	4	26	300	670	32.6
27	820	4	26	None	819	43.6
28	820	6	26	None	819	65.4
29	1024	5	26	None	1023	68.0
30	1024	8	26	None	1023	108.9
31	1024	9	26	None	1023	122.5
32	1024	15	26	None	1023	204.2
33	969	5	34	None	968	84.2
34	969	7	34	None	968	117.9
35	969	9	34	None	968	151.6
36	1224	11	34	None	1023	234.1
37	1224	15	34	None	1023	319.3
38	823	10	34	None	822	143.0
39	1024	5	34	None	1023	89.0
40	1024	8	34	None	1023	104.4
41	1024	9	34	None	1023	160.2
42	1024	15	34	None	1023	267.1

Continued

Standard Type Code	Number of Cylinders	Heads	Sectors	Precomp	Landing Zone	Formatted Capacity
43	1024	16	17	None	1023	142.4
44	969	18	17	None	968	151.8
45	823	20	17	None	822	143.2
46	1224	22	17	None	1023	234.3
47	1224	30	17	None	1023	319.6

appendix f

Hard Drive Types by Manufacturer

Important low-level formatting information may be found here by looking up the manufacturer and model of the hard drive in question. This information is important when using the manual method of low-level formatting. While every effort has been made to ensure the accuracy of this information, it is meant only as a guide, not as the final authority.

ATASI

Model	Cylinders	Heads	Sectors	Precomp	Landing Zone	Total Bytes
3046	645	7	26	323	644	60,103,680
3051	704	7	26	352	703	65,601,536
3051 +	733	7	26	368	732	68,303,872
3085	1024	8	17	None	1023	71,303,168
3128	1024	8	26	None	1023	109,051,904

BULL

Model	Cylinders	Heads	Sectors	Precomp	Landing Zone	Total Bytes
D530	987	3	17	987	987	25,772,544
D550	987	5	17	987	987	42,954,240
D570	987	7	17	987	987	60,135,936
D585	1166	7	17	1166	1166	71,042,048

CDC

Model	Cylinders	Heads	Sectors	Precomp	Landing Zone	Total Bytes
9420X-30	989	3	17	0	989	39,496,704
9420x-51	989	5	26	0	989	65,827,840
9420x-77	989	5	26	0	989	65,827,840
9415x-21	697	3	26	0	697	27,835,392
9415x-25	615	4	17	300	615	21,411,840
9415x-36	697	5	26	0	697	46,392,320

Continued

Model	Cylinders	Heads	Sectors	Precomp	Landing Zone	Total Bytes
9415x-38	733	5	17	0	733	31,900,160
9415x-48	925	5	26	0	925	61,568,000
9415x-57	925	6	26	0	925	73,881,600
9415x-67	925	7	26	0	925	86,195,200
9415x-77	925	8	26	0	925	98,508,800
9415x-85	1024	8	17	0	1024	71,303,168
9415x-86	925	9	26	0	925	110,822,400
9415x-96	1024	9	17	0	1024	80,216,064
9415x-135	960	9	26	0	960	115,015,680

CMI

Model	Cylinders	Heads	Sectors	Precomp	Landing Zone	Total Bytes
CM-5410	256	4	17	256	256	8,912,896
CM-5616	256	6	17	256	256	13,369,344
CM-6426	615	4	26	300	615	32,747,520
CM-6426S	640	4	17	256	640	22,282,240
CM-6640	615	6	26	300	615	49,121,280

CMS

Model	Cylinders	Heads	Sectors	Precomp	Landing Zone	Total Bytes
K 40	1024	5	17	1024	1024	44,564,480
K 60	1024	7	17	1024	1024	62,390,272
K 40	1024	8	17	1024	1024	71,303,168
K 40	1024	9	17	1024	1024	80,216,064

Fujitsu

Model	Cylinders	Heads	Sectors	Precomp	Landing Zone	Total Bytes
M2226D2	615	6	17	0	615	32,117,760
M2226DR	615	6	26	0	615	49,121,280
M2227D2	615	8	17	0	615	42,823,680
M2227DR	615	8	26	0	615	65,495,040
M2230AS	320	2	17	0	320	5,570,560
M2230AT	320	2	17	0	320	5,570,560
M2233AS	320	4	17	0	320	11,141,120
M2233AT	320	4	17	0	320	11,141,120
M2234AS	320	6	17	0	320	16,711,680
M2235AS	320	8	17	0	320	22,282,240
M2241AS	754	3	26	375	754	30,111,744
M2242AS	754	7	26	375	754	70,260,736
M2243AS	754	11	26	375	754	110,409,728
M2243T	1185	7	17	0	1185	72,199,680
M2243TR	1185	7	26	0	1185	110,423,040

Hitachi

Model	Cylinders	Heads	Sectors	Precomp	Landing Zone	Total Bytes
DK511-3	699	5	26	300	699	46,525,440
DK511-5	699	7	26	300	699	65,135,616
DK511-8	823	10	26	400	822	109,557,760
DK521-5	823	6	26	None	822	65,734,656

IMI

Model	Cylinders	Heads	Sectors	Precomp	Landing Zone	Total Bytes
5006H	306	2	17	306	306	5,326,848
5012H	306	4	17	306	306	10,653,696
5018H	306	6	17	306	306	15,980,544

Irwin/Olivetti

Model	Cylinders	Heads	Sectors	Precomp	Landing Zone	Total Bytes
416	819	2	17	0	819	14,257,152
HD561	180	4	17	180	180	6,266,880

LaPine

Model	Cylinders	Heads	Sectors	Precomp	Landing Zone	Total Bytes
Titan20	615	4	26	None	615	32,747,520

Maxtor

Model	Cylinders	Heads	Sectors	Precomp	Landing Zone	Total Bytes
XT1065	918	7	17	None	918	55,931,904
XT1085	1024	8	26	None	1023	109,051,904
XT1105	918	11	26	None	1023	134,424,576
XT1120	1024	8	26	None	1023	109,051,904
XT1140	918	15	26	None	1023	183,306,240
XT1240	1024	15	26	None	1023	204,472,320
XT2085	1224	7	26	None	1223	114,057,216
XT2085 –	1024	7	26	None	1023	95,420,416
XT2140	1224	11	26	None	1223	179,232,768
XT2140 –	1024	11	26	None	1023	149,946,368
XT2190	1224	15	26	None	1223	244,408,320

Continued

Model	Cylinders	Heads	Sectors	Precomp	Landing Zone	Total Bytes
XT2190 –	1024	15	26	None	1023	204,472,320
XT3170	1224	9	26	None	1224	146,644,990
XT3280	1224	15	26	None	1224	244,408,320
XT4170E	1224	7	35	None	1223	153,538,560
XT4380E	1224	15	35	None	1223	329,011,200
XT8380E	1651	7	52	None	1650	307,693,568
XT8760E	1651	15	52	None	1650	659,343,360
EXT-4175	1224	7	35	None	1224	153,540,000
EXT-4280	1224	11	35	None	1224	241,270,000
EXT-4380	1224	15	35	None	1224	329,010,000

Micropolis

Model	Cylinders	Heads	Sectors	Precomp	Landing Zone	Total Bytes
1302	830	3	17	None	829	21,672,960
1303	830	5	17	None	829	36,121,600
1304	830	6	17	None	829	43,345,920
1323	1024	4	17	None	1023	35,651,584
1323A	1024	5	17	None	1023	44,564,480
1324	1024	6	17	None	1023	53,477,376
1324A	1024	7	17	None	1023	62,390,272
1325	1024	8	17	None	1023	71,303,168
1333	1024	4	17	None	1024	35,651,584
1333A	1024	5	17	None	1024	44,564,480
1334	1024	6	17	None	1023	53,477,376
1334A	1024	7	17	None	1023	62,390,272
1335	1024	8	17	None	1023	71,303,168
3650	809	6	17	None	808	42,249,216
3675	809	6	26	None	808	64,616,448

Microscience

Model	Cylinders	Heads	Sectors	Precomp	Landing Zone	Total Bytes
HH-312	306	4	17	None	306	10,653,696
HH-325	615	4	17	None	615	21,411,840
HH-330	615	4	26	None	615	32,747,520
HH-612	306	4	17	306	306	10,653,696
HH-725	612	4	17	612	612	21,307,392
HH-725	612	4	26	612	612	32,587,776
HH-738	612	4	26	None	612	32,587,776
HH-825	615	4	17	None	615	21,411,840
HH-830	615	4	26	None	615	32,747,520

Continued

Model	Cylinders	Heads	Sectors	Precomp	Landing Zone	Total Bytes
HH-1050	1024	5	17	None	1023	44,564,480
HH-1060	1024	5	26	None	1023	68,157,440
HH-1075	1024	7	17	None	1023	62,390,272
HH-1090	1314	7	17	None	1313	80,059,392
HH-1095	1024	7	26	None	1023	95,420,416
HH-1120	1314	7	26	None	1313	122,443,776
HH-2120	1024	7	35	None	1023	128,450,560

MiniScribe

Model	Cylinders	Heads	Sectors	Precomp	Landing Zone	Total Bytes
MS1006	306	2	17	0[a]	306	5,326,848
MS1012	306	4	17	0[a]	306	10,653,696
MS2006	306	2	17	0[b]	306	5,326,848
MS2012	306	4	17	0[b]	306	10,653,696
MS3053	1024	5	17	None	1024	44,564,480
MS3212	612	2	17	128[c]	612	10,653,696
MS3412	306	4	17	128[b]	306	10,653,696
MS3425	615	4	26	128[c]	656	32,747,520
MS3438	615	4	26	128	656	32,747,520
MS3650	809	6	26	300	852	64,616,448
MS4010	480	2	17	480[d]	480	7,102,464
MS4020	480	4	17	480[d]	480	14,204,928
MS6032	1024	3	26	512[e]	1023	40,894,464
MS6053	1024	5	26	512[e]	1023	68,157,440
MS6074	1024	7	26	512	1023	95,420,416
MS6079	1024	5	26	512	1023	68,157,440
MS6085	1024	8	26	512[e]	1023	109,051,904
MS6128	1024	8	26	512	1023	109,051,904
MS8212	615	2	17	128[c]	615	10,705,920
MS8425	615	4	17	128[c]	663	21,411,840
MS8438	615	4	26	128	663	32,747,520

[a]Reduced Write 153
[b]Reduced Write 306
[c]Reduced Write 612
[d]Reduced Write 480
[e]Reduced Write 1024

Mitsubishi

Model	Cylinders	Heads	Sectors	Precomp	Landing Zone	Total Bytes
MR522	612	4	26	300	612	32,587,776
MR533	971	3	26	None	971	38,777,856
MR535	971	5	26	None	971	64,629,760

NEC

Model	Cylinders	Heads	Sectors	Precomp	Landing Zone	Total Bytes
D5124	309	4	26	None	664	16,453,632
D5126	612	4	26	None	664	32,587,776
D5146	615	8	26	None	664	65,495,040

Newbury

Model	Cylinders	Heads	Sectors	Precomp	Landing Zone	Total Bytes
PENNY 340	615	8	17	615	615	42,823,680
NDR320	615	4	26	None	615	32,747,520
NDR340	615	8	26	None	615	65,495,040
XT-1065	918	7	17	918	918	55,931,904
NDR1085	1024	8	26	None	1023	109,051,904
NDR1105	918	11	26	None	1023	134,424,576
NDR1140	918	15	26	None	1023	183,306,240
XT-2085	1224	7	17	1224	1224	74,575,872
XT-2140	1224	11	17	1224	1224	117,190,650
NDR2190 –	1024	15	26	None	1023	204,472,320
NDR2190	1224	15	26	None	1223	244,408,320

PTI

Model	Cylinders	Heads	Sectors	Precomp	Landing Zone	Total Bytes
PT238R	615	4	26	410	614	32,747,520
PT251R	820	4	26	544	819	43,663,360
PT357R	615	6	26	410	614	49,121,280
PT376R	820	6	26	544	819	65,495,040
PT4102	820	8	26	544	819	87,326,720
PT225	615	4	17	410	614	21,411,840
PT234	820	4	17	544	819	28,549,120
PT338	615	6	17	410	614	32,117,760
PT351	820	6	17	544	819	42,823,680
PT468	820	8	17	544	819	57,098,240

Priam/Vertex

Model	Cylinders	Heads	Sectors	Precomp	Landing Zone	Total Bytes
V130	987	3	26	None	987	39,416,832
H150	1024	5	17	None	1024	44,564,480
V150	987	5	26	None	987	65,694,720
V160	1166	5	17	None	1166	50,744,320

Continued

Model	Cylinders	Heads	Sectors	Precomp	Landing Zone	Total Bytes
V160 –	1166	5	26	None	1166	77,608,960
V170	987	7	26	None	987	91,972,608
V185	1166	7	17	None	1166	50,744,320
V185 –	1024	7	26	None	1023	95,420,416
519 –	1024	15	26	None	1023	204,472,320
519	1224	15	26	None	1223	244,408,320

Quantum

Model	Cylinders	Heads	Sectors	Precomp	Landing Zone	Total Bytes
Q520	512	4	26	256	512	27,262,976
Q530	512	6	26	256	512	40,894,464
Q540	512	8	26	256	512	54,525,952

Rodime Drive

Model	Cylinders	Heads	Sectors	Precomp	Landing Zone	Total Bytes
RO101	192	2	17	None	193	3,342,336
RO102	192	4	17	None	193	6,684,672
RO103	192	6	17	None	193	10,027,008
RO104	192	8	17	None	193	13,369,344
RO201	321	2	17	None	321	5,587,968
RO202	321	4	17	None	321	11,175,936
RO203	321	6	26	132	321	25,638,912
RO204	321	8	26	132	321	34,185,216
RO201E	640	2	17	640	640	11,141,120
RO202E	640	4	26	0	640	34,078,720
RO203E	640	6	26	0	640	51,118,080
RO204E	640	8	26	0	640	68,157,440
RO3055	872	6	26	650	872	69,648,384
RO3065	872	7	26	650	872	81,256,448
RO5090	1224	7	26	None	1224	114,057,216

Seagate

Model	Cylinders	Heads	Sectors	Precomp	Landing Zone	Total Bytes
ST125	615	4	17	None	615	21,411,840
ST138	615	6	17	None	615	32,117,760
ST138R	615	4	26	None	615	32,747,520
ST157R	615	6	26	None	615	49,121,280
ST213	615	2	17	300	615	10,705,920

Continued

Model	Cylinders	Heads	Sectors	Precomp	Landing Zone	Total Bytes
ST225	615	4	17	300	615	21,411,840
ST238R	615	4	26	300	615	32,747,520
ST250R	667	4	31	None	667	42,346,496
ST251	820	6	17	None	820	42,823,680
ST251R	820	4	26	None	820	43,663,360
ST277R	820	6	26	None	820	65,495,040
ST412	306	4	17	128[a]	305	10,653,696
ST4026	615	4	17	300	615	21,411,840
ST4038	733	5	17	300	733	31,900,160
ST4038M	733	5	17	None	977	31,900,160
ST4051	977	5	17	None	977	42,519,040
ST4053	1024	5	17	None	1023	44,564,480
ST4096	1024	9	17	None	1023	80,216,064
ST4077R	977	5	26	None	977	65,029,120
ST4144R	1024	9	26	None	1023	122,683,392

[a]Reduced Write 128

Storage Dimensions

Model	Cylinders	Heads	Sectors	Precomp	Landing Zone	Total Bytes
AT-40	1024	5	17	None	1023	44,564,480
AT-70	1024	8	17	None	1023	71,303,168
AT-100	1024	8	26	None	1023	109,051,904
AT-120	918	15	17	None	1023	119,854,080
AT-133	1024	15	17	None	1023	133,693,440
AT-140	1024	8	34	None	1023	142,606,336
AT155E	1224	7	36	None	1223	157,925,376
AT-160	1224	15	17	None	1223	159,805,440
AT-200	1024	15	26	None	1023	204,472,320
AT-320	1224	15	35	None	1223	329,011,200
AT335E	1224	15	36	None	1223	338,411,520
AT650E	1632	15	52	None	1631	651,755,520

Tandon

Model	Cylinders	Heads	Sectors	Precomp	Landing Zone	Total Bytes
TM252	306	4	17	306	306	10,653,696
TM262	615	4	26	None	615	32,747,520
TM264	781	4	26	781	781	41,586,688
TM755	981	5	26	None	981	65,295,360
TM362	615	4	26	None	615	32,747,520
TAN501	306	2	17	153	306	5,326,848
TAN502	306	4	17	153	306	10,653,696

Continued

Model	Cylinders	Heads	Sectors	Precomp	Landing Zone	Total Bytes
TAN503	306	6	17	153	306	15,980,544
TM602S	153	4	17	153	153	5,326,848
TM603S	153	6	17	153	153	7,990,272
TM603SE	230	6	17	128	230	12,011,520
TM702AT	615	4	17	615	615	22,666,440
TM703	695	5	26	None	695	46,259,200
TM703AT	733	5	17	733	733	31,900,160
TM705	962	5	26	None	962	64,030,720
TM702AT	615	4	26	None	615	32,747,520
TM703AT	733	5	26	None	733	48,788,480
TM755	981	5	17	981	981	42,693,120

Toshiba

Model	Cylinders	Heads	Sectors	Precomp	Landing Zone	Total Bytes
MK-53F	830	5	26	512	830	55,244,800
MK-54F	830	7	26	512	830	77,342,720
MK-56F	830	10	26	512	830	110,489,600

Tulin

Model	Cylinders	Heads	Sectors	Precomp	Landing Zone	Total Bytes
TL226	640	4	26	None	640	34,078,720
TL326	640	4	26	None	640	34,078,720
TL240	640	6	26	None	640	51,118,080
TL340	640	6	26	None	640	51,118,080
TL238	640	4	26	None	640	34,078,720
TL258	640	6	26	None	640	51,118,080

appendix g

Hayes 2400 Modem Commands

Modem Commands

Command	Description
AT	Attention code; required before all of the following commands except the A/ command and the +++ (escape) code
A/	Repeat the entire command line given last (does not require an AT command prior; also, no carriage return is required)
A	Answer the phone (take the phone off hook)
B	Selects the CCITT V.22 bis mode when using 1200 baud
B1	Selects the normal, Bell 212A operating mode when using 1200 baud
D	Dial the following number
E	Do not echo (send back) typed characters to the computer
E1	Echo (send back) typed characters to the computer
H	Hang up the telephone
H1	Pick up the telephone
I	Request the product identification code from the modem
I1	Compute and return the CHECKSUM of the internal ROM chip
I2	Perform a CHECKSUM of ROM and return either an OK or ERROR message
L	Select the lowest speaker volume
L1	Same as above
L2	Select the medium speaker volume
L3	Select the highest speaker volume
M	Keep the speaker off at all times
M1	Leave the speaker on until a carrier is received
M2	Leave the speaker on at all times
M3	Disable the speaker when dialing and after a carrier is received
O	Return the modem to the on-line state
O1	Return the modem to the on-line state and start a retrain sequence
Q	The modem returns a result code (OK) after carrying out commands
Q1	The modem does not confirm performance of commands

Command	Description
Sr?	Return the decimal value currently within one of 27 internal registers, "r"
	Example: S7? (The command is "What is the current number of seconds to wait for a carrier before terminating?")
	6 (The answer returned by the modem)
Sr = n	Set internal register "r" to a decimal value of "n"
	Example: S7 = 16 (Command to reset the time to wait for a carrier to 16 seconds.)
V	Select numeric result codes to be sent from the modem to the computer
V1	Select "verbal" or word result codes to be sent from the modem to the computer
X	The modem does not wait for dial tone before dialing, sends CONNECT when connection is made with remote modem
X1	The modem does not wait for dial tone before dialing, sends CONNECT 1200 or CONNECT 2400 as appropriate when connection is made with remote modem, but does not detect a busy signal
X2	The modem waits for dial tone before dialing (sends NO DIALTONE if none detected within 5 seconds), sends CONNECT 1200 or CONNECT 2400 as appropriate when connection is made with remote modem, but does not detect a busy signal
X3	The modem does not wait for dial tone before dialing, sends CONNECT 1200 or CONNECT 2400 as appropriate when connection is made with remote modem, sends BUSY if busy signal is detected
X4	The modem waits for dial tone before dialing (sends NO DIALTONE if none detected within 5 seconds), sends CONNECT 1200 or CONNECT 2400 as appropriate when connection is made with remote modem, and sends BUSY if busy signal is detected
Y	Disconnecting on a long space is disabled
Y1	Enable the modem to hang up the telephone if the data terminal ready (DTR) line goes low (computer is turned off), an H0 command is given, or a BREAK signal is sent from the remote modem for more than 1.6 seconds
Z	Reset the modem to the default configuration as written in the modem's nonvolatile RAM
+ + +	An escape code that changes the modem from the on-line state back to the command state. There must be a delay of at least 1 second before and after this command for it to be effective.
&C	The data carrier detect (DCD) line from the modem is always ON
&C1	The DCD line from the modem indicates whether or not there is a carrier from a remote modem
&D	The modem ignores the DTR line signal from the computer
&D1	The modem goes from on-line to the command state if the computer drops the DTR line low
&D2	The modem goes from on-line to the command state if the computer drops the DTR line low. This option also disables the modem from automatically answering the telephone.

Continued

Command	Description
&D3	The modem automatically initializes from nonvolatile RAM when DTR goes from high to low
&F	Initialize the modem with the factory defaults from ROM
&G	Do not use guard tones
&G1	Use 550 Hz guard tone
&G2	Use 1800 Hz guard tone
&J to &J1	Used in some modems to select one of two installed telephone jacks
&L	Using dial-up lines (numbers must be dialed, can call any number)
&L1	Leased line operation (no dial-tone, no dialing of numbers, dedicated line use)
&M	Using asynchronous mode
&M1 to &M3	Special codes to switch from asynchronous to synchronous modes; often not available in modems
&P	Use 39/61 make/break ratio for pulse dialing, commonly used in the United States and Canada
&P1	Use a 33/67 make/break ratio for pulse dialing, as used in the United Kingdom and in Hong Kong
&R	The CTS signal from the modem mimics the RTS signal received from the computer
&R1	The modem ignores the RTS signal from the computer. The CTS signal from the modem is always held ON, indicating that the modem is ready to handle data.
&S	The DSR line from the modem is always held ON, indicating that the modem is ready for data transmission
&S1	The DSR line from the modem goes high when connection is made
&T to &T8	Various modem testing options
&W	Write the current configuration to nonvolatile RAM memory
&X to &X2	Options to select the carrier in the synchronous mode, not used in microcomputer applications
&Z	Store the telephone number in nonvolatile memory

Dialing Commands

Command	Description
P	Use pulse dialing, not tone dialing
R	Use reversed modem carrier, originate carrier used in the answer mode
S	Dial the stored telephone number
T	Use tone dialing, not pulse dialing
W	Wait for a second dial tone
,	Pause, used between commands in a string
;	Return the modem to the command state after dialing
!	The modem goes on-hook for ½ second, then off
@	The modem waits for silence, then continues with the command string

appendix h

Epson Printer Control and Escape Sequences

The Epson printer codes are perhaps the best "standard" of extended printer codes in common use today. Many printers advertise "Epson Emulation": The printer acts as though it were an Epson printer.

The following codes are by necessity abbreviated, but their summary in this appendix will be of help to the technician needing a quick reference. Detailed instructions can be found in an Epson printer manual.

All codes are in hex. Other numbers may be decimal, with a lowercase "d" following, such as 65d, for example. Conversion between numbering systems or to ASCII characters may be necessary in a given application.

Master Select

Code	Effect
1B 21 (n)	Values for (n) are as follows Elite = 1 Compressed = 4 Enhanced = 8 Double strike = 16 Enlarged = 32 Values of (n) can sometimes be combined. For instance, using 1 and 4 will result in compressed elite type.

Print Quality

Code	Effect
1B 78 (n)	Near letter quality (NLQ) (best appearance type) where values for (n) are as follows: Turn ON NLQ = 1d or 49d Turn OFF NLQ = 0d or 48d
1B 45	Turn ON enhanced print (between draft and NLQ).
1B 46	Turn OFF enhanced print. [Draft (fastest) print is default. Turn OFF both NLQ and Enhanced]

Print Size and Spacing

Code	Effect
0E or 1B 0E	Turn ON enlarged print for one line only
14	Cancel enlarged print in midline
1B 57 (n)	Turn enlarged print ON and OFF where values for (n) are as follows: Turn ON enlarged Type = 1d or 49d Turn OFF enlarged Type = 0d or 48d
0F or 1B 0F	Turn ON compressed print
12	Turn OFF compressed print
1B 4D	Switch to elite print size (12 characters per inch)
1B 50	Switch to pica print size (10 characters per inch)
1B 70 (n)	Turn proportional spacing ON and Off, where values for (n) are as follows: Turn ON proportional spacing = 1d or 49d Turn OFF proportional spacing = 0d or 48d
1B 53 (n)	Turn sub- and superscript ON and OFF, where values for (n) are Turn ON superscript = 0d or 48d Turn ON subscript = 1d or 49d
1B 54	Turn OFF either super- or subscript

Type Fonts

Code	Effect
1B 25 (n)	Switch source of type fonts, where values for (n) are as follows: Select internal ROM characters = 0d Select internal RAM characters = 1d Select plug-in ROM characters = 2d
1B 34	Use the high memory characters
1B 35	Use the low memory characters
1B 3D	Force high bit of all incoming bytes to "0" (force use of low character set in memory)
1B 3E	Force high bit of all incoming bytes to "1" (force use of high character set in memory)
1B 23	Do not change high bit of incoming bytes

Modifying or Creating Fonts

Code	Effect
1B 3A 00 00 00	Load ROM characters into RAM
1B 26 00	Character redefinition bytes follow (lead-in as follows)
1B 26 00 (n) (m) (a)	Load RAM from the computer, where (n) is the first character to be redefined (hex) (m) is the last character to be redefined (hex) (a) is the attribute; descender and proportional spacing information

Printing International Characters

Code	Effect
1B 36	Print 128d to 159d of high font memory (international symbols)
1B 37	Cancel 1B 36 command
1B 52 (n)	Use full international character set, where values for (n) are as follows: United States = 0d France = 1d Germany = 2d United Kingdom = 3d Denmark = 4d Sweden = 5d Italy = 6d Spain = 7d Japan = 8d

Printing Attributes

Code	Effect
1B 49	Print control codes
1B 2D	Turn underlining ON and OFF, where values of (n) are as follows: Turn ON underlining = 1d or 49d Turn OFF underlining = 0d or 48d
1B 47	Turn ON double strike
1B 48	Turn OFF double strike

Paper Movement

Code	Effect
0A	Line feed
1B 30	1/8 inch line spacing
1B 31	7/72 inch line spacing
1B 32	1/6 inch line spacing
1B 41 (n)	Variable spacing in 1/72 of an inch, where values of (n) are between 0d and 85d
1B 33	Variable spacing in 1/216 of an inch, where values of (n) are between 0d and 255d
1B 4A (n)	Advance paper (n)/216th of an inch
1B 6A (n)	Withdraw paper (n)/216th of an inch
0C	Go directly to top of next sheet
1B 43 (n)	Change length of sheets to (n) lines, where values of (n) are from 1 to 127

Continued

Code	Effect
1B 43 00 (n)	Change length of sheets to (n) inches, where values of (n) are from 1d to 22d
1B 4E (n)	Skip over perforations (at end of each sheet), and set the skip distance to (n) lines, where (n) is between 1d and 127d
1B 4F	Cancel skip over perforations
0B	Advance to next vertical tab
1B 42 (n1) (n2)....(n16) 00	Set vertical tab stops, where (nx) is between 1d and 254d (last command is a 00 hex)
1B 2F (n)	Select tab channel, where (n) is between 0d and 7d
1B 62 (n) (ms) (m2)...(m16) 00	Setting tabs in a vertical tab channel, where (n) is a value from 0d to 7d, and (m) is a value from 1 to 254

Printhead Movement

Code	Effect
08	Backspace printhead
0D	Return to left margin of page
09	Advance to next horizontal tab position
1B 44 (n1), (n2)...(n32) 00	Set horizontal tabs at column positions (mx); values of x may be from 0 to 31 (last command is a 00 hex)
1B 6C (n)	Set left margin at column (n)
1B 51 (n)	Set right margin at column (n)
1B 3C	Print left to right for one line only
1B 55 (n)	Print direction control, where values of (n) are as follows: Turn ON bidirectional printing = 0d or 48d Left-to-right printing only = 1d or 49d

Graphics Printing

Code	Effect
1B 4B (n1) (n2)	Switch into normal graphics mode, where values of (n) are as follows modulus of number of characters/256 = (n1) remainder of above = (n2) [(n1) values of 0 to 255 only]
1B 2A (m) (n1) (n2) (d1) (d2)...	Graphics master select command for 8-pin graphics, where values are as follows: Dot intensity = (m) Normal density = 60 dots per inch (DPI) = 0 Double density = 120 DPI = 1

Continued

Code	Effect
	High-speed double density = 120 DPI = 2
	Quad density = 240 DPI = 3
	CRT graphics = 80 DPI = 4
	Plotter graphics = 72 DPI = 5
	CRT graphics II = 90 DPI = 6
	Modulus of number of characters/256 = (n1)
	Remainder of above = (n2)
	[(n1) values of 0 to 255 only]
	Data bytes carrying specific pin firing data = (d1) (d2)...
1B 4B (n1) (n2) (d1) (d2)....	Normal density graphics [see above for values of (n) and (d)]
1B 4C (n1) (n2) (d1) (d2)...	Double-density graphics [see above for values of (n) and (d)]
1B 59 (n1) (n2) (d1) (d2)...	High-speed double-density graphics [see above for values of (n) and (d)]
1B 5A (n1) (n2) (d1) (d2)...	Quad-density graphics [see above for values of (n) and (d)]
1B 5E (a) (n1) (n2) (d11) (d12) (d21) (d22)...	9-Pin graphics, where values are
	Density = (a)
	Normal density = 60 DPI = 0
	Double density = 120 DPI = 1
	Modulus of number of characters/256 = (n1)
	Remainder of above = (n2)
	[(n1) values of 0 to 255 only]
	First pair of data bytes carrying specific pin firing data = (d11) (d12)
	Second pair of data bytes carrying specific pin firing data, etc. = (d21) (d22)
1B 40	Reset (initialize) the printer
07	Sound the "bell" (beeper)
18	Erase all data in printer buffer line
7F	Delete last character sent, place following character in its place
11	Enable (select) the printer (works only if parallel interface is used, software DIP switches 1 through 8 OFF, and line #36 of interface SCLCT IN is logic high)
13	Disable (deselect) the printer
1B 39	Enable paper out detect
1B 38	Disable paper out detect
1B 69 (n)	Switches immediate printing ON or OFF, where values of (n) are as follows:
	Immediate print ON = 1d or 49d
	Immediate print OFF = 0d or 48d

Continued

Code

1B 73 (n)

Effect

Switches print speed, where values of (n) are as follows:

Cut print speed by half = 1d or 49d
Resume normal print speed = 0d or 48d

appendix i

RS-232C Standard Explained

The Electronics Industry Association set the standard: Recommended Standard 232, modification C. While earlier versions used other voltages, version C specified + 12 and − 12 V and defined the lines to be used.

Data are sent, one bit ("1" or "0") at a time. They are grouped as either 7 or 8 data bits. (Microcomputers seldom use 7 bits for data transmission.) The number of stop bits to be used within the data stream between each 8-bit byte must be chosen, usually a single stop. See Figure I.1.

The original intent of the standard was to provide for all of the possible signals needed for a data terminal to communicate with a remote mainframe computer. See Figure I.2. The data terminal was called a data terminal equipment (DTE) and the modem was called a data communications equipment (DCE). When the terminal sent data on pin #2, they were received on pin #2 at the modem end. Data sent from the modem were received by the terminal on pin #3 in both cases, resulting in a straight pin-for-pin interconnection.

According to the standard, the connector should be a 25-pin connector. The DTE end should be a plug (male, DB-25P) and the DCE end should be a socket (female, DB-25S) connector.

The original RS-232C wiring table provided for many more functions than are used today with microcomputers. The following table is the original RS-232C wiring standard.

RS-232C Connections

Pin		Name	Direction DTE DCE \ /	Function
1	*	FG	None	Frame Ground
2	#	TD	--->	Transmitted Data
3	#	RD	<---	Received Data
4	#	RTS	--->	Request To Send
5	#	CTS	<---	Clear To Send
6	#	DSR	<---	Data Set Ready
7	#	SG	None	Signal Ground
8		DCD	<---	Data Carrier Detect
9	*		<---	Positive DC Test Voltage
10	*		<---	Negative DC Test Voltage

Continued

Pin		Name	Direction	Function
11		QM	<---	Equalizer Mode
12	*	(S)DCD	<---	Sec. Data Carrier Detect
13	*	(S)CTS	<---	Sec. Clear To Send
14	*	(S)TD	--->	Sec. Transmitted Data
		or NS	--->	New Sync
15		TC	<---	Transmitter Clock
16	*	(S)RD	<---	Sec. Received Data
		or DCT	<---	Divided Clock, Transmitter
17		RC	<---	Receiver Clock
18		DCR	<---	Divided Clock, Receiver
19	*	(S)RTS	--->	Sec. Request To Send
20	#	DTR	--->	Data Terminal Ready
21	*	SQ	<---	Signal Quality Detect
22		RI	<---	Ring Indicator
23			--->	Data Rate Selector
			<---	Data Rate Selector
24	*	TC	--->	Ext. Transmitter Clock
25			--->	Busy

The most important connections used with microcomputers. Other lines frequently not connected.

* Omitted connection on many computers, including the IBM PC.

Fortunately, only a few of the signal lines provided for in the original standard are used today between microcomputers and peripheral equipment. Thus, the serial communications port of a microcomputer has only about half of the lines actually wired in. The maximum number of lines are used when connecting to an external modem rather than any other serial device. The following table relates the signals to the use of a modem.

Microcomputer RS-232C Port Wiring Table

	Computer (DTE)		Modem (DCE)	Interpretation of Signal
FRAME	1	–	1	Frame or shield ground
TXD	2	–	2	Data out from computer (DTE)
RXD	3	–	3	Data input from modem (DCE)
RTS	4	–	4	Computer wishes to send data
CTS	5	–	5	Modem says OK for computer to send data
DSR	6	–	6	Modem is on and ready to transmit data
GND	7	–	7	Signal ground (power supply common)
DCD	8	–	8	Modem has detected a carrier from a remote modem
DCD	12	–	12	High-speed indicator (2400 baud?)
DTR	20	–	20	Computer is on, ready for work
RI	22	–	22	Ring indicator

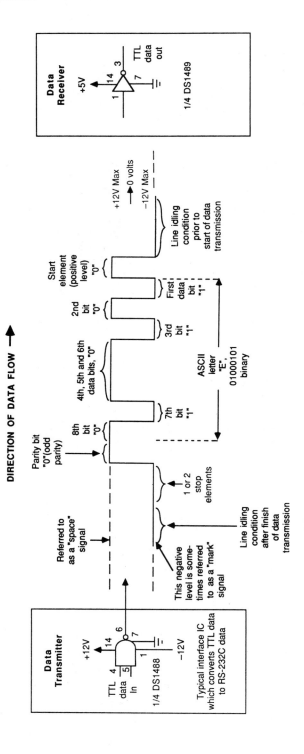

RS232C serial data transmission standards. Note the major points:
Data is inverted to a negative-true convention;
The least significant bit is sent first, most significant bit last;
Voltage levels are either positive or negative, not zero;
Line level idles at a negative voltage.
Control signals, not shown, are positive-true convention and use the
same voltage levels as above.

Figure I.1 Serial data transmission parameters are determined by the software used.

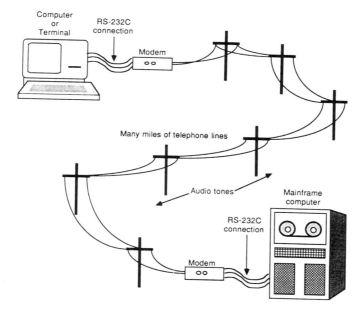

Figure I.2 Serial data communications were first used to pass information over telephone lines between data terminals and mainframe computers. The standard for connecting the modems at either end gave rise to the RS-232C standard of today.

The connection of a microcomputer to a modem is shown in Figure I.3.

It is imperative to know the configuration of both the ports to be connected via a serial communications cable. If the ports are of different configurations, a simple extension cable will do the job. If they are of the same type (both DTE or both DCE), a crossover cable must be used. See Figure I.4 for three common types of crossover (null-modem) cables.

Labels on the back panel near a port indicating DTE or DCE may mean what it is internally OR what it is to be connected to! End result: Back panel labeling is no help at all! Schematics in instruction books can help determine the configuration of a port; if the output of the data is being sent out to pin #2 of the standard DB-25P, then it is a DTE device.

Figure I-5 shows how two DTE devices might be connected using a null-modem cable.

Most microcomputer serial ports are configured as they would be on a DTE. If there is any doubt, a breakout box can be used to determine the configuration. Simply insert the breakout box, which is basically a series of LEDs attached to each of the RS-232C data lines, into the circuit. Disconnect one end of the cable from a serial port, connect the breakout box, and reconnect the cable into the breakout box on the other side. The box will show lighted LEDs where there are logic "1" levels and flickering lights when data are passed on a line. To determine whether the microcomputer is a DTE device, use the COPY command of DOS and copy any file to the port. If the #2 line shows a flickering light, this is a DTE microcomputer port [memory aid: DTE Transmits on Two (note the three "T's")]. If the #3 line shows the flickering light, however, the microcomputer is configured as a DCE port.

The microcomputer is usually configured as a DTE device. A straightforward connection to a DCE device such as a modem requires the use of a straight-through extension cable, where each wire connects to identical pins on each end: The #2 pin is connected to #2 on the opposite end, etc.

The configuration of both the microcomputer and the peripheral port must be determined before they are connected. Although serial ports are very forgiving by design, why take the chance of a wrong connection? See the above note on breakout boxes if there is any doubt as to the configuration of either of the ports. Since a printer with a keyboard could be used as a "terminal," both sending and receiving data just like a data terminal, printers are often wired in a DTE configuration.

A printer will generally accept a certain number of characters before filling up, often only a single line of text. This line is then placed on the paper character by character. Compared to the operating speed of the microcomputer, the process of printing characters can take thousands of times longer than the generation and transmission of the data to the printer. Thus, the printer must have some means of telling the microcomputer to stop sending data until the contents of the printer's buffer can be emptied onto the paper. This process is called *handshaking*. There are two ways of handshaking: using a wire from the printer to the microcomputer to signal whether the printer is busy or by sending a special ASCII character to the microcomputer to tell it to stop sending data for a moment.

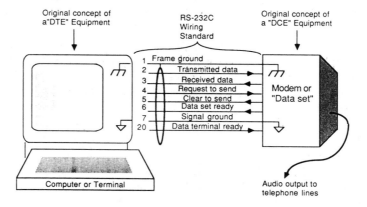

Figure I.3 A modem connected to a microcomputer port uses all of the lines wired to the port within the computer.

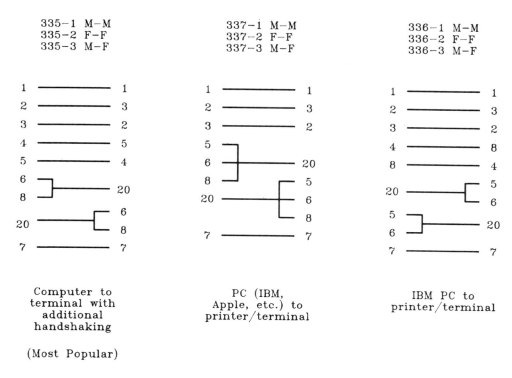

335-1 M-M
335-2 F-F
335-3 M-F

337-1 M-M
337-2 F-F
337-3 M-F

336-1 M-M
336-2 F-F
336-3 M-F

Computer to
terminal with
additional
handshaking

PC (IBM,
Apple, etc.) to
printer/terminal

IBM PC to
printer/terminal

(Most Popular)

Figure I.4 Wiring of common null-modem cables for microcomputer use.

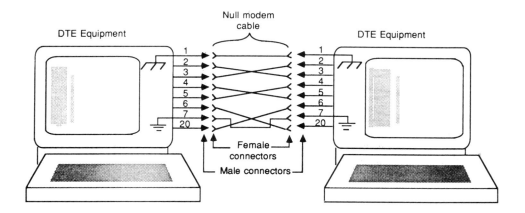

Figure I.5 Two DTEs such as these computers can be cross-connected with a null-modem cable with female connectors on each end.

Less wiring is required from a serial port to a printer than is required for connection to a modem. An abbreviated RS-232C wiring table for hardware handshaking printer use is as follows:

RS-232C Wiring Table for Hardware Handshaking

	Computer (DTE)		Modem (DTE)	Interpretation of Signal
FRAME	1	–	1	Frame or shield ground
TXD	2	–	3	Data out from computer (DTE)
RXD	3	–	2	Data input from printer (DTE)
RTS	4	–	5	May be used as auxiliary handshaking
CTS	5	–	4	May be used as auxiliary handshaking
DSR	20	–	6	Printer is on and ready to receive data
GROUND	7	–	7	Signal ground (power supply common)
BUSY	6	–	20	When logic is low, printer is busy (often connected at printer to #11, this enables use of either #11 or #20 at the printer end to be used as BUSY line)

Note that both the microcomputer and the printer are represented as DTE devices, thus requiring pin #2 of one connector to be wired to pin #3 at the opposite end. This is, therefore, a null-modem cable.

Sending data to a printer that uses XON and XOFF handshaking required only three wires, as shown in the following table:

RS-232C Wiring Table for Software Handshaking Printer

	Computer (DTE)		Modem (DTE)	Interpretation of Signal
TXD	2	–	3	Data out from computer (DTE)
RXD	3	–	2	Data input from printer (DTE)
RTS	4			4 must be jumpered to 5 at computer end
CTS	5			
GND	7	–	7	Signal ground (power supply common)

The actual hookup might be as in Figure I.6.

Note that there is no provision to tell whether the printer is on and ready for characters. Characters must now be sent by the microcomputer "in the blind," awaiting a software character of XOFF to tell the microcomputer when to wait for the printer to catch up. The software at the microcomputer end must be set up so that it is controlling microcomputer output in accordance with the incoming serial characters XON (DC1 on the ASCII chart) and XOFF (DC3 on the ASCII chart) from the printer.

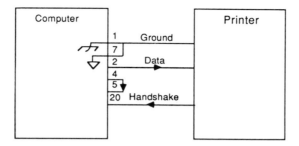

Figure I.6 Using software handshaking, only three lines are necessary to send data to a printer.

Answers to Odd-Numbered Questions

Chapter 1

1. In the computer's read-only memory (ROM) chip
3. An XT is a PC with a hard disk drive.
5. By writing the information into special battery-maintained RAM memory
7. First from the "A" floppy diskette drive, then from the hard drive is no diskette is in the "A" drive
9. For most applications programs; some games, however, do not use an operating system
11. Assembly language

Chapter 2

1. Operator error, power line problem, floppy diskette failure, improper setup of software
3. The metal oxide varistor (MOV)
5. One or both of the drives have drifted out of alignment.
7. Diagnostic software

Chapter 3

1. The complete failure
3. In their original containers
5. CMOS
7. See "Safety and cautions to be Observed During computer Repair."
9. The mechanical, thermal, and erratic intermittents
11. See the list of "Check the Simple Things First."
13. Accidental turning down of the brightness control, making the screen completely blank

15. Reduce the system to the minimum configuration necessary for operation by removing unnecessary boards and options, then see if the problem is still there.

17. The 9th bit is used for parity checking of the remaining 8 bits.

19. Use of a diagnostic program

Chapter 4

1. A "compatible" computer is one that will run the programs originally written for the IBM microcomputer based on the 8088 central processor.

3. The addition of a hard disk drive to a PC makes it an XT.

5. Write down the original settings.

7. Changing the CPU master clock to a higher frequency; increasing its "heart-beat" rate to make it operate faster

9. About 200 watts is sufficient

11. An XT can have more than 640K, accessible with special software. This memory is called *expanded* memory. The AT additional memory is called *extended* memory.

13. On the system board

15. DOS version 3.3, for instance, will recognize only two serial ports. Special software must be used to utilize a third serial port, and the functions provided by DOS will not be available for that port.

Chapter 5

1. Base memory

3. Nine, all of which must be either the 64K or the 256 kilobit type, depending on the wiring of the sockets in which they will be installed. 64 kilobit chips must be used for 64K banks, 256 kilobit chips in 256K banks.

5. No! The CGA monitor has poor resolution compared to the monochrome monitor.

Chapter 6

1. The floppy diskette controller (adapter) and at least one, most often two, diskette drives

3. 112

5. The bottom, or opposite side from the label

7. Formatting a diskette will destroy all data on the diskette.

9. Switch the signal/control cables between the drives. If the problem switches, the controller is at fault.

11. Usually both drives should be set up for the second drive of the series, "1" if the drives are designated "0" and "1," or drive "2" if they are numbered "1" and "2."

Chapter 7

1. Getting the hard disk ready to be used, correctly setting up the low-level format, partitioning and then performing the high-level format of the drive

3. Always park the drive heads before turning off the power. Always park the drives when transporting the computer. Never move or jar a computer containing a hard disk while the hard disk is turning (while power is applied).

5. Only if the drive will never be used again

7. 17.

9. Use commercial formatting software to speed and ease the job.

11. With the present DOS in general use, version 3.3, you cannot install three drives. Only two drives, physical or logical, are supported by DOS.

13. All new cylinder and sector information is placed upon the disk, and all data areas are written into during a write/verify routine. Bad sectors are locked out of use permanently.

15. FORMAT establishes the file allocation table (FAT) to keep track of the sectors of information on the hard drive. It sets aside the directory area for 512 entries. It can also, with the proper option codes, transfer the operating system and COMMAND.COM to the hard disk, preparatory to making the hard disk able to boot up the computer.

17. The FILES and BUFFER lines:
    FILES=20
    BUFFERS=40

19. Not really. All that happens with severe fragmentation is that the computer apparently slows down due to the frequent movement of the heads necessary to retrieve the scattered information.

21. BACKUP and RESTORE

Chapter 8

1. The switching power supply

3. DC, an AC squarewave, DC

5. NO! DO NOT arbitrarily connect these plugs. Be sure that "P8" is to the rear of the system board.

7. No. The supply will refuse to oscillate, merely going to a self-protecting, idle state.

9. Eliminate printed circuit boards and/or drives by disconnecting them, one at a time. Try operating the computer after each removal. When the supply begins to work, the last unit disconnected was causing the problem.

Chapter 9

1. System CPU
3. True
5. A television screen
7. One, a coaxial cable
9. By slightly rotating the deflection yoke on the neck of the CRT
11. Adjustment of the two magnetized rings near the rear of the CRT, on the rear of the deflection yoke

Chapter 10

1. Simplicity, inexpensive, may be capable of graphics, is relatively fast
3. NLQ stands for "near letter quality" and is produced by a dot-matrix printer making more than one pass over the letters, filling in between the dots of the previous pass. NLQ is almost as pleasant to read as letter-quality printing.
5. The laser printer
7. LPT1, the first parallel output port
9. Issue the following command:
   MODE LPT1:
11. By toggling the printer on with a CTRL-PrtSc, then, while holding the ALT key down, key in the decimal equivalent for the desired character on the right-hand number pad, then releasing the ALT key. The special combination is then passed to the printer.
13. No. All they do is occupy space. Only the drivers actually used need be present. Some programs have no further use for the drivers once the configuration (setup) is complete.
15. Parallel or serial
17. DTE (DTE Transmits on Two)
19. The use of a hardware or a software printer spooler
21. Probably not. The new software must first be configured for the printer being used. The printer, also, must be set for the proper defaults if in conflict with the new software.

Chapter 11

1. Between the computers and the telephone line
3. The Hayes Company
5. Setting of the internal DIP switches or jumpers inside an external modem or on an internal modem card
7. The answer modem. The originate modem does the dialing
9. Communications protocols
11. YMODEM BATCH, using wild cards
13. The block is sent again from the beginning
15. Some protocols do not use error-detection routines because special hardware is capable of actually correcting data that is received with errors.
17. Configuration of the hardware and the software used

Chapter 12

1. Those for the computer (executable, command files) and those for humans (data files)
3. ASCII files, 8th bit word processor files, and graphics files.
5. The power supply is not working.
7. The system files in the hard drive root directory have been removed, moved, or damaged.
9. The file COMMAND.COM is missing.
11. The RECOVER program. This program should ONLY be used in an EMERGENCY, however, since it renames all of the files on the entire disk!
13. Copy the diskettes, keeping the backups in a different, safe place.
15. Run the diskette in another, identical computer.
17. The diskette program has become damaged.

Glossary

Active low Negative logic. When the voltage is at minimum or zero, the logic condition is satisfied to activate the circuit in question.

Active high Positive logic. When the voltage is at maximum or high, the logic condition is satisfied to activate the circuit in question.

Adapter card A card inserted into a microcomputer to interface the systems address, data, and other lines to a specific purpose such as providing signals to and from the computer and an external port, or to put characters on a monitor screen.

Address A name, label, or number identifying a register, or location in memory.

ANSI American National Standards Institute, the agency responsible for setting all manner of standards in the United States.

Append Add information onto the end of an existing file. This does not alter the existing information.

Applications program A program that uses the operating system to perform a specific task for an operator. Examples are word processing and data management programs.

ASCII American Standard Code for Information Interchange. A standard code used in transmitting text information. Upper- and lowercase letters, numbers, symbols, and communications control information are represented. ASCII uses only 7 of the 8 bits available in a byte.

Assembly language A means of programming a computer that is one step removed from manipulating instructions and data at the machine, or binary, level. Uses mnemonic codes to symbolize operations. Final assembly language code must be assembled by a computer program called an assembler to produce an intermediate hex code result. This hex code is then converted into a binary (executable) file by another computer program called a linker or a loader.

Asynchronous Without synchronism, not in step with a clocking signal. Describes the transmission of digital information that can arrive at any time and that uses start and stop bits to signify the beginning and ending of characters.

Auto answer A feature of a modem that allows it to answer a telephone ring, responding by sending a received carrier back to the originating modem.

AUX Alternate name for the first serial communications port of a computer. Also called COM1.

Azimuth   In floppy diskette drives, the alignment of a read/write head around its own center as one views the head from the top, through the surface of the diskette. **Azimuth misalignment** causes the head to meet the oncoming data on the rotating diskette at other than 90 degrees.

Backplane   The collection of connectors into which additional boards are plugged.

Backup   A copy of a working diskette kept in a safe place to be used as a master in case of damage to the primary working diskette.

BASIC language   Beginners All-purpose Symbolic Instruction Code. A powerful computer language that is intended to be easy to learn.

Baud rate   A measure of serial communications speed equal to the reciprocal of the shortest signal element (usually one bit interval). For synchronous data transmission, the baud rate is equal to the clock period. The same is true for asynchronous transmission if there is only one stop bit.

Bidirectional   Moving in two directions, such as a printer that can print in either direction, right to left or vice versa, an advantage in printing speed.

Binary   A numbering system based on the number 2. This numbering system, converted to on or off states of circuitry, allows a computer to carry out all its complex tasks.

BIOS   Basic Input/Output System. Software used to enable communications between a monitor, keyboard, and disk drives. The BIOS lies between the programs and the actual hardware of the computer.

BIOS.COM   The file that, when executed by the computer, provides the BIOS functions.

Bit   Abbreviation for *binary digit*.

Block diagram   A simplified overall diagram of system operation represented by interconnected blocks, each of which indicates a single task.

Blooming   Presentation on a CRT that is dimmer and larger in size than normal. Usually caused by lack of high voltage to the tube.

Boot record   A short machine language routine that starts the loading of the operating system from a diskette into memory for execution.

Booting up   The process of loading the operating system into the computer memory and executing it.

Bootstrap   A routine that, once begun, loads the rest of itself into memory.

BPS   Bits per second. A measure of serial data transmission rate, often used with K for thousands of bits (Kbps) or M for millions of bits (Mpbs).

Buffer   A storage area in memory used to temporarily hold information on its way to another computer device. Often a specially designated portion of memory.

Bug   An error in a program that causes undesired results.

Bus   One or more connections, commonly eight, used for transmitting data between many sources and destinations.

Byte   Eight bits of information as a unit. Can be used to represent 256 different values.

"C"   A high-level language that is relatively easy to learn and has the advantage of being highly portable, able to operate on different computers.

Card extender   A plug-in card with parallel conductors used to raise a printed circuit up away from other cards for troubleshooting purposes.

Carrier   A relatively high frequency signal on which lower frequency intelligence is then superimposed.

Cassette interface   A port provided for the saving and loading of computer programs and data from an audio cassette.

CCITT   Comite Consultatif Internationale de Telegraphie et Telephonie. An international committee responsible for setting international communications standards.

Centering   The accuracy of rotating a diskette from its true center, thus making the data tracks available to the read/write heads without wobbling.

Centronics   A wiring standard pioneered by the Centronics Company for the purpose of interfacing a parallel feed printer to a computer.

Character   A single printable letter, number, or symbol.

Checksum   A number derived from a block of data to be transmitted that is used to verify the validity on receipt.

CHKDSK   A command file that is used to test a diskette for gross errors.

Cleared   (1) Set to logic 0. (2) A state where all data buffers are set to zero and operations begun from a new beginning.

CMOS   Complimentary metal oxide semiconductor. A family of logic chips characterized by very low power requirements but high sensitivity to static damage.

COBOL   COmmon Business Oriented Language. A programming language used principally for business applications.

Cold reboot   Turning off the computer and turning it back so that all of the registers and the RAM memory are begun again from a totally fresh start. Often the only way to gain control of a computer that has crashed. Also called a *hardware reset*.

COM1, COM2   Designations for the first and second serial communications ports of a computer. When used in commands to the computer, they must usually be followed with a colon, e.g., COM1: The COM refers to COMmunications.

Command files (.COM)   Files stored on floppy diskettes or a hard disk that are intended to be loaded into the computer and executed as a program. Examples are a BASIC.COM file or a LOTUS.COM file. These files are in 8-bit binary format. Another type of command file is the .EXE file, which may also be loaded and executed directly.

COMMAND.COM   A file used as part of the operating system of an MS-DOS or PC-DOS computer. This file contains interpreters for commands such as COPY, RENAME, DIR, and ERASE, and it must be present to operate a computer with these operating systems.

Commands Typed words that mean that the computer is to carry out a specific task. Example: DIR. This command, when typed on the keyboard of a computer, is a command for the computer to display the directory of one of the diskette drives.

Communications port One of the serial input/output ports of a computer. Usually used to operate a modem or a serial printer.

Compatibility Standardized in order to work with or just like something else. Software may be called compatible if it works on all of a specific group of computers, such as IBM-compatibles. Hardware may also be termed compatible if it is usable on all of a similar group of computers.

Component level Part of the term "troubleshooting to the component level." This is troubleshooting beyond the level of replacing equipment circuit cards and extends to the replacement of individual components such as ICs, resistors, and capacitors.

CON: Designation of the control console consisting of the keyboard and the screen of a computer. Sometimes used in more advanced commands to manipulate data directly. For example, typing CON: B:TEST.DOC at the operating system level allows the keyboard input (seen on the screen, too) to be filed directly onto the B diskette in a file called TEST.DOC. (To stop the keyboard input you must use a Control-Z character.)

Concatenate Combine several files into a single file or combine strings of characters into one string. This is done by appending each one onto the end of the last.

Configuration A specific collection of hardware devices that work together. For instance, a monitor, keyboard, disk drives, and the system unit make up a basic computer configuration. A different configuration might include a hard disk drive and only one floppy disk drive.

Console The console consists of the keyboard and monitor display used by the computer operator. It allows the control and feedback of computer status to the operator.

Control C The control character used by a computer operator to abort a program and return to the operating system.

Control character A keystroke used to control rather than to pass data to a computer. It is invoked by holding down the Control key while hitting one of the character keys. This clears the D5 and D6 bits of the character key. For instance, the ASCII code for the letter H is 01001000. The code for h is 01101000. If either of these keys is hit while holding down the control key, the result is 00001000, the control code for backspace.

Controller A microcomputer chip dedicated to the control of a mechanical device. The floppy disk controller is an example of this type of chip, intended for the specific purpose of coordinating all of the control signals and directing data flow to and from a floppy disk drive.

Coprocessor A microprocessor chip that specializes in a particular function, intended for use with another more general purpose processor. An example is the 8087 math coprocessor used with the 8088 or 8086 general-purpose microprocessors.

Copy protection Use of one or more of several different schemes to prevent the duplication of software. Prevents the unpaid proliferation of valuable software to those who don't pay for it. These schemes may consist of using deliberately misnumbered or duplicate numbers of floppy diskette sectors, deliberate manipulation of the CRC numbers on each sector of a diskette, or punching a tiny laser hole in the diskette. Despite these obstacles, many copy protection methods can be bypassed using sophisticated duplicating software programs.

CP/M An operating system originally written for 8-bit computers. An acronym for control program and monitor. Since it was intended for 8-bit computers with a maximum addressable memory of 64KB, CP/M made the most efficient use of the limited memory available. Sixteen-bit operating systems such as MS-DOS, on the other hand, make operating a computer a bit easier at the expense of using more memory.

CPU Central processor unit. The "brain" of the computer. Eight-bit computers often use the Z-80 CPU or the 8088 CPU, 16-bit computers use the 80286 CPU.

Crash A condition of the computer where control has been lost and further operation of the computer is impossible. Symptoms include random characters and symbols on the screen and inability of the keyboard to respond to operator keystrokes. May be corrected by a warm boot in some cases. In others, only a cold boot will regain control.

CRC Cyclic Redundancy Check. A binary number placed at the end of a block of binary data that represents that block of data. While a parity bit checks a byte of data, the CRC checks the validity of an entire block of information.

CRT Cathode ray tube. The monitor's picture screen, or TV tube.

CRTC Cathode ray tube controller. The sophisticated IC that takes the data from video memory and breaks it up into the pulses needed to control the electron beam of the CRT. Also generates the pulses necessary to initiate the horizontal and vertical scanning waveforms, called *sync pulses*.

Cursor The present active character position on the monitor screen; the place marked by the blinking dashed line or block on the monitor screen.

Daisy-wheel printer A printer that uses a spoked wheel, each of which has a fully formed character die. Striking this die against the ribbon, then against paper produces a single letter.

Data Information. May consist of numbers, letters, or symbols. The information used by a *program* to accomplish a task. Example: A word processing program uses keyboard input to record *data* such as business letters. Both programs and data are stored together as *files* on a floppy diskette or hard disk.

Data base management system A program used to store, manipulate, and retrieve data. An example would be all of the personal checking accounts at a particular bank. All of its branches would have access to the data base, which has each account's information recorded within it. Each account would be a file and each item within the file such as the current balance would be a *record* within that file.

Debugging The process of removing errors from computer programs.

Decimal A system of counting based on the number 10. An example is our use of dollars and cents (1/100th of a dollar).

Default The value or location used if nothing else is provided. For instance, the default diskette drive of a computer may be shown at the system prompt as A>. Files may be accessed on either the A or the B drives, but the absence of a drive designator (such as B:) results in the file being sought on the A drive only.

Device driver A program used to interface between a computer and the hardware of a peripheral device. A device driver receives computer commands and generates the proper signals for the hardware of the peripheral device.

Diagnostics Programs to assist in troubleshooting the computer and its peripherals. Consists of the ROM diagnostics that are executed at each power up and, for more detailed troubleshooting, the diskette diagnostics.

DIN Deutsche Industrie Normenausschuss. The association in West Germany that sets standards for electronic equipment there.

DIP Dual in-line plastic. Often used to refer to tiny switches that can be plugged into an IC socket: DIP switches. Also used to describe the packaging method for many ICs.

Directory A table containing the names and other data related to the files on a diskette or hard disk.

Disk drive The mechanism that rotates a diskette, monitors the passage of the index hole, moves the read/write head to a specified position, and reads and writes data to the diskette.

Diskette A specially coated mylar material cut into a circle and placed within a protective envelope for the purpose of storing digital computer data.

Display Either the presentation observed on a monitor or the row of digits shown on a device such as a calculator.

DMA Direct memory access. A method of getting data out of memory without involving the CPU, allowing faster access.

DOS Disk operating system. The software necessary to allow the writing and reading of data to and from a diskette drive. Since the retrieval and storage of data is a major function of a computer, the DOS portion of an operating system is a major portion of the software necessary to operate a computer.

DOS.COM The command program in a computer, often loaded from a diskette or a hard disk, that allows communications with the diskette drives.

Dot-matrix printer A printer that prints characters and sometimes graphics. Printing is done by coordinated firing of tiny wires (pins) against the ribbon and paper. The most common are 7-, 9-, and 24-pin printers.

Double-sided drive A drive outfitted with two heads rather than the one required for a single-sided drive. The two heads are on the bottom (side 0) and the top (side 1) of the diskette.

Downtime Time that a piece of equipment is not available for use due to a failure within the system.

Drive exerciser A device used to generate appropriate commands to operate the mechanisms of a diskette drive for alignment or test purposes. Such commands include movement of the heads in and out along the diskette radius and the operation of the diskette rotating motor.

Dump Place machine-level data from RAM onto an external device such as storage or to an output device such as a printer for examination by a programmer.

Duty cycle A measurement of the time a device is actually working. A percentage obtained by dividing the on time by the time of an entire cycle. For example, if a soldering iron is operated for 2 minutes out of every 10, the duty cycle is 2/10 times 100 (to make it a percentage), or 20 percent.

Dynamic RAM Random access memory that operates by virtue of short-term storage of electrical charges. Dynamic memory must be automatically "refreshed" many times a second in order to retain memory data. Characterized by small chip size for the number of memory cells available.

EIA Electronics Industries Association. A large group of manufacturers that develops serial data communications standards such as RS-232C, RS-422, and RS-423. The "RS" stands for "Recommended Standard," the number is a "serial number" for that standard, and the "C" is the minor variation of the basic standard.

Emulate "To act like...." An emulator can be hardware or software. A software example is a program that would allow an 8088 microprocessor to run a program that was originally written for a Z80 microprocessor. A hardware example might be a Z80 microprocessor physically removed from its circuit and replaced by a cable and a larger piece of equipment that not only runs a Z80 program, but also allows the setting of breakpoints, printing of the program as it executes, etc. as a software development tool.

Erratic intermittent The worst kind of intermittent problem. Apparently will not respond to heating or mechanical stresses. Problem appears and disappears at random.

Error codes   Binary or ASCII numerical codes generated by a computer as a shorthand means of informing of an error condition.

Executable files (.EXE)   Files intended to be executed by a computer. Similar in structure (binary files) to a command file but occupies more disk storage space and runs slightly slower.

Expansion unit   A means of providing additional expansion slots for a computer that has too many option cards to install in the system unit. The expansion unit basically consists of additional sockets in an appropriate chassis, with a cable that plugs into one of the system board expansion sockets. Additional cards are then installed in the sockets within the expansion unit.

Expansion sockets   Sockets provided in a microcomputer for the purpose of installing optional printed circuit cards. These sockets, in a typical IBM-compatible computer, have 62 connections and include the address, data, and control lines from the CPU.

FAT   File allocation table. One of two tables placed on a diskette for the purpose of keeping track of the chains of sectors belonging to a file and to mark bad sectors of the diskette to prevent their use. The FATs (two copies) are located on track 0 of a diskette.

FDC   See *Floppy disk controller*.

FDD   Floppy diskette drive. The mechanisms necessary to rotate the diskette, locate the read/write heads on the diskette, and monitor passage of the index hole. Often includes a printed circuit card for some of the control functions.

FET   Field effect transistor. An amplifying semiconductor with very high input impedance and high gain. Remotely similar to the common bipolar transistor.

FIFO   First in, first out. Refers to a type of memory organization that stores data in a stack. Reading that data results in the last item written being the first data read out of the stack. Often compared to a stack of plates in a cafeteria that is loaded and unloaded from the top.

File   A collection of information treated as a unit. May be a program or data file.

Filename   An alphanumeric identification assigned by an operator to identify a file recognized by both the operator and the operating system of the computer.

Firmware   Programming residing in ROM, rather than in RAM or on a recorded medium such as a diskette or tape.

Floppy disk controller   The large-scale integrated circuit that takes commands from the CPU and converts them to signals for the floppy diskette drive. Includes coding and decoding of track, sector, and side. Returns the data requested to the CPU.

Font   A group of printable characters that are styled alike. For example, a standard roman text font is different from an italic font.

Format   The arrangement of the individual elements that make up a field, record, file, or volume. A standardized form in which data are put together.

Full-duplex Having information flowing in both directions between two points simultaneously. See also Half-duplex.

FORTRAN FORmula TRANslation, a high-level language principally for mathematics, used by scientists and engineers.

Graphics An information-passing mode in which pictures and other graphic information is processed, rather than ASCII characters. An example would be the production, storage, and printout on a graphics printer of a blueprint-style drawing.

Half-duplex Transmission of data in one direction, alternating with verification and handshaking signals in the opposite direction on the same line.

Hall effect The voltage produced by application of a current and a magnetic field through a special semiconductor.

Handshake Signals used to control the flow of data. Data can be sent too fast for the receiving end. Handshaking is used to temporarily stop the transmission of data when necessary to prevent the overflow of the receiving equipment. Handshaking can be done using a separate signal line such as those used between a modem and a terminal, or they can be digital signals sent over the telephone lines between two modems. The first method is called hardware handshaking and the second is software handshaking.

Hard copy A printed copy on paper, usually in readable form.

Hard disk A storage medium consisting of one or more specially coated plates rotating at high speed, read by read/write magnetic heads. In microcomputers, a hard disk may be installed with the system unit. Common rotational speed is 3600 rpm with a storage capacity of 10 or 20 MB.

Hard errors Errors detected in reading data from a diskette or hard disk that cannot be corrected by repeatedly reading the data.

Hard-sectored Referring to diskettes that have multiple index holes. These holes fix the location of the sectors on the disk. Declining in popularity as soft-sectored diskettes become more common.

Hardware Something you can handle: the physical portions of a computer such as the chassis, printed circuits, and IC chips.

Hidden files Diskette files not shown on a listing of the diskette directory, hidden to help prevent their erasure during normal file manipulation.

High impedance A relative term indicating a high internal resistance that limits the amount of current available from a given voltage source. A low impedance source, on the other hand, can supply relatively large currents. As an example, a series of penlight cells equaling 12V is a high impedance voltage source when compared to a 12V car battery.

High-level programming Programming utilizing a language far removed from the machine language level. Generally speaking, higher level languages are easier to learn and use, but result in slower running of the processor for which they are written.

Home position The beginning position to which a servo system such as the carriage of a printer moves when powered up. This position is then used as the starting point for all further incremental counting of the carriage movements back and forth on the carriage bars.

IC Integrated circuit. A collection of many transistors and circuits at a microscopic level, sealed within a plastic or ceramic package through which pins extend for connection to external circuitry. Commonly available with 14, 16, 20, 24, and 40 connections.

IEEE Institute of Electrical and Electronics Engineers. A professional society that issues its own standards, yet is a member of ANSI and ISO.

IEEE-488 A byte-wide wiring standard for interconnecting one- or two-way digital equipment to a computer. An example is an automated electronic testing station.

Index hole A small hole through a diskette near the center spindle hole, used to monitor the rotation of the diskette and as a starting point for the sectors recorded on the diskette.

Index width The width of the pulse resulting from the reading of a light beam through an index hole in a diskette.

Initialize To "start from scratch." The loading of special registers within LSI IC chips to required values for using the chips in computer operations. Also the setting of other registers to zero for the same purpose.

Inputs Signals that provide information to electronic circuitry. May be either analog or digital.

Interface A collection of electronic hardware and/or software necessary between two pieces of digital equipment to enable one- or two-way communication of commands and data signals.

Interleaf factor The recording of successive data segments on a hard disk surface. Recording of data on every fourth sector is an interleaf of 4, common on XT computers. The AT computers can sometimes handle a tighter interleaf of 2, with every other sector being written as the disk turns, without having to wait for more than a full turn of the platter to read the next record.

Intermittents Problems in electronic equipment that come and go. They may be thermal, mechanical, or erratic.

Interrupt A single signal sent to a CPU, which results in a jump to a specified location in memory required to service that interrupt.

ISO International Standards Organization. A voluntary international organization similar to CCITT.

Jumper A piece of wire or a small shorted connector to place on specific pins for the purpose of shorting them out. Used to select functions that are seldom changed.

Keyboard The set of switches used by a computer or terminal operator, often called a QWERTY keyboard for the first keys on the upper left of the keyboard.

LAN Local area network. The interconnection of microcomputers to share resources such as printers or mass storage media.

Language A means of providing humans a way to direct the operation of a computer with less effort than working directly with binary numbers. Common examples are assembly language, one step above binary programming. A more sophisticated, slower, but easier way to program is to use a higher level language such as BASIC.

Laser printer A printer that uses a laser to imprint an image on paper, utilizing methods of a copier machine to fix the image on paper.

Light pen A light-sensitive attachment for a computer that tells it where the human operator is touching it on the screen. It does this by noting when the light pen is activated versus the position of the CRT sweep at that instant. Coincidence of the light pen and the cursor is done by the CRTC.

Loading (1) Placing a resistance across a source of voltage. (2) Placing a program in RAM for CPU execution. (3) Converting a .HEX file into an executable form such as a .EXE file.

Logical drive A drive that exists entirely through software. A physical drive, on the other hand, is what is purchased. A physical drive can be divided into two or more logical drives.

Logic levels The voltages within the acceptable high and low limits for a specific digital family. Voltage levels between these levels are not acceptable but are bad levels, not "nothing" levels.

Logic probe An electronic instrument that detects and indicates the voltages within the acceptable ranges of high and low logic levels, and those within the bad level range.

LPT1, LPT2, LPT3 The names assigned to the three parallel ports of a typical microcomputer to identify the three parallel ports used principally for printers. LPT refers to Line PrinTer.

LQP Letter-quality printer. A printer that produces print quality similar to that of a typewriter.

LSI Large-scale integrated circuit. A microscopic, dense array of transistors, resistors, and other circuit elements necessary to perform a complex task. Examples: A Z-80 microprocessor and an 8255A I/O chip.

Machine language The series of "1"s and "0"s that make up the actual instructions that a microprocessor executes. The most fundamental programming language. The closest practical language is assembly language.

Memory chips ICs that are used for the storage of digital data. There are two types, RAM and ROM.

Microcomputer A small computer with many of the features of a minicomputer and even some of the mainframe computer capabilities. Commonly a desktop computer.

Microprocessor The central processor LSI chip of a microcomputer. Examples include the 8-bit Z-80 and 8085 and the 16-bit 8086 and 8088 microprocessors.

Modem An electronic unit that sends or receives digital information over standard telephone lines.

Monitor A visual means of providing digital information to an operator, most commonly a CRT.

Monochrome Having only one color. Refers to a black-and-white, green, or amber CRT screen as opposed to a color monitor.

Mouse An analog device used to input positional data to a computer faster than manipulating keyboard switches. By positioning the mouse, the cursor on the monitor changes position. When the desired cursor position is reached, the computer is notified to take the action requested at that position on the screen by pressing a button also located on the mouse.

MOV Metal oxide varistor. A discrete electronic component that clamps voltages at a defined level in either direction of current flow. Acts very much like a pair of zener diodes wired in series. Used to limit the amplitude of voltages.

MS-DOS Microsoft™ Disk Operating System. Similar to PC-DOS, the Personal Computer Disk Operating System. One of the popular disk-operating systems used on 16-bit microcomputers.

MTBF Mean time between failures. The average time a device can be expected to operate before failing.

Multiplexed Carrying bidirectional data flow one way at a time or carrying different signals one way at different times.

Negative logic When a logic low is the required level to activate a logic circuit.

Network Two or more computers linked together to use a common source of data. Each computer in this configuration may be called a node.

Noise Any unwanted, generally random, electrical signals on a circuit.

Nonvolatile Describes data that will not be lost if power is lost. Characteristic of ROMs, EPROMs, EEPROMs, and floppy disk and hard disk data.

Null modem A cable used in place of a modem when two digital equipments are located close enough together that telephone lines are not necessary. For instance, when two microcomputers in the same office need to communicate between themselves, a null modem would be used. Neither of the computers would "know" that a modem was missing.

Octal A numbering system based on the number 8. Numbers up to 7 appear the same as a decimal number, but 8 is shown as a 10, or one 8 plus no digits; 9 appears as 11, or one 8 plus 1 digit.

Off-line Not connected to the incoming data lines, often used to describe the status of a printer. When on-line, the printer is accepting commands and data from a computer. When off-line, some degree of local control may be possible, but all control from the computer is disabled.

Offset In addressing, the application of a positive or negative amount from a given base location in memory. For instance, an offset of three applied to a memory location of 0F231H would point to an address of 0F234H.

OK The prompt used in BASIC. The presence of an OK indicates that you are at the command level of BASIC. As a contrast, an A> is an example of the operating system prompt for most microcomputers.

On-line Equipment that is under the control of the computer's CPU.

Operating system A program or collection of programs that organizes a CPU and all peripheral devices, including the operating console, into a working unit for the execution of application programs.

Operator problem An apparent failure of electronic equipment that is caused by inadvertent misoperation of the equipment by the system operator. A common problem in microcomputer operation.

Option cards Printed circuit cards that perform one or more functions not provided for in a basic microcomputer unit. For example, an option card might provide both additional memory for the computer and an additional parallel port for a printer.

Parameters Constraints used by a microcomputer system. For instance, the baud rate parameter for many microcomputers is set at 1200 baud.

Parity A method of checking the validity of 7 bits of data. This is done by using the most significant (eighth) bit to make the total number of set bits always come out to be even or odd, a parameter that is defined prior to a transfer of digital data.

Parity bit The most significant bit of an 8-bit byte. See *Parity*.

Parity error An error condition detected by using the parity bit system of data checking.

Parser A software routine that "filters out" certain bytes or combinations of bytes. An example is the parser used in a printer that "catches" control code bytes used to control the printer directly. All other bytes of data are sent to the print buffer for eventual printing on paper.

PC-DOS Personal computer disk operating system. An outgrowth of the MS-DOS, bought by IBM for use in its personal computers.

Peripheral A device used with a computer that can either accept or provide input to the computer's central processor.

Physical device An I/O device or storage device connected to a CPU.

Physical drive The hardware of a single hard disk drive. The hard disk drive that is purchased, as opposed to a virtual or logical drive.

Pin feed A type of paper, often used with computer printers, that has holes along the paper edge. The holes provide precise alignment and indexing of the paper through the printer even after many sheets pass through it.

Pinout A listing of the connecting pins of a device, often either an IC or a connector.

Plotter A hardware device that produces finished drawings from computer data, generally using special pens.

Port An access connector that provides data input to and/or output from a computer.

Port collision   Installing options cards in such a manner that two or more ports have the same address. This usually results in the computer "locking up" when that port is accessed. Correct this situation by changing one or more of the conflicting addresses.

Positive logic   When a high represents a true. In other words, the most logical way of thinking about logic circuits where, if a voltage is present (from 2.4 to 5VDC for TTL, 70 to 100 percent of Vcc for CMOS circuits), the circuit is satisfied. As an example, an AND gate requires that both inputs be high at the same time for a high output. This is pure positive logic. A NAND gate, however, has a negative logic output that is true low.

Precompensation   A method of writing data or the synchronizing signal to a hard disk slightly out of normal place because of data "drift" caused by certain bit patterns.

Print to disk   An option of an applications program, the printing of a document or a graphic image to a file rather than to a printer or plotter. This file is the necessary data with printer or plotter codes appropriately embedded. Files thus saved may be printed or plotted at the DOS level without using the original applications program.

Priority   A number for a particular task that determines how important it is in relationship to the numbers assigned other tasks. The higher the priority number, the more preference is given.

PRN   Standard designation for the printer connected to a computer. Also may be referred to as LPT1 or LPT2.

Processing   Manipulation, consolidation, and the like of information to change it from one form to another or to make it more manageable.

Program   A string of instructions that gives a CPU instructions to carry out a task.

Prompt   A symbol used by a computer to indicate that it is awaiting input from the operator.

Proportional spacing   A feature of advanced printers that spaces letters next to one another according to the space actually required for the character, wasting no space. This results in print that looks as though it is typeset.

Protocol   An agreed-upon set of parameters that, when used by both ends of a communications transfer, govern the exchange of data between two digital equipments.

Radial alignment   The position of a diskette read/write head in relationship to the position in which it should be. If the head is exactly where it should be along a radial line to the center of a diskette, it is in radial alignment.

RAM   Random access memory. Now inaccurately taken as a term for static and dynamic memory in a modern computer, wherein data may be written and read at any location directly, without having to scan intervening data. Although also technically random access, ROM cannot be written into and is never referred to as RAM.

Random access   A method of accessing computer memory data that does not depend on the location of the previously accessed data.

Read/write heads The magnetic head assembly (or assemblies) of either a floppy diskette drive or a hard disk drive that puts magnetic data onto the recording surface of the media and later retrieves it for use by the computer.

Rectifier An electronic device that converts alternating current into pulses of direct current.

Relative drive Term used to differentiate between the first and the second of two hard disk drives during a low-level format procedure. The first relative drive is 0, the second is 1.

RF modulator In microcomputer applications, a very small oscillator that is modulated by a computer's composite digital information for the purpose of sending monitor signals through the normal tuner circuits of a television receiver. This enables the use of a television for a monitor, saving the cost of a separate monitor.

RGB Red, green, blue. An abbreviation commonly used to describe a color monitor that has direct drive (separate lines for each of these colors) as opposed to a composite color monitor in which the colors are combined into a single signal.

Risetime The time required for a waveform to go from 10 percent of maximum amplitude to 90 percent.

ROM Read only memory. Usually an IC chip, the ROM contains the necessary programs for a computer to begin loading the operating system. May also contain diagnostic routines.

Rotational speed The speed with which a diskette or hard drive turns. Common speeds are 300 rpm for a 5 1/4 inch diskette, 360 rpm for an 8 inch diskette, and 3600 rpm for a hard disk drive.

RS-232C A standard of interconnecting lines to pass serial digital data between a terminal or computer and a modem. Parts of this standard are commonly used for serial data transfer between other digital equipment such as printers and computers.

Scope Common abbreviation for *oscilloscope.*

Secondary storage Mass storage media such as floppy disk drives and hard disk drives. May also be tape or cassette storage.

Seek time Time allowed for the read/write head of a floppy diskette drive or hard disk drive to come to a stop after moving to a new track.

Sequential access A method of data storage in which data must be accessed from one end toward the other when accessing specific addresses. An example is data storage on tape drives.

SET A binary value of high, as opposed to RESET or CLEAR, where the value is low.

Setup switches Switches set by a technician during system configuration that are later read by the computer at each power-up. These switches provide the means of letting the computer know what resources are available, such as the number of disk drives, amount of memory, type of monitor, and the like.

Shipping diskette   A cardboard dummy diskette used to prevent a glass-to-glass contact of one read/write head against another during transportation. Prevents chipping of the heads. Must be removed before operation of the drive is attempted.

Skew   The departure of the path of a read/write head from an exact radial line to the center of a diskette drive.

Soft errors   Errors detected in reading data from a diskette or hard disk that may be recovered by repeatedly reading that data.

Soft-sectored   Description of a diskette that has a single index hole and uses software to determine the number and location of sectors.

Software   Computer programs stored on floppy diskettes or other secondary storage media. *Firmware* is software contained in a ROM.

Solid-state tester   An instrument that provides an E/I curve of components and circuits during power-off circuit testing.

Static   Without motion. Describes circuit operation wherein the voltage levels remain the same until manually tripped or incremented by the troubleshooting technician.

Static RAM   The memory cells of a computer that retain data once written into them until those data are rewritten or the power is turned off. A series of many flip-flop circuits to accomplish this purpose.

Static stimulus tester   A troubleshooting instrument that injects static DC logic levels into the CPU socket of a computer for the purpose of static testing of the control, address, and data buses.

Step rate   The time required between stepping pulses that position the read/write heads radially on a floppy diskette drive or hard disk drive.

Strobe   A pulse of short duration used to indicate that data are stable and ready for use.

Subscript   A letter or number below the normal level of printing, such as in the chemical formula for water, H_2O.

Superscript   A letter or number above the normal level of printing, such as in a formula for squaring a number, $3^2 = 9$.

Suppressors   Electronic components designed to clamp the incoming AC voltage below a specified value.

Surge   A momentary increase in voltage, such as a power line surge.

Sync pulse   A short pulse indicating the proper timing for an event to begin. For example, the horizontal sync pulse provided to a monitor indicates when the horizontal sweep should begin.

System board   The main circuit board of a computer, sometimes called a mother board. The circuitry of a microcomputer exclusive of any optional boards.

Technoid   A technically inclined person who consistently and eloquently overestimates his knowledge and/or ability.

Terminal   Equipment that provides the input and output functions to enable an operator to communicate with a computer. Often monitor and keyboard, but may also be a printer with keyboard.

Terminating resistor   A resistor connected to the end of a log line intended to minimize reflections by closely matching the characteristic impedance of that line.

Thermal intermittent   An intermittent problem that is controlled by the amount of heat present in or on the circuitry. Either heating or cooling can affect the thermal intermittent.

Timer chips   Integrated circuits used to provide digital waveforms or to provide timing functions through their counting ability.

Tractor feed   The small pegs, used to drive the paper through a printer, that engage the holes in the edges of the printing paper. The mechanism that drives the pegs.

Transients   Signals of short duration that are undesirable and may cause computer damage by puncturing semiconductor materials and circuit insulation.

TTL   Transistor-transistor logic. Integrated circuits that depend mostly on interconnected transistors to perform circuit tasks. Characterized by ruggedness, speed, and operation at exactly 5VDC.

UART   Universal asynchronous receiver-transmitter. An IC that is used to convert parallel data bytes into serial strings, send that information over two or three lines, and at the other end reassemble the serial data into parallel again, using another of the same chips.

Utility   A program for general use. An example is the utility program used to format new diskettes.

Varistor   An electronic component that acts like two zener diodes wired in series. Used to clamp transients on power lines to safe level, it is often referred to as an MOV, or metal oxide varistor.

Video display card   An option card that gets information from the system bus, places it into its video memory, then outputs it in a form suitable for use by a monitor.

Virtual drive   Same as a logical drive.

Warm reboot   Resetting of a computer from the keyboard to begin computer initialization from the beginning.

Word processing   A program specializing in the manipulation of text data. Such a program makes text typing and editing much easier than typing with a typewriter.

Index

Answers to questions, Appendix J
Applications programs, 156, 200
Archiving of files, 232
ASCII (American Standard Code
    for Information
    Interchange), 242
  chart, 265
  explained, Appendix C
Assembly language, 16
AT
  battery cable, Appendix A
  clock, 96
  CPU chip, 80
  defined, 7
  expansion slot, Appendix A
  memory, 89
  setup, 90, 96, 148, 153, 157
  troubleshooting, 157
  upgrading PC/XT to, 105
Audio error codes, 37
AUTOEXEC.BAT, 37, 91, 97, 250,
    Appendix B
Azimuth checks, 113

BACKUP, 156
Bad tracks, 138
  See also FORMAT
BASIC, 9, 16, 36, 123, 124
Basic input/output system
    (BIOS), 10
Batch files, 249
Battery backup. See UPS
Binary files, 241
Board level troubleshooting, 41
Boot-up, 8, 38
Buffer, 138, 211
Bulletin boards, 68

"C" language, 16

Cable problems, 55
Cases, computer, 77
CCB option byte, 137
Central processor unit (CPU),
    7, 10
Centering, 110
CHKDSK, 33, 245, 247
Clock, 90, 96
COBOL language, 20
Columns, printed, 197
COMMAND.COM, Appendix B
Communications problems, 233
  See also Modem
Communications programs, 14
Communications protocols, 229
Compatible, 75
Complete failures, 48
Component level troubleshooting,
    41
Composite video, 171
Computer aided drafting
    programs, 14
Computer problems, Chapter 2
COMx, 91, 103, 209
  addresses, 104
CONFIG.SYS, 154, Appendix B
Configuration
  AT, 9, 99
  drivers, 201
  hard disk, 141
  PC/XT, 99
  software, 200
  See also, AT setup
Control codes, 199
Control panel, 77, 97
Co-processor, 90
  installing, 106
CORE, 154
Crash, 26, 34, 62

CRT (Cathode ray tube), 173

Data
  loss prevention, 245
  recovery, 246
  restoration. *See* RESTORE
Data base programs, 12
Data files, 242
DCE, 209, Appendix I
Debug, 16, 149
Diagnostics, 9, 36, 37, 62, 67, 69
Digitizer
  pad, 108
  See also Mouse
DIP Switches
  Printer, 209
  See also System switches
DIRSORT, 155
Diskette drives, 38, 43
Diskettes, floppy, 32, 45
DOS (disk operating system), 10,
      36, 103, 105, 146, 148, 197, 200
  Commands for the technician,
      Appendix B
DTE, 209, Appendix I
Dumb printers, 198
Dynamic configuration, 150

EGA video adapter, 97
  See also Monitors
Eighth-bit files, 242
Elite, 197
Epson printer codes, Appendix H
Error codes, 9, 62
  listing, Appendix D
Error correction code, 137
Escape sequences, 199, Appendix H
ESD (electrostatic discharge), 43,
      70, 93
Expanded memory, 87, 102
Extended memory, 89, 102

FDISK, 146, 147, 152
Floppy diskette controller, 84, 110,
      112, 119
  handling, 121
  troubleshooting, 124
Floppy diskette drives, 84, 110

  capacities, 115
  data loss prevention, 248
  handling, 120
  installing additional, 107, 121
  jumpers, 127
  preventive maintenance, 128
  problems, 123, 125, 127, 247
Floppy diskettes
  3-1/2", 117
  5-1/4", 115
  capacities, 84, 112, 116
  data storage, 114, 118
  handling, 32
  write protecting, 118
FORMAT, 114, 121, 152
Fortran language, 19
Fragmented files, 155
Fully populated, 87

Game port, 92, 105
Glossary, 310
Graphics files, 242

Hardcards, 136
Hardcopy, 197
Hard disk
  boot-up, 9, 244
  capacities, 133
  cylinders, 134
  drive number designation, 134
  failures, 33, 244
  formatting, 139
  handling, 131, 134
  installing, 107, 141, 143
    checking, 153
  jumpers, 142
  parking, 34, 43
  platters, 135
  power requirements, 132
  read/write heads, 135
  recording data, 135
  standard types, Appendix E
    by manufacturer, Appendix F
  terminating resistor, 141
  tracks, 134
  troubleshooting, 156
  types, Appendixes E, F
Hard disk controller, 131

installation, 144
jumpers, 141
Hardware problems, 36, 243
HAYES, 218
    codes, Appendix G
High density, 116
Host mode, 103

IBM compatible, 75
    system board note, 81
Index hole, 112
Index width, 112
Initialize
    computer, 9
    software, 25
Installing
    See individual units, e.g.
        Monitors, Printers, etc.
Interconnections, Appendix A
Interleaf, 138, 154
Interlock switches, 208
Intermittent problems
    erratic, 49
    mechanical, 48
    thermal, 48
I/O ports
    See Ports

Joystick, 92, 108
Jumper cables, 140
Jumpers
    hard drive controller, 141
    multifunction card, 104
    system board, 81, 95

Keyboards, 105
    cables, Appendix A
    installation, 83
    problems, 59

Labels, printing, 212
Landing zone, 137
Landscape, 197
Light pen, 107
Logical drive, 146
Low-level format, 139, 146
    automatic method, 148
    commercial program, 139, 148

failure of, 151
manual method, 140, 149
LPTx, 91, 103, 198, 200, 209
    addresses, 104

MACE-plus, 153
Mainframe computer, 6
Math co-processor. See
        Co-processor
Memory
    additonal, 86, 102
    map, 88, 89
    problems, 62
    See also ROM, RAM
MFM (modified frequency
        modulation), 135, 139
Microcomputers
    block diagram, 6
    defined, 3
Minimum system, 35, 61
MODE, 180, 198
Modem, 98
    answer mode, 227
    block diagram, 216
    codes, Appendix G
    communications, 217
    external, 219
    initializing, 234
    installing, 216
    internal, 219
    operation, 219
    originate mode, 223
    problems, 233
    setup switches, 220
    software setup, 222
Modules, 76
Monitors
    cables, Appendix A
    CGA, 171, 175
    comparison of, 174, 177
    composite, 177
    direct drive, 178
    dual, 92, 179
    EGA,ECD, 170, 176
    hercules, 175
    installation, 82, 170
    internal adjustments, 182
    MDA, 174

MGCA, 171, 176
monochrome. *See* Monitors,
    MDA
problems, 57, 170
television as, 175
troubleshooting, 180
upgrading, 106
VGA, 176
Mouse
installing, 107
MOV (metal oxide varistor), 29
MS-DOS, 5
Multifunction cards, 92, 96, 104
Multiple problems, 51

New software. *See* Software
    installation
NLQ (near letter quality), 191
Normal operation, 7
Null-modem cable, 209
Numerical error codes, 37

Operating system, 9, 10, 153
Operator problems, 25
OPTIMIZE, 155
Option cards, 75
adding, 102
installing, 98
See also Multifunction cards
Out of alignment, 115, 123
Overheated parts, 53

Packing for shipment, 70
Paperwork, 69
Parallel port
Cables, Appendix A
See also LPTx
Park program, 137, 138
Parity errors, 37, 62, 103
Partitioning. See FDISK
PC (personal computer)
CPU chips, 79
defined, 7
expansion slots, Appendix A
PCPLUS, 103
Personal log, 69
Physical drive, 145
Pica, 197

PKARC, 232
Plotter, 210
Portrait, 197
Ports, 91, 99, 103
Power problems, 26, 48
Power supplies, 35, 84
cables, Appendix A
connectors, 164
failure symptoms, 166, 243
fuses, 166
inadequate, 165
installation, 95
internal failures, 165
replacing, 168
specifications, 162
troubleshooting, 160
Power-up. *See* Boot-up
Precompensation, 136
Primary Format. *See* Low-level
    format
Print to disk file, 201
Printer spooler, 211
Printers
carriages, 204
codes (Epson), Appendix H
daisy wheel, 202
dot matrix, 189, 202
fully formed character, 192
inkjet, 192
laser, 194
line, 196
paper feed, 203
preventive maintenance, 213
printheads, 202
problems, 55, 212
self-test, 212
software, 213
thermal, 192
Programming, 16
Prompt, 10, 36, 38
Proportional spacing, 205

Quad density, 116

Radial alignment, 112
RAM (random access memory),
    62, 65
RAM disk, 88, 103

Reassembly, 69
RECOVER, 33
Reduced write current, 137
Relative drive, 146
Repair options, 66
Resistor pack. *See* Terminating
   resistor
RESTORE, 156
Ribbon cables, 98, 99, 144
Ribbon feeds (printer), 206
RLL (run length limited), 135, 139
ROM (read only memory), 7, 10,
   65
   diagnostics, 37, 62
Rotational speed, 112
RS-232C, 217, Appendix A

Safety, 45, 173, 188
Serial port
   cables, Appendixes A, I
   See also COMx
Setup program. *See* AT setup
Simple things, 53, 124
Skew, 115
Smart printers, 199
Software installation, 145, 249
Software problems, 36, 38, 241, 248
Speaker, 78
   Cable, Appendix A
SPEEDSTOR, 139, 148, 154
Spikes, voltage, 29
Spooler. *See* Printer spooler
Spreadsheets, 12
Standard hard drive types,
   Appendix E

Step pulse rate, 137
System board, 35, 79
   installing, 94
   problems, 61
System switches, 9, 62, 91, 94,
   103, 106

Tampered equipment, 48
Terminating resistor, 127, 143
Transient, 28
Tough problems, 52
Turbo Board, 106
Turbo mode, 81

UPS (uninterruptable power
   supply), 26
Utility programs, 14

Video adapter, 82, 170
   installing, 97
   troubleshooting, 180
   See also Monitors
Virtual drive, 146
Viruses, 236
Voltage in wrong place, 50
Voltage transient, 28

Wait states, 81, 90, 95
Word processing, 11
Write precompensation, 136

XT
   defined, 7